BROOKLANDS BOOKS

HIGH PERFORMANCE ESCORTS

Mk 1   1968-1974

Compiled by
R.M. Clarke

ISBN 0 946489 62 9

Booklands Books Ltd.
PO Box 146, Cobham, KT11 1LG
Surrey, England

Printed in Hong Kong

BROOKLANDS BOOKS

BROOKLANDS ROAD TEST SERIES

AC Ace & Aceca 1953-1983
Alfa Romeo Alfasud 1972-1984
Alfa Romeo Alfetta Coupes GT. GTV. GTV6 1974-1987
Alfa Romeo Giulia Berlinas 1962-1976
Alfa Romeo Giulia Coupes 1963-1976
Alfa Romeo Giulietta Gold Portfolio 1954-1965
Alfa Romeo Spider 1966-1990
Allard Gold Portfolio 1937-1959
Alvis Gold Portfolio 1919-1967
American Motors Muscle Cars 1966-1970
Armstrong Siddeley Gold Portfolio 1945-1960
Aston Martin Gold Portfolio 1972-1985
Austin Seven 1922-1982
Austin A30 & A35 1951-1962
Austin Healey 100 & 100/6 Gold Portfolio 1952-1959
Austin Healey 3000 Gold Portfolio 1959-1967
Austin Healey Sprite 1958-1971
Avanti 1962-1990
BMW Six Cylinder Coupes 1969-1975
BMW 1600 Col. 1 1966-1981
BMW 2002 1968-1976
Buick Automobiles 1947-1960
Buick Muscle Cars 1965-1970
Buick Riviera 1963-1978
Cadillac Automobiles 1949-1959
Cadillac Automobiles 1960-1969
Cadillac Eldorado 1967-1978
High Performance Capris Gold Portfolio 1969-1987
Chevrolet Camaro SS & Z28 1966-1973
Chevrolet Camaro & Z-28 1973-1981
High Performance Camaros 1982-1988
Camaro Muscle Cars 1966-1972
Chevrolet 1955-1957
Chevrolet Corvair 1959-1969
Chevrolet Impala & SS 1958-1971
Chevrolet Muscle Cars 1966-1971
Chevelle and SS 1964-1972
Chevy Blazer 1969-1981
Chevy EL Camino & SS 1959-1987
Chevy II Nova & SS 1962-1973
Chrysler 300 1955-1970
Citroen Traction Avant Gold Portfolio 1934-1957
Citroen DS & ID 1955-1975
Citroen SM 1970-1975
Citroen 2CV 1949-1988
Shelby Cobra Gold Portfolio 1962-1969
Cobras and Cobra Replicas Gold Portfolio 1962-1989
Cobras & Replicas 1962-1983
Chevrolet Corvette Gold Portfolio 1953 1962
Corvette Stingray Gold Portfolio 1963-1967
High Performance Corvettes 1983-1989
Daimler SP250 Sport & V-8250 Saloon Gold Portfolio 1959-1969
Datsun 240Z 1970-1973
Datsun 280Z & ZX 1975-1983
De Tomaso Collection No.1 1962-1981
Dodge Charger 1966-1974
Dodge Muscle Cars 1967-1970
Excalibur Collection No.1 1952-1981
Facel Vega 1954-1964
Ferrari Cars 1946-1956
Ferrari Dino 1965-1974
Ferrari Dino 308 1974-1979
Ferrari 308 & Mondial 1980-1984
Ferrari Collection No.1 1960-1970
Fiat-Bertone X1/9 1973-1988
Fiat Pininfarina 124 + 2000 Spider 1968-1985
Ford Automobiles 1949-1959
Ford Bronco 1966-1977
Ford Bronco 1978-1988
Ford Consul. Zephyr Zodiac MkI & II 1950-1962
Ford Cortina 1600E & GT 1967-1970
Ford Fairlane 1955-1970
Ford Falcon 1960-1970
Ford GT40 Gold Portfolio 1964-1987
Ford RS Escorts 1968-1980
Ford Zephyr Zodiac Executive MkIII & MkIV 1962-1971
High Performance Capris Gold Portfolio 1969-1987
High Performance Escorts Mk1 1968-1974
High Performance Escorts Mk II 1975-1980
High Performance Escorts 1980-1985
High Performance Escorts 1985-1990
High Performance Fiestas 1979-1991
High Performance Mustangs 1982-1988
Holden 1948-1962
Honda CRX 1983-1987
Hudson & Railton 1936-1940
Jaguar and SS Gold Portfolio 1931-1951
Jaguar XK120 XK140 XK150 Gold Portfolio 1948-1960
Jaguar MkVII VIII IX X 420 Gold Portfolio 1950-1970
Jaguar Cars 1961-1964
Jaguar Mk2 1959-1969
Jaguar E-Type Gold Portfolio 1961-1971
Jaguar E-Type 1966-1971
Jaguar E-Type V-12 1971-1975
Jaguar XJ12 XJ5.3 V12 GIold Portfolio 1972-1990
Jaguar XJ6 Series II 1973-1979
Jaguar XJ6 Series III 1979-1986
Jaguar XJS Gold Portfolio 1975-1990
Jeep CJ5 & CJ6 1960-1976
Jeep CJ5 & CJ7 1976-1986
Jensen Cars 1946-1967
Jensen Cars 1967-1979
Jensen Interceptor Gold Portfolio 1966-1986
Jensen Healey 1972-1976
Lamborghini Cars 1964-1970
Lamborghini Countach Col No.1 1971-1982
Lamborghini Countach & Urraco 1974-1980
Lamborghini Countach & Jalpa 1980-1985
Lancia Stratos 1972-1985
Land Rover Series I 1948-1958
Land Rover Series II & IIa 1958-1971
Land Rover Series III 1971-1985
Land Rover 90 & 110 1983-1989
Lincoln Gold Portfolio 1949-1960
Lincoln Continental 1961-1969
Lincoln Continental 1969-1976
Lotus and Caterham Seven Gold Portfolio 1957-1989
Lotus Cortina Gold Portfolio 1963-1970
Lotus Elan Gold Portfolio 1962-1974
Lotus Elan Collection No.2 1963-1972
Lotus Elite 1957-1964
Lotus Elite & Eclat 1974-1982
Lotus Turbo Esprit 1980-1986
Lotus Europa Gold Portfolio 1966-1975
Marcos Cars 1960-1988
Maserati 1965-1970

Maserati 1970-1975
Mazda RX-7 Collection No.1 1978-1981
Mercedes 190 & 300SL 1954-1963
Mercedes 230/250/280SL 1963-1971
Mercedes Benz SLs & SLCs Gold Portfolio 1971-1989
Mercedes Bens Cars 1949-1954
Mercedes Bens Cars 1954-1957
Mercedes Bens Cars 1957-1961
Mercedes Bens Cars Compention Cars 1950-1957
Mercury Muscle Cars 1966-1971
Metropolitan 1954-1962
MG TC 1945-1949
MG TD 1949-1953
MG TF 1953-1955
MG Cars 1959-1962
MGA & Twin Cam Gold Portfolio 1955-1962
MGB MGC & V8 Gold Portfolio 1962-1980
MGB Roadsters 1962-1980
MGB GT 1965-1980
MG Midget 1961-1980
Mini Cooper Gold Portfolio 1961-1971
Mini Moke 1964-1989
Mini Muscle Cars 1961-1979
Mopar Muscle Cars 1964-1967
Morgan Three-Wheeler Gold Portfolio 1910-1952
Morgan Cars 1960-1970
Morgan Cars Gold Portfolio 1968-1989
Morris Minor Collection No.1
Mustang Muscle Cars 1967-1971
Oldsmobile Automobiles 1955-1963
Old's Cutlass & 4-4-2 1964-1972
Oldsmobile Muscle Cars 1964-1971
Oldsmobile Toronado 1966-1978
Opel GT 1968-1973
Packard Gold Portfolio 1946-1958
Pantera Gold Portfolio 1970-1989
Plymouth Barracuda 1964-1974
Plymouth Muscle Cars 1966-1971
Pontiac Tempest & GTO 1961-1965
Pontiac Firebird and Trans-Am 1973-1981
High Performance Firebirds 1982-1988
Pontiac Fiero 1984-1988
Pontiac Muscle Cars 1966-1972
Porsche 356 1952-1965
Porsche Cars in the 60's
Porsche Cars 1960-1964
Porsche Cars 1964-1968
Porsche Cars 1968-1972
Porsche Cars 1972-1975
Porsche Turbo Collection No.1 1975-1980
Porsche 911 1965-1969
Porsche 911 1970-1972
Porsche 911 1973-1977
Porsche 911 Carrera 1973-1977
Porsche 911 SC 1978-1983
Porsche 911 Turbo 1975-1984
Porsche 914 Gold Portfolio 1969-1976
Porsche 914 Collection No.1 1969-1983
Porsche 924 Gold Portfolio 1975-1988
Porsche 928 1977-1989
Porsche 944 1981-1985
Range Rover Gold Portfolio 1970-1988
Reliant Scimitar 1964-1986
Riley 11/2 & 21/2 Litre Gold Portfolio 1945-1955
Rolls Royce Silver Cloud 1955-1965
Rolls Royce Silver Shadow 1965-1981
Rover P4 1949-1959
Rover P4 1955-1964
Rover 3 & 3.5 Litre Gold Portfolio 1958-1973
Rover 2000 + 2200 1963-1977
Rover 3500 1968-1977
Rover 3500 & Vitesse 1976-1986
Saab Sonett Collection No.1 1966-1974
Saab Turbo 1976-1983
Shelby Mustang Muscle Cars 1965-1970
Stubebaker Gold Portfolio 1947-1966
Stubebaker Hawks & Larks 1956-1963
Sunbeam Tiger & Alpine Gold Portfolio 1959-1967
Thunderbird 1955-1957
Thunderbird 1958-1963
Thunderbird 1964-1976
Toyota Land Cruiser 1956-1984
Toyota MR2 1984-1988
Triumph 2000. 2.5. 2500 1963-1977
Triumph GT6 1966-1974
Triumph Spitfire Gold Portfolio 1962-1980
Triumph Stag 1970-1980
Triumph Stag Collection No.1 1970-1984
Triumph TR2 & TR3 1952-60
Triumph TR4-TR5-TR250 1961-1968
Triumph TR6 1969-1976
Triumph TR7 & TR8 1975-1982
Triumph Herald 1959-1971
Triumph Vitesse 1962-1971
TVR Gold Portfolio 1959-1990
Valiant 1960-1962
VW Beetle Collection No.1 1970-1982
VW Golf GTi 1976-1986
VW Karmann Ghia 1955-1982
VW Kubelwagen 1940-1975
VW Scirocco 1974-1981
VW Bus. Camper. Van 1954-1967
VW Bus. Camper. Van 1968-1979
VW Bus. Camper. Van 1979-1989
Volvo 120 1956-1970
Volvo 1800 1960-1973

BROOKLANDS ROAD & TRACK SERIES

Road & Track on Alfa Romeo 1949-1963
Road & Track on Alfa Romeo 1964-1970
Road & Track on Alfa Romeo 1971-1976
Road & Track on Alfa Romeo 1977-1989
Road & Track on Aston Martin 1962-1990
Road & Track on Auburn Cord and Duesenburg 1952-1984
Road & Track on Audi & Auto Union 1952-1980
Road & Track on Audi 1980-1986
Road & Track on Austin Healey 1953-1970
Road & Track on BMW Cars 1966-1974
Road & Track on BMW Cars 1975-1978
Road & Track on BMW Cars 1979-1983
Road & Track on Cobra, Shelby & GT40 1962-1983
Road & Track on Corvette 1953-1967
Road & Track on Corvette 1968-1982
Road & Track on Corvette 1982-1986
Road & Track on Datsun Z 1970-1983

Road & Track on Ferrari 1950-1968
Road & Track on Ferrari 1968-1974
Road & Track on Ferrari 1975-1981
Road & Track on Ferrari 1981-1984
Road & Track on Fiat Sports Cars 1968-1987
Road & Track on Jaguar 1950-1960
Road & Track on Jaguar 1961-1968
Road & Track on Jaguar 1968-1974
Road & Track on Jaguar 1974-1982
Road & Track on Jaguar 1983-1989
Road & Track on Lamborghini 1964-1985
Road & Track on Lotus 1972-1981
Road & Track on Maserati 1952-1974
Road & Track on Maserati 1975-1983
Road & Track on Mazda RX7 1978-1986
Road & Track on Mercedes 1952-1962
Road & Track on Mercedes 1963-1970
Road & Track on Mercedes 1971-1979
Road & Track on Mercedes 1980-1987
Road & Track on MG Sports Cars 1949-1961
Road & Track on MG Sprots Cars 1962-1980
Road & Track on Mustang 1964-1977
Road & Track on Nissan 300-ZX & Turbo 1984-1989
Road & Track on Peugeot 1955-1986
Road & Track on Pontiac 1960-1983
Road & Track on Porsche 1961-1967
Road & Track on Porsche 1968-1971
Road & Track on Porsche 1972-1975
Road & Track on Porsche 1975-1978
Road & Track on Porsche 1979-1982
Road & Track on Porsche 1982-1985
Road & Track on Porsche 1985-1988
Road & Track on Rolls Royce & B'ley 1950-1965
Road & Track on Rolls Royce & B'ley 1966-1984
Road & Track on Saab 1955-1985
Road & Track on Toyota Sports & GT Cars 1966-1984
Road & Track on Triumph Sports Cars 1953-1967
Road & Track on Triumph Sports Cars 1967-1974
Road & Track on Triumph Sports Cars 1974-1982
Road & Track on Volkswagen 1951-1968
Road & Track on Volkswagen 1968-1978
Road & Track on Volkswagen 1978-1985
Road & Track on Volvo 1957-1974
Road & Track on Volvo 1975-1985
Road & Track - Henry Manney at Large and Abroad

BROOKLANDS CAR AND DRIVER SERIES

Car and Driver on BMW 1955-1977
Car and Driver on BMW 1977-1985
Car and Driver on Cobra, Shelby & Ford GT 40 1963-1984
Car and Driver on Corvette 1956-1967
Car and Driver on Corvette 1968-1977
Car and Driver on Corvette 1978-1982
Car and Driver on Corvette 1983-1988
Car and Driver on Datsun Z 1600 & 2000 1966-1984
Car and Driver on Ferrari 1955-1962
Car and Driver on Ferrari 1963-1975
Car and Driver on Ferrari 1976-1983
Car and Driver on Mopar 1956-1967
Car and Driver on Mopar 1968-1975
Car and Driver on Mustang 1964-1972
Car and Driver on Pontiac 1961-1975
Car and Driver on Porsche 1955-1962
Car and Driver on Porsche 1963-1970
Car and Driver on Porsche 1970-1976
Car and Driver on Porsche 1977-1981
Car and Driver on Porsche 1982-1986
Car and Driver on Saab 1956-1985
Car and Driver on Volvo 1955-1986

BROOKLANDS PRACTICAL CLASSICS SERIES

PC on Austin A40 Restoration
PC on Land Rover Restoration
PC on Metalworking in Restoration
PC on Midget/Sprite Restoration
PC on Mini Cooper Restoration
PC on MGB Restoration
PC on Morris Minor Restoration
PC on Sunbeam Rapier Restoration
PC on Triumph Herald/Vitesse
PC on Triumph Spitfire Restoration
PC on VW Beetle Restoration
PC on 1930s Car Restoration

BROOKLANDS HOT ROD 'MUSCLECAR & HI-PO ENGINE SERIES

Chevy 265 & 283
Chevy 302 & 327
Chevy 348 & 409
Chevy 350 & 400
Chevy 396 & 427
Chevy 454 thru 512
Chrysler Hemi
Chrysler 273, 318, 340 & 360
Chrysler 361, 383, 400, 413, 426, 440
Ford 289, 302, Boss 302 & 351W
Ford 351C & Boss 351
Ford Big Block

BROOKLANDS MILITARY VEHICLES SERIES

Allied Mil. Vehicles No.1 1942-1945
Allied Mil. Vehicles No.2 1941-1946
Dodge Mil. Vehicles Col. 1 1940-1945
Military Jeeps 1941-1945
Off Road Jeeps 1944-1971
Hail to the Jeep
US Military Vehicles 1941-1945
US Army Military Vehicles WW2-TM9-2800

BROOKLANDS HOT ROD RESTORATION SERIES

Auto Restoration Tips & Techniques
Basic Bodywork Tips & Techniques
Basic Painting Tips & Techniques
Camaro Restoration Tips & Techniques
Chevrolet High Performance Tips & Techniques
Chevy-GMC Pickup Repair
Custom Painting Tips & Techniques
Engine Swapping Tips & Techniques
Ford Pickup Repair
How to Build a Street Rod
Mustang Restoration Tips & Techniques
Performance Tuning - Chevrolets of the '60s
Performance Tuning - Ford of the '60s
Performance Tuning - Mopars of the '60s
Performance Tuning - Pontiacs of the '60s

CONTENTS

5	Ford Escort Twin Cam Road Test	*Autocar*	June	6	1968
10	Clark Wins Tulip Rally	*Motor*	May	4	1968
13	Escort Gammon 1600 GT	*Cars & Car Conversions*	June		1968
14	Escort Broadspeed	*Cars & Car Conversions*	June		1968
15	Escort Allard Blown 1300 GT	*Cars & Car Conversions*	June		1968
16	Ford Twin Cam Escort Preview Test	*Car & Driver*	Sept.		1968
18	Ford Escort 1300 GT Brief Test	*Motor*	Nov.	30	1968
21	Broadspeed Escort Stage 2 1300 GT Road Test	*Cars & Car Conversions*	Feb.		1969
22	Pirana Escort 1600 GT	*Cars & Car Conversions*	Feb.		1969
24	Inside Rally Information	*Autocar*	Feb.	27	1969
28	The LuMo Pirana Sprint	*Autosport*	Mar.	14	1969
29	Crayford's 3-litre Escort Eliminator	*Motor*	May	31	1969
30	Dashing Broadspeed Escort	*Car*	May		1969
31	Ford Escort RS 1600 Brief Test	*Motor*	May		1970
34	Escort 1600 T/C Road Test	*Sports Car World*	May		1970
38	Escort 1300 GT Road Test	*Wheels*	June		1970
43	Twin Cam Escort Without Gas Road Test	*Wheels*	Oct.		1970
48	Mexico	*Car*	Jan.		1971
50	Ford Escort Mexico	*Motor*	Jan.	2	1971
52	Escort Super Speed 2000 GT Brief Test	*Autocar*	June	24	1971
54	Mexico, the Instant Motor Racer	*Motor Sport*	Oct.		1971
56	Ford Escort 1300 Road Test	*Autocar*	Dec.	2	1971
60	Taking Stock — Mexico	*Autocar*	June	15	1972
62	Navajo, Émigré from Mexico	*Motor*	June	30	1973
64	Ford Escort 1300 E Brief Test	*Motor*	June	30	1973
67	Favo's Escort RS 2000	*Autosport*	July	5	1973
68	Ford Escort RS 1600 & Dolomite Sprint	*Car*	July		1973
72	Ford Escort RS 2000	*Autocar*	July	5	1973
74	Two-litre Tiger RS 2000	*Modern Motor*	Sept.		1973
76	Escort RS 2000 Road Test	*Rally Sport*	Oct.		1973
77	Ford RS 2000 Road Test	*Wheels*	April		1974
80	Hi Ho Pinto!	*Motor*	June	22	1974
83	Road Impressions of RS 2000	*Competition Car*	Sept.		1974
84	Ford Escort RS 2000 Road Test	*Motor*	Oct.	19	1974
88	A Hot Escort	*Asian Auto*	March		1977
91	Collector's Corner — Escort Mark I	*Motor*	Nov.	8	1980
94	Escort Mexico & Mk. I RS 2000	*Thoroughbred & Classic Car*	July		1982
98	Rather Special RS 2000	*Classic & Sportscar*	Aug.		1982

BROOKLANDS BOOKS

ACKNOWLEDGEMENTS

Two years ago we read Graham Robson's Osprey Auto History 'Ford Escort RS' and this prompted us to research these small muscular vehicles and the outcome was 'Ford RS Escorts 1968-1980'.

Through this book our series has become known to a whole new group of mainly young owners who with vigour prepare and tune their Escorts for a variety of sporting events. Those we have met personally have urged us to return to the subject and if possible to be more specific. Fortunately this marque featured prominently in the motoring press of the period and we have been able to cover the Mk. I in this volume and devote a second to the later Mark IIs.

Our cover photograph is of Colin Walker taking his Mexico over one of the more rugged stages of the 1973 Avon Tour of Britain and we are indebted to Ford for this attractive action shot. We would also like to thank Mr. Pelby, owner of the beautifully kept 1974 RS 2000 VGY 66M, whom we met recently at a Knebworth gathering.

This book is a good example of what Brooklands Books are all about. We endeavour to satisfy the needs of groups of enthusiasts by making available lost or hard-to-find information about their cars. Due to the narrowness of subject they are produced in small numbers and rarely reprinted.

The publishers of the world's leading motoring journals understand both our motives and the feelings of these owners and have for many years generously allowed us to include their copyright stories. Our thanks in this instance go to the management of Asian Auto, Autocar, Autosport, Car, Car & Car Conversions, Car and Driver, Classic & Sportscar, Competition Car, Modern motor, Motor Sport, Rally Sport, Sports Car World, Thoroughbred & Classic Cars and Wheels for their continued support.

R.M. Clarke

Autocar
Road test
NUMBER 2187

FORD ESCORT TWIN CAM

2187

1,558 c.c.

MANUFACTURER
Ford Motor Co. Ltd., Warley, Brentwood, Essex.

PRICES

Basic	£910 0s. 0d.
Purchase Tax	£252 15s. 7d.
Seat Belts	£8 6s. 2d.
Total (in GB)	**£1,171 1s. 9d.**

EXTRAS (inc PT)

Ford radio (fitted in production)	£34 3s. 8d.
Special chrome wheels	£29 12s. 0d.

PERFORMANCE SUMMARY

Mean maximum speed . . .	113 mph
Standing start ¼-mile . .	17.2 sec
0-60 mph . . .	9.9 sec
30-70 mph (through gears) .	9.2 sec
Typical fuel consumption .	24 mpg
Miles per tankful . . .	260

CORTINA-LOTUS power in much lighter body-shell gives startling performance for such a small car. Vigorous torque delivery and wide power range, limited at high revs by ignition cut-out. Well chosen gear ratios and excellent gear change. Delicately balanced roadholding with predictable final oversteer, dead though sensitive steering, and poor ride for normal road use. Fuel economy poor if full performance used. Trim and fittings identical with Escort GT. Rather cramped driving position and poor seat adjustment. Unobtrusive and rapid road car, quickly converted to competition use.

EVER since Ford started their performance programme, their sporting saloons have been getting fiercer. The new Ford Escort Twin-Cam, announced only in January this year and already in the thick of competition successes, is the fiercest yet. Other sporting Fords could be called saloons capable of being raced or rallied, but the Twin-Cam Escort is unashamedly a racing saloon de-tuned for road use. In production form, with quantity sales needed to justify its homologation as a Touring Car, the Twin-Cam gives the customer exactly what he expects; a high performance competition car that can be converted into a real projectile by spending a bit more money on approved Ford equipment. Allowing for the noise, vibration and harshness, the Twin-Cam is still incredible fun to drive in crowded Britain, and is guaranteed to take years off any jaded motorist who gets his hands on one. Apart from the artillery-style road wheels (an extra on our test car) and the black painted grille, the car is hardly recognizable as such, often astounding other road users by its remarkable acceleration and handling.

To understand the Twin-Cam Escort, one must first understand the need. Ford wanted a new model for outright successes in racing and rallying to replace the Cortina-Lotus, preferably using the well-known twin cam engine and transmission in a much lighter car. The Escort, called the 1968 Anglia, has been under development for some time, but it was not until last summer that the Competitions Department was finally given the go-ahead to develop a road version of their future competition car. The whole car is based on the Escort GT's bodyshell, and it is a credit to Ford's forward planning that the only real changes forced upon them have been to flare out the wheel arches slightly to accommodate much wider wheels (and to allow for even wider racing wheels to be fitted), and to mount the Twin-Cam engine slightly askew in the shell to improve alignment of the power line and cut down vibrations. The major drawback of the Escort GT bodyshell is that Ford are stuck with unsatisfactory rectangular headlamps on their competition car, a definite handicap in rallies and long-distance saloon car racing where control of the beam pattern counts.

As one would expect with such a compact little sports saloon, the performance is pretty startling. Mechanically—engine, gearbox, final drive and brakes—the Escort Twin-Cam is identical with the Cortina-Lotus; since it is also lighter than the bigger car, the acceleration is very much better throughout. The bodyshell has less frontal area and a better shape aero- ◊

Ford Escort Twin Cam (1,558 c.c.)

PERFORMANCE

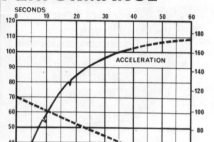

MAXIMUM SPEEDS

Gear		mph	kph	rpm
Top	(mean)	113	182	6,300
	(best)	113	182	6,300
3rd		81	130	6,300
2nd		56	90	6,300
1st		38	61	6,300

MOTORWAY CRUISING

Error (ind. speed at 70 mph)	66 mph
Engine (rpm at 70 mph)	3,930 rpm
(mean piston speed)	1,880 ft/min
Fuel (mpg at 70 mph)	30.7 mpg
Passing (50-70 mph)	4.8 sec
Noise (per cent silent at 70 mph)	25 per cent

Standing ¼-mile 17.2 sec 81 mph
Standing Kilometre 31.9 sec 98 mph

TIME IN SECONDS

	3.8	5.2	7.2	9.9	13.0	16.8	24.2	33.6
TRUE SPEED MPH	30	40	50	60	70	80	90	100	110
INDICATED SPEED	28	37	47	57	66	76	86	96	105

Mileage recorder 5.5 per cent under-reading

SPEED RANGE, GEAR RATIOS AND TIME IN SECONDS

mph	Top (3.78)	3rd (5.27)	2nd (7.59)	1st (11.22)
10-30	—	7.7	4.7	3.6
20-40	10.6	6.2	3.8	—
30-50	9.8	6.0	3.6	—
40-60	9.7	6.2	—	—
50-70	9.9	6.5	—	—
60-80	10.6	7.1	—	—
70-90	12.4	—	—	—
80-100	16.5			—

HOW THE CAR COMPARES

Maximum Speed (mph)

80	90	100	110

Ford Escort Twin-Cam
BMC Mini-Cooper S
Ford Cortina-Lotus
Renault Gordini 1300
Triumph Vitesse 2-litre

0-60 mph (sec.)

20	10	0

Ford Escort Twin-Cam
BMC Mini-Cooper S
Ford Cortina-Lotus
Renault Gordini 1300
Triumph Vitesse 2-litre

Standing Start ¼-mile (sec.)

30	20

Ford Escort Twin-Cam
BMC Mini-Cooper S
Ford Cortina-Lotus
Renault Gordini 1300
Triumph Vitesse 2-litre

MPG Overall

0	20	30

Ford Escort Twin-Cam
BMC Mini-Cooper S
Ford Cortina-Lotus
Renault Gordini 1300
Triumph Vitesse 2-litre

PRICES

Ford Escort Twin-Cam	£1,171
BMC Mini-Cooper S	£921
Ford Cortina-Lotus	£1,171
Renault Gordini 1300	To special order
Triumph Vitesse 2-litre	£872

CONSUMPTION

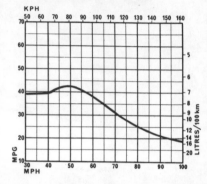

FUEL

(At constant speeds—mpg)

30 mph	.	39.2
40 mph	.	40.0
50 mph	.	42.5
60 mph	.	38.1
70 mph	.	30.7
80 mph	.	25.8
90 mph	.	21.7
100 mph	.	18.9

Typical mpg	24 (11.8 litres/100km)
Calculated (DIN) mph	27.9 (10.1 litres/100km)
Overall mpg	21.5 (13.1 litres/100km)
Grade of fuel : Premium, 5 star Super (min 100RM)	

OIL

Miles per pint (SAE 10W/40) . . .	350

TEST CONDITIONS Weather: Dry, blustery. Wind: 5-15 mph. Temperature: 18 deg. C. (65 deg. F). Barometer: 29.8in. Hg. Humidity: 58 per cent. Surfaces: Dry concrete and asphalt.

WEIGHT Kerb weight: 16.7 cwt (1,872lb-849kg) (with oil, water and half-full fuel tank). Distribution, per cent F, 51.6; R, 48.4. Laden as tested: 20.9 cwt (2,343lb-1,063kg).

Test distance 1,323 miles.
Figures taken at 7,800 miles by our own staff at the Motor Industry Research Association proving ground at Nuneaton.

TURNING CIRCLES
Between kerbs L, 31ft 9in.; R, 30ft 3in.
Between walls L, 33ft 3in.; R, 31ft 11in.
Steering wheel turns, lock to lock, 3.0

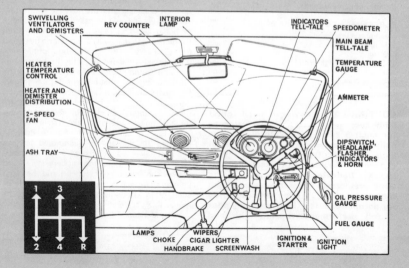

BRAKES

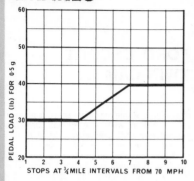

PEDAL LOAD (lb) FOR 0·5 g — STOPS AT ¾ MILE INTERVALS FROM 70 MPH

(from 30 mph in neutral)

Load	g	Distance
20lb	0.25	120ft
40lb	0.65	46ft
50lb	0.86	35ft
60lb	1.05	28.6ft
Handbrake	0.42	72ft

Max. Gradient 1 in 3
Clutch Pedal 30lb and 4.75in.

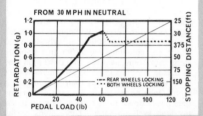

FROM 30 MPH IN NEUTRAL

RETARDATION (g) — PEDAL LOAD (lb) — STOPPING DISTANCE (ft)

- - - REAR WHEELS LOCKING
—— BOTH WHEELS LOCKING

SPECIFICATION

FRONT ENGINE, REAR-WHEEL DRIVE

ENGINE

Cylinders	4, in line
Main bearings	5
Cooling system	Water, pump, fan and thermostat
Bore	82.55mm (3.25in.)
Stroke	72.8mm (2.87in.)
Displacement	1,558 c.c. (95.2 cu.in.)
Valve gear	Twin overhead camshafts
Compression ratio	9.5-to-1 : Min. octane rating : 5 star, 100 RM
Carburettor	Two double choke Weber 40DCOE
Fuel pump	AC mechanical
Oil filter	Fram or Tecalemit full flow, renewable element
Max. power	109.5 bhp (net) at 6,000 rpm
Max. torque	106.5 lb.ft. (net) at 4,500 rpm

TRANSMISSION

Clutch	Borg and Beck, diaphragm spring, 8.0 in. dia
Gearbox	4-speed, all-synchromesh
Gear ratios	Top 1.00
	Third 1.40
	Second 2.01
	First 2.97
	Reverse 3.32
Final drive	Hypoid bevel, 3.78-to-1

CHASSIS and BODY

Construction	Integral, with all-steel body

SUSPENSION

Front	Independent, MacPherson struts, bottom wishbone, coil springs, telescopic dampers, anti-roll bar
Rear	Live axle, half-elliptic leaf springs, radius arms, telescopic dampers

STEERING

	Burman and Cam Gears, rack and pinion
Wheel dia.	14.9in.

BRAKES

Make and type	Girling, disc front, drum rear
Servo	Girling vacuum
Dimensions	F. 9.62in. dia., ; R. 9.00in. dia., 1.75in. wide shoes
Swept area	F. 190 sq.in.; R. 96 sq.in.; Total 286 sq.in. (283 sq.in./ton laden)

WHEELS

Type	Pressed steel disc, four-stud fixing 5.5in. wide rim
Tyres—make	India on test car
type	Autoband Radial tubeless
size	165-13in.

EQUIPMENT

Battery	12 volt 38 Ah
Generator	Lucas C40/1 22-amp d.c.
Headlamps	Lucas rectangular sealed beam, 120/80-watt (total)
Reversing lamp	None
Electric fuses	6
Screen wipers	Two speed, self-parking
Screen washer	Standard, foot button
Interior heater	Standard, air-blending
Heated backlight	Not available
Safety belts	Extra, anchorages built-in
Interior trim	Pvc seats, pvc headlining
Floor covering	Carpet
Starting handle	No provision
Jack	Screw scissors
Jacking points	4, under body
Windscreen	Zone toughened
Underbody protection	Phosphate treatment under paint

MAINTENANCE

Fuel tank	9 Imp. gallons (no reserve) (41 litres)
Cooling system	12.5 pints (including heater)
Engine sump	7.2 pints (4.1 litres) SAE 10W 30. Change oil every 2,500 miles. Change filter every 2,500 miles
Gearbox	1.75 pints SAE 80 EP. No change needed.
Final drive	2.0 pints SAE 90 EP. No change needed.
Grease	No points
Tyre pressures	F. 24 ; R. 24 p.s.i. (all conditions)

PERFORMANCE DATA

Top gear mph per 1,000 rpm	17.8
Mean piston speed at max power	2,867 ft./min
Bhp per ton laden	104.7

STANDARD GARAGE 16ft x 8ft 6in.

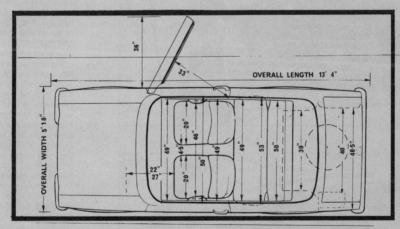

OVERALL LENGTH 13' 4"
OVERALL WIDTH 5'18"

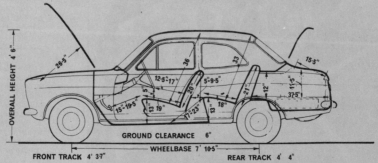

OVERALL HEIGHT 4' 6"
GROUND CLEARANCE 6"
FRONT TRACK 4' 3?"
WHEELBASE 7' 10·5"
REAR TRACK 4' 4"

SCALE
0.3in. to 1ft
Cushions uncompressed

1

2

3

FORD ESCORT TWIN-CAM . . .

dynamically so the maximum speed is appreciably higher as well. The ignition distributor cut-out that Ford have always fitted to their Lotus-built engines is a nuisance; set nominally for 6,500 rpm, that on our test car cut out at 6,300 rpm, limiting the engine's range when there was clearly lots of lusty breathing still in reserve. Removing the cut-out invalidates the warranty, but we would be prepared to take this risk and respect a red-line instead. As it is, the rev-counter reads unmarked to 8,000 rpm and the engine spends a lot of its time cutting out which can only be bad for it, considering the stress reversals produced. Undoubtedly better acceleration figures could have been achieved without the cut-out, and maximum speed would have been higher; even so, the car achieved a spluttering 113 mph both ways.

Plenty of spare grip from the fat 165—13in. India Autoband tyres means that wheelspin sprint starts are possible only on low friction surfaces and then only by letting in the clutch viciously from about 5,000 rpm. Wheelgrip and clutch grip combined are so firm that standing starts took some learning. The 0-30 mph time of 3.8sec is not as quick as the power/weight ratio would suggest, but then bottom gear is high. Once on the move, the twin-ohc engine gets busily down to its task, rushing up to the rev limit with no torque curve steps or flat spots, and an unusual eagerness.

Not long ago the Cortina-Lotus was considered the ultimate in road cars, but the Escort Twin-Cam beats its performance on all counts except initial getaway. The Twin-Cam sprints to 60 mph in 9.9sec (Cortina-Lotus, 11.0sec), to the quarter-mile in 17.2sec (18.2sec), and to 100 mph in 33.6 (44.0sec). The Cortina-Lotus was good for only 104 mph.

Big engines in small cars usually give effortless performance, and the deep-lunged Lotus unit makes light work of high speed. The unit itself is by no means smooth nor silent, but the pleasantly refined camshaft chain whine makes up for the low-speed gobblings of Webers, the rumbles and the odd vibrations. Throttle response is immediate once the engine is warmed through from cold, there being strong and vigorous torque from as low as 1,000 rpm, but transmission judder usually encourages a down-change as soon as the revs drop to 2,000. The choke's never needed when starting from cold, provided one remembers the stab-the-throttle dodge of priming Webers before turning the key. The engine and gearbox are bolted down fairly rigidly, so hard driving brings a lot of clamour with it; to a keen driver this is music but less enthusiastic passengers might be overwhelmed by the deep-throated roar. Purely as a

1. *The relatively fat spare wheel takes up a lot of boot space*
2. *In spite of the big carburettors, accessibility is not too restricted. Dipstick is now a flexible one behind the air cleaner; note the brake booster on the right*
3. *Twin-Cam Escorts use an instrument panel similar to that of the GT; it is very neat. A standard Escort steering wheel is used; a handsome leather-covered wheel is extra*

"Chucking" the Twin-Cam on a MIRA track. From right to left:—at first, marked understeer in front partially offset by slight rear end breakaway; then by lifting off momentarily the tail slides wide and a front wheel lifts; the delightfully quick steering and good lock make correction of even the worst slide easy

traffic-lights symbol, the Twin-Cam plays well-bred and exciting tunes without offending too much.

We noticed that the engine is mounted askew, with the nose at least 1½in. offset to the left-side of the car. This alleviates all manner of minor clearance problems from the steering rack and bodyshell.

The gearbox and transmission is very nicely matched to the 110 bhp engine. The close gear ratios now common to the Cortina-Lotus, Cortina GT and Corsair 2000 are used along with the 3.78-to-1 Cortina final drive. Useful maxima of 38, 56 and 81 mph seem to provide a gear for every situation, and the remote control is one of the very best we know. The gate is narrow and absolutely precise, with a very nice feel, and the synchromesh is unbeatable. It is also a very "quick" change that feels right for this sort of car.

Suspension and Handling

In view of the Twin-Cam's performance potential, and because most of us tended to treat it like the instant-rally car it is, our overall fuel consumption is 21.5 mpg is not too un-reasonable. The constant-speed fuel graph shows just what sort of economy is possible from this engine if the thirsty accelerator pump jets are not overworked. The 9-gallon fuel tank, identical with all the other Escorts, is too small for the Twin-Cam; it is no consolation to know that an extra tank (at extra price) can be fitted in the other side of the boot after delivery. On a compression ratio of 9.5-to-1, Ford like Twin-Cam owners to use 5-star 100-octane fuel. Some examples run quite well on ordinary 4-star premium but we chose not to chance it. Oil consumption (350 miles per pint) was reasonable enough.

So far as suspension and handling are concerned, the Twin-Cam has a very definite character; most owners who recognize the delicate set-up as a semi-rallying one will be happy, but it might be a bit too "nervous" for others. Compared with basic Escorts, the suspension is lowered and stiffened all round, with twin radius arms to assist the rear axle location. Very wide (5.5in.) roadwheels, radial-ply tyres and a front anti-roll bar are all special to the Twin-Cam; the Lotus hubs and brakes help to ensure that there is a modicum of negative camber to the front wheels; the steering rack has a more direct ratio than the basic Escort and there are only three turns lock-to-lock.

Helped by these factors, which are the results of careful development by the Ford Competition Department, the Twin-Cam has almost neutral handling characteristics at normal speeds. Just a touch on the wheel is needed to send the car scurrying round long main road corners with hardly a trace of roll. But if the corner suddenly tightens up, a bit more steering wheel movement produces more roll and just enough roll over-steer to change the car's attitude, and—if the car is really pressed—the inside rear wheel lifts and spins to limit the speed. In the wet, rear wheel spin occurs fairly readily, but the changes of attitude are caught very quickly and somehow feel right and proper to the character of the car.

A penalty of this set-up is the extreme sensitivity to side winds, in which the car tends to dart around a lot. Road camber changes affect it quite strongly, enough for instance to discourage us from flat-out speeds on MIRA's steep and rough bankings. There is very little suspension feed-back to the steering wheel, but out-of-balance vibrations on the test car shook the column.

Ride is hard and jolty, making front seat belts almost compulsory wear for comfort as well as safety. Rear suspension movement is limited.

The complete Cortina-Lotus braking system has been adapted to the Twin-Cam Escort (there is ample room within the same 13in. wheels) and it is well able to deal with the vigorous performance. Fade tests at MIRA showed that effort increased slightly during persistent use, but on the road, even when driving very hard, we noticed no loss in efficiency. Helped by the servo and the fat tyres, braking figures achieved were superb. With only about 60lb pedal load, the car pulled up four-square without locked wheels and with the manometer reading well over 1.0g. The handbrake, a sturdy pull-up lever between the seats, was also powerful, holding the car easily facing either way on the 1-in-3 test hill, just managing to lock the rear wheels and being good for 0.42g as an emergency brake. Front disc and rear drums are all self-adjusting so the only servicing checks are to replace pads and linings at infrequent intervals.

GT Trimmings

Inside the car, the trim and furnishings are exactly the same as the Escort GT; in fact Twin-Cams start life as GT bodies before being plucked off the assembly lines for final assembly in Halewood's special little Twin-Cam shop, where they are now in volume production. The only really significant body modification is to flare the wheel arches slightly to give more clearance. On our test car (an early Boreham-built production car) the extra flaring was rather crude, and the front wheels still contacted bodywork on lock and bump.

The instrument panel and seats are the same as in the Escort GT, a battery condition meter being a significant newcomer. Only the standard plastic Escort steering wheel is fitted; though nicely small at 14¾in. dia it still looked out of place on a £1,170 sports saloon. Snap checks of the rev counter showed it to be almost exactly accurate, while the speedometer was consistently under-reading right through. The oil pressure gauge—very important in this application—is completely obscured by the steering wheel rim, and there is no low-pressure warning light.

The Escort is a small car despite the advertisements and seat adjustment is none too generous. All our drivers put the seat right back, and then complained about the angle of the back rest. The seat itself is comfortable enough, but should have adjustable backrests.

Control switches all work on the rocker principle and look nice and safe in case of accidents. With the seat belts tugged up good and tight, it was not easy even for a tall driver to reach the lighting and wiper switches without a

stretch. The washer control is conveniently on the floor in the "dipswitch" position, and dipping is incorporated in the multi-action steering column stalk which also works the indicators and sounds the unworthy horn. Heel-and-side-of-foot pedal operation is easy.

The ventilation system took some learning, especially as the facia vents can be twisted to face windscreen, occupants, or the side windows across the car. The through-flow was efficient and a steamed-up rear window cleared very quickly; there was a good supply of hot air when needed.

Under the bonnet, the twin-ohc Lotus engine and the big air-cleaner really fill the available space, so that servicing and checking need some patience. The distributor, as always on this engine, is masked by the big Weber carburettors, and the oil filler cap (a type that is prone to work loose) is rather hidden behind the air cleaner tube. An oil cooler is standard, mounted to the right of, and parallel with, the water radiator in the nose. The dipstick is now at the back of the engine and clearly marked.

The battery has had to be moved into the boot because of the bulky twin-ohc engine, but it lives in the left-side rear wing recess and has a protective cover; it would, of course, have to be moved yet again if the optional extra fuel tank were added. It has also displaced the spare wheel which is now bolted direct to the boot floor, making what was a roomy boot rather an uneven shape; the wheel is not covered to protect luggage, but one would hardly class the Twin-Cam as a potential holiday tourer. There is no tool kit as such, only jack and wheelbrace, plus a wheelnut spanner.

Viewed as a potential competition car, the Twin-Cam Escort is well-conceived. As a regular road car it lacks refinement in certain respects but has nothing to be ashamed of. It will probably work wonders for Ford's already excellent performance campaign, and we will respect it all the more for that. As a new model that brings back just a little of that ever-so-elusive fun into driving, we can award it top marks.

The chromium plated wheels are extra and as on the 1600E need regular care to avoid deterioration

Escort escorts Escort

Clark wins Tulip Rally
by five seconds from Andersson

by Hamish Cardno: pictures by Paul Skilleter

Eventual winner Roger Clark with Jim Porter hurtles round a corner on Mont Clergeon in the Escort Twin-Cam.

Ove Andersson clips the verge on Mont Clergeon on the way to taking second place in the Twin-Cam Escort.

FORD again, Clark again—for the second time in just over a week. Fresh from his outright win in the Circuit of Ireland over Easter, Roger Clark romped to victory in last week's Tulip Rally in a Twin-Cam Escort, and finished five seconds ahead of team-mate Ove Andersson in the other works Escort after four days of fast but uninspiring rallying. And in notching up this sensational debut for a competition car, the Boreham team have scotched one of the main criticisms of international rallying—that there is too much service—for Clark's car proved utterly reliable, and in 3,500 km. of rallying the only parts replaced were brakes and tyres.

In third place—and first in the Group 2 category—came Julien Vernaeve and Mike Wood in a works Mini Cooper S, followed by local hero and Tulip veteran Rob Slotemaker in a BMW 2002.

But it is doubtful if works teams will compete in next year's Tulip Rally, which in turn throws doubt on whether the rally will be held. Sponsorship problems were rife this year, and with a complete withdrawal of works entries it seems unlikely that many firms will put up money for next year's event.

Start

A month before the start of the 20th Tulpen-rallye few people were sure if it would take place. But the Dutch RAC West found sufficient firms to provide the money, and three weeks before the start the regulations appeared, along with rumours of works teams from Porsche and Lancia; Ford and BMC had already committed themselves for the event. When the cars—a mere 75—assembled at Noordwijk for scrutineering on Sunday, however, there were no works Porsches and no Lancias. Contesting the Group 3 classification were the works Escorts of Roger Clark/Jim Porter, Ove Andersson/John Davenport, with Belgian Gilbert Staepelaere/Andre Aerts making up the team; Alpine Renaults for Gerard Larrousse/Marcel Callewaert, Jean-Claude Andruet/Jean Escudier, Freddy Krause/Michel Godichard; two Datsun Fairladys driven by Finns Hannu Mikkola/Anssi Jarvi and Jorma Lusenius/Klaus Letho; and the private entrants including Norman Harvey/Hywel Thomas (Porsche 911S), Jack Tordoff/Donald Griffiths (Porsche 911T), and Brian Petch/Harold Miller (Austin-Healey 3000).

Running in the combined Group 1 and Group 2 class were works Minis for Timo Makinen/Paul Easter, Julien Vernaeve/Mike Wood, with privateers David Friswell/Mike Merrick making up the team; Rob Slotemaker/Rob Janssen in a BMW 2002 with Harry Bierman/

Sid Brandsma (BMW 2000TI) and Ad Haans/Marcel Verbunt (BMW 1600TI) making up their team; and works entries of one Daf 55 and two 44s; Trabants from East Germany and Wartburgs.

Private entries were down on previous years—partly because of the lateness of the regulations, partly because of an entry fee which had been increased to £70, and partly, for British competitors, because of the proximity of the Circuit of Ireland. Among the more unlikely entries which did set off, however, were a Shelby Mustang GT350, a Steyr Puch and a Honda N360.

Noordwijk-Annecy

One of the problems of being a Dutch club running an International rally is that there is practically nowhere in Holland to run the event. For this reason the Tulip—like other Internationals—heads for the French Alps, via routes through Holland and Belgium, special stages with target times and two flat-out eliminating tests. This section took 24 hours bringing the competitors to Annecy on a beautiful sunny morning, but with their numbers depleted by 10—including the Harvey/Thomas Porsche, Ford's number three Escort, Krause's Alpine, a Matra, an Alfa, two BMWs, and British private entrants

Action scene at the Flumet time control during the Alpine loop. Car on the right is the Vernaeve/Wood Mini which came third.

Unusual angle adopted by Makinen's Mini is due to a punctured rear tyre—but he didn't have time to stop.

Some friendly advice for Roger Clark at the start from Ford competitions manager Henry Taylor.

Miss Jean Crossley/Mrs. Margaret Lowrey (MG 1100), who had a front wheel bearing go very early on.

Already an air of dissatisfaction was building up, particularly among the works entries who disliked a rather "club rally" aspect of the timing, where there were tight road sections between stages, no waiting was allowed at time controls and so competitors had to accept the time given them by the marshal—even if this made the next tight road section ridiculously tight. Works people much prefer to have the deciding done on special stages where there is no other traffic and not have a situation where one control is reached and the car given a time of, say, 1.53, when the clock reads 1.53.59, then reach the next time control at 2.10.1 (2.11)—meaning that on a 17 minute section they have taken, on paper, 19 minutes, yet lost marks for the two minutes over.

All three Minis had problems. The two works cars were down on power, and at a service point before they reached Annecy the timing was advanced on both cars. Friswell's car had been rebuilt in 24 hours after going out of the Circuit of Ireland with clutch trouble, and on this event was having overheating and gearbox snags. The only Imp in the rally, an ex-Rosemary Smith car being

run in Group 3 by Dennis Greenslade/Frank Bilk, arrived at the Annecy parc ferme with a useless alternator. It retired that night.

At Annecy the Rally stopped for 10 hours for the competitors to get some well-earned (and needed) sleep before starting off on the Alpine loop in the evening. The overall position at Annecy was—**Group 3: 1** J-C. Andruet/J. Escudier (Alpine), 300; **2** R. Clark/J. Porter (Ford Escort), 305; **3** Ove Andersson/J. Davenport (Ford Escort), 312. **Groups 1 and 2: 1** T. Makinen/P. Easter (BMC Mini), 313; **2** H. Greder/E. Stalpaert (Opel Rallye Kadett), 376; **3** R. Slotemaker/R. Janssen (BMW 2002), 403.

Annecy-Noordwijk

One of the major bones of contention during this enforced halt was that the results given above were not known—they only became available when the Rally returned to Holland. Team managers and competitors nursed their nerves in hotels and slept the sleep of the innocent—or the uninformed—knowing only that their cars had completed the route so far, but not knowing how they were faring in the classification beyond what they knew of their own times, and what others had said they had done—those that said anything.

The Tulip's Alpine loop is more than 400 km

of special stages which takes the cars in the space of seven hours from the lakeside resort over some of the most tortuous roads in the shadow of Mont Blanc to Rumilly, a small town on the west side of the hills. This section always seems to contain some surprise element—last year it was ice in the tunnel on the Col des Aravis, which drastically restyled some of the entry, this year it was a rough section on the nearby Col de la Croix-Fry. Only a few yards of this stretch of road had been poorly surfaced last year, but traffic associated with the Winter Olympics had taken its toll, and the surface was more reminiscent of that on a forestry stage than an Alpine one. Several cars had "moments" there, some appeared at Rumilly with slight body damage and others complained of tyres being torn open.

After a rest halt at Rumilly, the Rally set off on what was probably the tightest test in the area—over Mont Clergeon, a hill-climb and descent of a road which even on the map looks like a cross-section of a tin of spaghetti. In fact it was worse, because the local authority had decided to do some road mending the previous day, and there were little patches of tar with loose gravel chippings on top, the whole way over the mountain.

Continued on the next page

End of the road. This is where the Sheffield and Hallamshire Club's hopes for the team prize finished, when the Wilson/Pryor Mini went grape tramping.

Above: Suspension well down on the Mikkola/Jarvi Datsun Fairlady which finished fourth overall.

Right: Local hero Rob Slotemaker cornering hard in the BMW 2002. He was fifth overall.

Far right: Alpine in home country. This is the Larrousse/Callewaert car on Mont Clergeon.

Escort escorts Escort

The first few cars naturally removed the chippings from the tar, and from then on it was even more hairy. Makinen lost time here when a tyre punctured 6 km. from the start of the 18 km. test—he carried on, ruined a wheel and lost 44 points. Another victim here was the Tom Wilson/Ken Pryor Mini, which went off in a big way on one gravel-strewn corner and finished up most of the way down a vineyard (leaving a clear path through the vines to show its route). The combination of the position of the car, damage to the body shell and a twisted rear sub-frame put the Mini out of the Rally—a double tragedy in that it robbed the Sheffield and Hallamshire MC, whose team it was in, of a chance of the Club team prize; it could have been their fourth in a row.

It just wasn't the Mini's morning, for on Ballon d'Alsace, the last stage before the lunch halt, the Friswell Mini, which had previously got over its gearbox and over-heating problems, had a front wheel bearing go, and it was out.

By lunchtime, at St. Maurice-sur-Moselle, Anduet's Alpine had dropped out, the similar Larrousse car had dropped 56 points, so that Clark led the Group 3 classification, with Andersson seven points behind. Makinen was leading Groups 1 and 2 with 357 points lost, Slotemaker was behind him with 439, and Vernaeve third with 473.

The positions were not to stay like this for long—not in the Groups 1 and 2 combine. On the 12th special stage, the Col du Brabant, Makinen went straight through a hedge. The Mini landed on soft ground and was un-damaged but, as Paul Easter put it: "We had to wait until sufficient Frenchmen had gathered to carry it out". This took some time, and instead of doing the 7.2 km. stage in 6 minutes 10 seconds, the car took 1 hour, 9 minutes, 4 seconds—and lost 3,816 points. The most incredible thing about the incident is that Timo carried on from the end of the stage to reach the next time control 100 km. away inside the maximum permitted 30 minutes lateness—and the average necessary if you *didn't* go off the road was 55 k.p.h.

Weather conditions had deteriorated sharply by this point, and the Rally wound its way back through Belgium into Holland to be greeted early on Thursday morning by a real pea-soup fog. By this time the battle was between Slotemaker and Vernaeve for Groups 1 and 2 (Makinen's excursion had put him right out of the running), with Larrousse trying to catch Clark and Andersson in the Escorts.

One last eliminating test remained—on military testing ground near Leusden—and here Larrousse in the incredibly noisy Alpine failed to catch the Escorts. One who did, however was Timo Makinen—it didn't make any difference to the results, but he went round eight seconds quicker than Clark.

And so the cars made their way back to the Huis ter Duin Hotel at Noordwijk for the traditional bouquet of tulips (of course), and two nights' sleep to catch up on. When the

provisional results were announced, Clark had won by five seconds from Andersson, Lusenius in the Datsun had overtaken Larrousse to take third place in Group 3, the Alpine was in fourth place, the other Datsun fifth, and British clubman Jack Tordoff brought his Porsche in to sixth place.

Provisionally Slotemaker was listed as leader of the Groups 1 and 2 class, with Vernaeve second and the Alfa Romeo GTA of N. Koob/A. Kridel third. The BMC team successfully protested about being given a wrong minute, however, and this put them head of the group with the local hero relegated to second place.

But it was a comparatively easy win for Ford—Roger Clark's car only had brake pads and tyres changed, Andersson's had the crown wheel and pinion changed when it made noises although it had by no means started to give trouble—and it would be wrong to think that the Escorts are *bound* to clean up every event this year. They can still be caught. . . .

Provisional results

Overall: 1 R. Clark/J. Porter (Ford Escort Twin-Cam), 663.5 points lost: **2** O. Andersson/J. Davenport (Ford Escort Twin-Cam), 668.6; **3** J. Vernaeve/M. Wood (BMC Mini-Cooper S), 790; **4** J. Lusenius/K. Letho (Datsun Fairlady), 809.7; **5** R. Slotemaker/R. Janssen (BMW 2002), 525.2; **6** N. Koob/A. Kridel (Alfa Romeo GTA), 893.3. **Group 3: 1** Clark/Porter; **2** Andersson/Davenport; **3** Lusenius/Letho; **4** G. Larrousse/M. Caellewaert (Renault Alpine), 1,070.6; **5** H. Mikkola/A. Jarvi (Datsun Fairlady), 1,192.9; **6** J. Tordoff/D. Griffiths (Porsche 911T), 1,536.9. **Groups 1 and 2: 1** Vernaeve/Wood; **2** Slotemaker/Janssen; **3** Koob/Kridel; **4** A. Sigurdson/I. Strom (Saab V-4), 957.5; **5** G. Kolwes/H. Heine (Volvo 122S), 1,139.7; **6** Mlle. M. C. Beaumont/Mlle. C. Beckers (NSU TT1200), 1,178.0. **Private Owners' Trophy:** Koob/Kridel. **Ladies' Prize:** Mlle. Beaumont/Mlle. Beckers.

ESCORT
GAMMON 1600 G.T.
YOU CAN GET IT RIGHT NOW !

WELL, if you can't buy a Twin Cam for love nor money, there's an alternative—Gammon Racing's 1600 GT Escort based on the 1300 GT. At the time of our test the price was £875; it still is, but this is now the starting price and does not include lowered suspension; if you want this done it will cost an extra £15. You can thank happy 'Arold and his laughing axemen for this extra charge, as you can for all the other tortures applied to motorists since 1964. Before that you can cuss the other lot!

The conversion is usually fitted to a new car supplied by Gammon but if you want an existing motor "Gammonised" he'll be delighted to oblige. When we wrote this the cost of a big-engine job was £111.

As you probably gathered from our articles on swopping Cortina engines into Escorts, things aren't so simple as they look, mainly because of the Escort's rack and pinion steering, which means that the sump has to be reshaped. Another point to remember is that you must fit a flexible dip stick—the one on "ours" was nigh on impossible to replace. Peter Gammon assures us that this will not be present on later versions.

One of our optional extras was a lightened flywheel. Although this makes the car more responsive to virile feet, (how many have you got?) we weren't very taken with it as it makes the idling a series of hunting jerks. Once on the move this little problem is lost. Motoring gently, there's an impressive amount of urge in 4th gear, even with a cam, which on "our" car was designed to "come" in at 4000 RPM. Another optional extra (£10 fitted as part of the big-engine job, or £8 on its Todd), this cam goes under the name Sprint. With a Sprint fitted, total power output is claimed to be 102 (gross) at 5800 RPM. "Our" car also had the standard 1300 GT axle ratio installed (3.7) which means that you're flat out at 98 MPH.. As Mr Gammon had told us to observe the normal rev limit we therefore recorded a two-way top wizz of 98 MPH. The car gets to this speed pretty quickly, too.

Even with the low slung suspension we had handling problems if the car was exposed to a crosswind at anything over 80. You need a bit of elbow room at these speeds on a track, or at a true 70 on public roads. If it's any compensation we can tell you that the standard 1300 GT has this problem too.

A 1600 GT Escort can be made to go a lot faster than the ton by fitting a numerically lower axle ratio, which the car can easily pull. It would also give you a more relaxed cruising speed without sacrificing much of the acceleration.

While mumbling on about performance may we mention that "our" car had only covered 1400 miles and that by special request we restrained ourselves from using anything over 4500 RPM before letting the clutch in. In spite of this, the Gammon machine did 0-70 in 14.2 secs.

It's this instant "go", combined with the compact dimensions, that make the car such fun in traffic, together with the dirty looks you get from S type Cooper owners! In case you're interested, you get the same look from the same people when minding thy business in a 1650 Anglia, as we found out when we tried one recently.

To be honest (don halo and beam) we didn't find any perceptible difference in the roadholding with lowered suspension. The angle of roll on sharp roundabouts was slightly longer in turning up but it always did show up. (As you can see if our art dept have used that pic of it taking a sharp bend!) As on all the GT and other Escorts the brakes deserve a special mention for being so powerful and so light to use, without locking up. On wet surfaces the brakes will lock with clumsy use but we still think that this disc on front, drums at back combination is among the best in its class. It's significant that the anchors are not tweaked on Gammon's car—and they never let us down. Fuel economy was good at 26 MPG overall, which included some hard thrashes at over 90 and performance testing.

For those of you who think you've heard the name Peter Gammon before but can't place it, we will fill you in. Mr Gammon Esq., was a sports car driver in the early fifties with an MG-Lotus hybrid (among others); he did very well in this 'un, defeating many bigger cars and running in close company with Colin Chapman's similar streamlined motor. In the late fifties Peter became one of the first to exploit the potential of the 1100 c.c. Lola sports racer—in fact he bought the prototype. In 1959 he collected 14 wins and 4 track records with the Lola-Climax before he was forced to retire by the heavier demands of his drapery business.

So if you see an Escort with a 1600 GT label on its behind, think very carefully before doing anything rash!

Peter Gammon's address is: Eagle Caravan and Boats Ltd., Woodbridge Road, By Pass, Guildford, Surrey. It's worth dropping him a line if you have any Escort or Anglia queries, 'cos he stocks many Good Things for 'em.

ACCELERATION	
MPH	Secs.
0-30	4.0
0-40	6.0
0-50	8.0
0-60	10.1
0-70	14.2

I knew you'd forget a spanner.

ESCORT BROADSPEED

FITZ stuffs the three-wheeling 1300GT through Copse during the group 5 thrash at Silverstone. On the 12th lap he was leading the class by 9 secs; during the last lap the diff melted and Rhodes got by. Mike Walker came third, using Broad's BG3 clubman's motor giving 130 b.h.p. You could make an Escort to the same specification for about £1,200.

Broad's Angle-Box won at Thruxton against those invincible Abarths and at Silverstone Craft walked it, winning the class by 36 secs.

The Group 5 1300 GT motor contains forged steel crank and pistons, whirring round in company with Hepolite slipper pistons and Vandervell VP 3. Urge churns through a Hewland 5 speed box, a limited slip and 8½-in. Minilites. (They use 8-in. width up front.) Lots of urge gets to the tarmac—ask Rhodes.

Top: Look at all those suckers! Engine of the Group 5 145+ BHP Escort. Downdraught head (12.1 CR) and T/J fuel injection help out on the urge scene. Right: Fitz looks pleased after a Castle Combe sorting session.

ESCORT

ALLARD BLOWN 1300 G.T.

FANFARE! We are proud to present the saga of an Escort 1300 GT with a £60 tuning kit that does the 0–60 bit in 9·2 secs! Cold figures don't mean a lot, so if we tell you that this 'un tramps up from nought to 80 in 17·2 secs, which is as long as the old 997 Cooper takes to churn up to 60, you'll begin to understand why we liked it. But you'll only begin to comprehend because unlike every other small motor machine that we've tried, this one has FLEXIBILITY. Oodles of it in fact. We just couldn't get over the fact that for £60 you've got what feels like 2·5 litres under the hatch—and 2·5 litres in an Escort means low-down go. On crowded British roads it is quicker to overtake in fourth slot than it is in most other car's second or third. Of course if you want to grind people into the ground, then thrust it into third and grind 'em.

If you are a Drag-racing addict the standing quarter-mile times may interest you more than the above. This Escort GT has covered the quarter at Santa Pod in 17·2 secs. If you are wicked, and sneak over the red line momentarily this can be reduced to 16·2 secs. According to a contemporary mag, this is two-tenths of a second slower than the Elan Plus 2.

The Escort Allard lent us had the following equipment:— Shorrock C.75B blower (£60); suspension lowered by 1½ in. all round (£6 5s.); anti-tramp bars (£7 17s.) (very important, more on that later); Aeon bump rubbers (£9); five-eighth wheel spacers all round (neat way of getting round the Escort's wide wheel problem) which cost £6 10s.; small splash shields on the wheel arches at the front only, 17s. 6d. Finally, to decorate the job, there was a matt-black grille and sidewinders.

The suspension on the test car was a bit too harsh for road use but excellent for the circuit, where we found that there was very little roll. The tramp bars play an important part in the acceleration figures, keeping the back wheels from playing silly B——s. We are convinced that they help out on tight hairpins as well, because the inside back wheel stays down on the deck transmitting urge. We had a lot of fun hurling this car through hilly hairpin terrain. There's enough torque to save the bother of changing cogs all the time, and the same torque helps shove the tail out whenever you're feeling brave. Driven like this (on a private test track) the SP41s squeal like hell but stay remarkably cool. Having established that the handling is A Good Point, we now move on to roadholding. This is improved over the standard Escort GT, and in the dry is surprisingly high. However, in the wet one has to keep a very sharp 'feel' of what the tail end is up to. That low-down punch that is so welcome for overtaking can easily turn into an embarrassment, dumping thee through the hedge smartly. We suggest getting to know the beast on some non-public damp road so that you get the feel of it. In the dry, the breakaway point (tail first) is at a higher speed than most people are likely to travel at and when the break comes, it is quite gradual. The bump stop rubbers played their part when we went down to Lydden for the Rallycross final; with the equivalent of three adults on board the suspenders didn't bottom at all on the rough entry track.

On our test car there was one snag that seemed to us very serious but shouldn't bother others: the car wouldn't run over 98 true miles an hour in top gear, and this speed was accompanied by small bangs. All very exciting, but we could do without it, and so can you if you have either/or both of the two mods that we didn't have. First a low compression head, or special low comp pistons. Second, a large bore exhaust system all the way through, to carry away all that gas. The latter would be the cheaper method (about £15) and we hope Allards can let us have the car back with a large bore system fitted so that we can see that problem coped with. This pre-detonation problem hampers the cruising speed too, as the vibration gets too much beyond 85. The point about this is that Allard lent us a car with just the kit fitted, so that it was running on the standard 9·1 C.R. plus the blower! We strongly recommend that you go into this before buying.

If you are still trying to work out what it all costs here are the details:—parts on our car totalled £92 9s. 6d. Labour is free if you buy a car fitted with these bits but if you are adding them to an existing one, labour charges come to £21. With just the blower installed on to a brand spankers 1300 GT charges start at 865 quid; a 1600 GT engine job starts another 30 quid up the scale under the name Escortina.

We didn't use much oil during our test but we did get through an average 22·5 m.p.g. on a run down to Lydden and back. Mr. Allard reckons that with normal driving the car should return 26 m.p.g. As with all blown engines, it is advisable to use five star go juice.

Starting from cold in summer-type weather was very simple; hardly use any choke, just press the urge pedal and turn the key.

Allard does blower kits and loads of other gear for all popular models from The Performance Centre, 51 Upper Richmond Road, Putney, London S.W.15.

The big bit that looks like a second engine is in fact the blower.

PERFORMANCE

m.p.h.	secs.
0–30	3·0
0–40	4·8
0–50	6·8
0–60	9·2
0–70	12·2
0–80	17·2
0–90	24·2

Top speed 98 m.p.h.; solve the compression problem and there's more safe revs to come in top.
Overall m.p.g. 22·5
Price as tested £897 9s. 6d.

Preview Test: Ford Twin Cam Escort

Ford of England's slick little Q-ship might become the biggest thing in underground cars since the Mini Cooper S.

Gone is the Ford Lotus Cortina, a victim of cruel business practicality. Precisely, the men who make such decisions concluded that the cost of redesigning and testing such a limited-appeal car to meet current U.S. safety and smog regulations was just too far out of sight. But friendly old Ford of England just might have some help on the way for that vociferous band of enthusiasts who loved the little Q-ship. The recently introduced Ford Escort (FYI, April) shows signs of becoming the biggest thing in underground cars since the advent of the Mini Cooper S.

The Escort range begins with a modest little 1100cc version intended strictly for the home market, includes a pair of 1300cc models—which are slated to become mainstays of the export range—and, currently, ends with a 1600cc Twin Cam (the same engine that was in the beloved Lotus Cortina). But, lurking just a little below the horizon, there is a real-racer model which could shake up things in the under-two-liter division of the Trans-Am series. The latter is to be equipped with the 16-valve, 4-cylinder Ford FVA engine which has been almost invincible on the Formula Two circuits and speculation is that Keith Duckworth, who designed the engine as well as the Formula One Cosworth-Ford, will be called in to help

Car Craft (Ford's own race preparation shop), prepare a couple of cars for next year's Trans-Am.

While information like this is enough to get small-bore racing enthusiasts reaching for their wallets, the comparatively mundane Twin Cam version has been making a name for itself by recording several impressive finishes in the rugged European Touring Car Championship events (including firsts in the Tulip Rally and Scottish Rally). But perhaps an even more significant cachet in the eyes of those practical, salesmen-types who gave the axe to the Lotus Cortina is the auspicious list of hero-drivers (Dan Gurney, John Surtees, Jackie Ickx) who have bought Escort Twin Cams and whose implied stamp of approval ensures acceptance by the general public—not necessarily as a racer but as a road car that offers performance plus prestige.

And, after an unusual press introduction in Morocco, we can say that a standard Twin Cam Escort would make a pretty nice road car—when and if Ford will sell you one. (Actually it would not be very difficult to make it comply with both safety and smog regulations, and the Escort's enthusiastic reception in Europe just might be enough to make those guys with the green eye shades and armgarters loosen up on the purse strings.)

Outwardly, except for the matte black grille, the sporty wheels and the quarte bumpers, the Twin Cam looks very much like any other Escort. Mechanically— and that includes engine, gearbox, rea axle and brakes—it is a Lotus Cortin but it's over 200 lbs. lighter and, conse quently, it goes a whole bunch better Ford claims a maximum speed of 11 mph, but we think it would actually d more than this without the distributor cu out. We had an opportunity to find out i Morocco, where there was a straight 2 miles long, but the damn distributor cu out was set at 6000 rpm (107 mph) an we did just that for 24 miles. Howeve even 107 mph (an indicated 110) is fair quick for a small family sedan, and woul be positively dangerous if the tires, brake and suspension were not suitable for eve higher velocities.

The tires, brakes and suspension of th Twin Cam Escort were developed wi competition in mind, and thus have plent in reserve. The car sits firmly on the roa at all times, takes most corners in a ve neutral attitude (although it is possible get increasingly out of shape on a seri of ess-bends), and maintains a straigl course even on capriciously cambere roads with primitive surfaces. It also a celerates very strongly, even at the upp end of the speed range.

All right, you say, what are the snag The ride? Noise? Inflexibility in tow Well, the ride is only a little firmer tha in the push-rod version, and with a thi front roll bar and radius arms at the re (neither of which are used on the tam cars) there is much less roll on corne There is a little more noise, mainly fro the suspension and tires, but there's ve little mechanical noise—not even the cha acteristic Lotus timing chain whine. for flexibility, it is possible to start off second and do almost everything else top, should that whim overtake you.

The interior of the Twin Cam is iden cal with that of the 1300 GT (the test c even had a GT badge in the center of steering column), which means that t minor instruments are poorly calibrat and difficult to read at a glance—in fa you have to take your hand off the ste ing wheel in order to see them proper The gearbox is as in the Lotus Corti and Cortina GT—and therefore there's very little complaint. The rack and pinion steering feels slightly heavier than in the pushrod Escort—due to the wider wheels and tires and the anti-roll bar—but is still light enough for the most delicate female wrist.

At the press introduction we were lucky enough to get hold of the one-and-only Twin Cam for the longest stage of the Moroccan escapade—the 330 miles from Marrakesh to Meknes—and with a few off the route excursions we managed to cover 350 miles in just over five hours at something in the region of 17 mpg.

The important thing to remember when driving in Morocco is *priorité à droite*. Even if you are doing 100 mph along the main road to Casablanca, a donkey coming out of a field gate has right of way. We even encountered a disoriented donkey who thought he had the right of way when coming from the left—at full gallop. Unfortunately for the Moroccan donkeyburger industry we missed it.

Apart from donkeys, camels and cyclists—all unlit at night—the only real hazard is the King of Morocco and the police patrols which precede the royal fleet of Mercedes 600s, forcing all oncoming traffic off the road (the police don't bother to escort the numerous Checker Aero Buses in which the King's wives travel).

Eventually we got into the foothills of the Ablas Mountains, where we discovered that second was too low to be of much use, particularly with a redline limit of 6000 instead of the normal 6500. However, despite repeated hard use, we failed to reveal any weakness in the braking system. We also failed to discover any serious flaws in the suspension, although we did get the rear hopping sideways once or twice—not an altogether forgotten sensation for old Lotus Cortina drivers. Not even full-throttle standing starts would promote axle tramp.

Our sojourn in Morocco gave us ample opportunity to evaluate the Twin Cam over a variety of surfaces and an even wider variety of traffic conditions. And, we found the Lotus Cortina's little brother is a much better car than its predecessor—just ask Dan, or John, or Jackie.

—H. H. Hathaway and David Phipps

FORD TWIN CAM ESCORT

VEHICLE TYPE
Front-engine, rear-wheel-drive, 4-passenger sedan

ENGINE
Type: Water-cooled, four-in-line, cast iron block, alloy head
Bore x stroke . 3.25 x 2.87 in, 82.6 x 72.8 mm
Displacement . . . . 95.2 cu. in., 1558 cc
Compression ratio . . . . 9.5 to one
Carburetion . . . . . . 2 x 2-bbl Weber 40 DCOE
Valve gear . . . Chain-driven double overhead camshafts
Power . . . . 115 bhp @ 6000 rpm
Torque . . . . 106 lbs/ft @ 4500 rpm
Max. recommended engine speed . 6500 rpm

DRIVE TRAIN
Transmission . . . . Four-speed, all-synchro
Final drive ratio . . . . 3.77 to one

SUSPENSION
F . . . . Ind., McPherson strut type
R . Rigid axle semi-elliptic springs, trailing links and Panhard rod

BRAKES
F . . . . 9.6 in solid disc
R . . . . 9.0 in solid disc
Swept area . . . . 285.6 sq in

WHEELS AND TIRES
Wheel size and type . . . . 13 x 5½-in
Tire make, size and type . . . Goodyear G800, 165 x 13

STEERING
Type . . . . Rack and pinion
Turns lock-to-lock 3.5
Turning circle . . . . 30 ft

DIMENSIONS AND CAPACITIES
Wheelbase . . . . 94.5 in
Track . . . . F: 51.0 in, R: 52.0 in
Length . . . . 156.6 in
Width . . . . 61.8 in
Height . . . . 54.5 in
Curb weight . . . . 1730 lbs
Weight distribution 54/46%
Fuel capacity . . . . 10.8 gal
Oil capacity . . . . 3.9 qts
Water capacity . . . . 5.4 qts

PERFORMANCE*
Zero to	Seconds
40 mph	4.9
60 mph	9.0
80 mph	15.4

*Performance figures for cars sold in the United States may vary due to installation of mandatory anti-smog equipment.

CHECK LIST

ENGINE
Starting . . . . Very Good
Response . . . . Very Good
Noise . . . . Good
Service accessibility . . . . Fair

DRIVE TRAIN
Shift linkage . . . . Very Good
Synchro action . . . . Very Good

STEERING
Effort . . . . Good
Response . . . . Very Good

SUSPENSION
Ride comfort . . . . Good
Roll resistance . . . . Very Good
Cornering ability . . . . Very Good
Predictability . . . . Very Good

BRAKES
Fade resistance . . . . Very Good
Directional stability . . . . Good

INTERIOR
Ease of entry/exit . . . . Good
Front seating comfort . . . . Good
Rear seating comfort . . . . Fair
Driver controls . . . . Very Good
Instrument comprehensiveness . . Very Good
Instrument legibility . . . . Poor
Heater/defroster . . . . Very Good
Ventilation . . . . Very Good

CONVENIENCE AND PROTECTION
Trunk space . . . . Good
Interior storage space . . . . Good
Bumper protection . . . . Fair
Visibility . . . . Good
Wiper effectiveness . . . . Good

CONSTRUCTION QUALITY
Sheet metal . . . . Very Good
Paint . . . . Good
Upholstery . . . . Good

PHOTOGRAPHY: DAVID PHIPPS

Brief test ● Ford Escort GT

MOTOR TESTED

A gem for £833

Family fun car par excellence; outstanding performance, handling and controls; fair economy; transmission changes improve mechanical refinement; quite comfortable despite hard ride.

IN our Rolls-Royce Silver Shadow report two weeks ago, we suggested that small specialist manufacturers must find it increasingly difficult to match the standards set by wealthy giants who can spend millions on the research and development of relatively mundane cars. There's a strong case for extending this theme still further. Cast aside for a moment the sort of whims—perhaps quite expensive ones—that can make buying a new car such an enthralling, even exciting, exercise. Consider instead that unless you *need* exceptional space or performance (a large estate or a "Continental express," perhaps) there is really little need to spend more than £850 to get a fast, civilised and comfortable four seater. Were we all condemned to purchase compact, small capacity cars, the sentence on people accustomed to bigger things would be a lot less severe than they might think. The Ford Escort GT, for instance, is so good in so many ways that, overall, we rate it more than a match for a great many more expensive machines. In other words, price is becoming an increasingly poor guide to merit—as, indeed, engine capacity, body size and brochure specification have long since been.

It is the appealing combination of a smooth, lively engine with an outstanding gearbox and near impeccable handling that make the Escort GT something of a gem if you enjoy driving. The GT engine differs from other 81-bore Fords of the same capacity in having a higher (9.2:1) compression, larger valves, a high-lift

camshaft, a Weber carburetter and a four-branch fabricated exhaust—the only external clue to its factory tune-up. Power and torque are both considerably increased (to 75 b.h.p. and 91 lb. ft.) without in any way impairing mechanical refinement.

In "go" through the gears, this efficient 1300 will comfortably out-perform many 2-litre saloons such as the Volvo 144 featured in this week's other test, a Ford Corsair, Rover, Triumph and Vauxhall 2000—none of which have a sluggardly reputation. The 0-50 time of 8.8 seconds puts the GT on a par with a BMW 1800, Mercedes 230SL and fuel injected Peugeot 404.

Although there is no lack of low-rev pull (witness the 20-40 m.p.h. top gear time of 10.6 seconds) a booming judder deters the use of top gear below about 23 m.p.h. At the other end of the scale at the red-lined 6,500 r.p.m. limit, the muffled wail of the engine is on the verge of becoming hysterical but then there is a useful surge of smooth torque throughout the rev range in between, so sky-high revs are not necessary for fast driving. In contrast to one of the earlier Escort GTs we tried (see Group Test No. 1, *Motor*, May 18, 1968) neither the engine nor transmission feels at all harsh or rough at high speeds. This dramatic improvement stems directly from the introduction of a divided prop shaft (phased quietly into production some months ago on all Escorts above the 1100) which, through shorter, more rigid revolving masses, more effectively camouflages any out-of-balance forces. (We shall probably see more twin prop-shaft installations on other marques and models, incidentally, for the same smoother-running reasons.) In the earlier car, 80 m.p.h. cruising was harsh and strained; in the latest one, it's just a smooth relaxed hum, still well within the all-out maximum of

Price: £652 plus £181 purchase tax equals £833.
Insurance: AOA group rating 4; Lloyds 4.

Performance

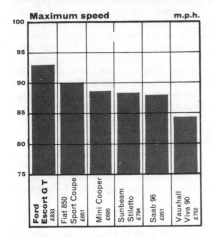

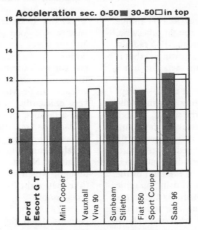

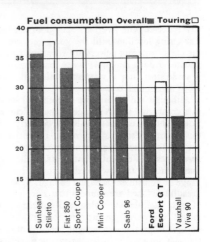

Performance tests carried out by *Motor's* **staff at the Motor Industry Research Association proving ground, Lindley.**
Test Data: World copyright reserved; no unauthorised reproduction in whole or in part.

Conditions

Weather: Good—calm and cool, wind 0-8 m.p.h.
Temperature: 40-41°F.
Barometer: 29.55 in. Hg.
Surface: Dry asphalt and concrete.
Fuel: 98 octane (RM) 4 star rating.

Maximum speeds

	m.p.h.	k.p.h.
Mean lap banked circuit	93.4	150.5
Best one-way ¼-mile	95.8	154.3
3rd gear	70	113
2nd gear	50	80
1st gear	30	48

"Maximile" speed: (Timed quarter-mile after 1 mile accelerating from rest)
Mean 91.9
Best 92.8

Acceleration times

m.p.h.	sec.
0-30	4.0
0-40	6.2
0-50	8.8
0-60	12.5
0-70	17.4
0-80	25.9
0-90	41.2
Standing quarter-mile	18.9

m.p.h.	Top sec.	3rd sec.
10-30	—	7.2
20-40	10.6	6.6
30-50	10.1	6.5
40-60	10.2	6.8
50-70	11.6	8.5
60-80	14.2	
70-90	24.0	

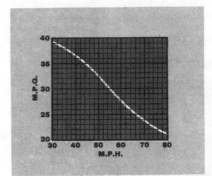

Fuel consumption

Touring (consumption midway between 30 m.p.h. and maximum less 5% allowance for acceleration) 31.8 m.p.g.
Overall . . . . 25.3 m.p.g.
(= 11.15 litres/100 km.)
Total test distance . . . . 1,180 miles

Speedometer

Indicated	20	30	40	50	60	70	80	90
True	19	28	37	46	55½	65	75	85

Distance recorder . . . . 6% fast

Weight

Kerb weight (unladen with fuel for approximately 50 miles) . . . . 15.5 cwt.
Front/rear distribution 53.5/46.5
Weight laden as tested . . . . 19.2 cwt.

Specification

Engine

Block material	cast iron
Head material	cast iron
Cylinders	4
Cooling system	Water
Bore and stroke	80.98 mm. 62.99 mm.
Cubic capacity	1,298 c.c.
Main bearings	Five
Valves	o.h.v. pushrod
Compression ratio	9.2:1
Carburetter	Weber compound
Max. power (net)	58.6 b.h.p. at 5,400 r.p.m.
Max. power (gross)	75 b.h.p. at 5,400 r.p.m.
Max. torque (gross)	91 lb.ft. at 2,500 r.p.m.

Transmission

Internal gearbox ratios
Top gear	1.0:1
3rd gear	1.418
2nd gear	1.995
1st gear	3.337
Reverse	3.867

Final drive 4.125
M.p.h. at 1,000 r.p.m. with 155 x 12 SP41 tyres:
Top gear	15.1
3rd gear	10.7
2nd gear	7.7
1st gear	4.5

Brakes

Type . . . . 8.6 in. front discs. 8 in. rear drums. Servo assisted.

Suspension and steering

Front . . . . . Independent by MacPherson struts and coil/spring damper units. Anti-roll bar doubles as longitudinal location.
Rear . . . . . Live axle on semi-elliptic leaf springs.
Shock absorbers:
Front: . . . . telescopic
Rear: . . . . telescopic
Steering type . . . . rack and pinion
Tyres . . . . Dunlop SP41 155 x 12
Wheels . . . . pressed steel
Rim size 4½J

---

around 95 m.p.h. High speed cruising on our test car was further enhanced by particularly low wind noise.

On a 600-mile run to Wales and back, the GT averaged 27.3 m.p.g. on four-star petrol (surprisingly, it doesn't seem to need the best five-star grades) which, if nothing special for a 1300, is quite respectable when weighed against other four-seaters of comparable performance—a more cogent comparison. Commuting use in and around London subsequently dropped the overall figure to 25.3 m.p.g.

If the engine is good on results (it's a rather drab, dull piece of machinery to look at) the gearbox—designed by Ford of Cologne, incidentally—is really outstanding. The gearchange is perhaps the best that money can buy as the lever slices through a very positive gate with such oily ease, speed and precision, and with no baulking at all from the effective synchromesh. The ratios are stacked closer together than in other 1100 and 1300 Escorts,

giving neat red-line limits of 30, 50 and 70 m.p.h. At 15.1 m.p.h. per 1,000 r.p.m. 70 m.p.h. in top is an easy 4,640 r.p.m.

The Escort GT's third fun-car ingredient is its excellent handling. Like the gearchange, the rack-and-pinion steering is very light and quick, rubber mounting of the rack and spring loading of the pinion by a Neoprene slipper effectively masking kick-back but not feel. The fairly stiff, well damped suspension doesn't do very much for the ride but it does prevent roll or lurch so that the car feels particularly taut and responsive to the steering. It is a very agile, swervable car. Replacement of the leading locating links for the MacPherson struts by the more familiar Ford set-up of an anti-roll bar doubling as longitudinal location (another quietly phased-in change) does not seem to have made much difference to the handling; if anything, we thought that understeer is slightly increased and transient lurch fraction-

Continued on the next page

Ford Escort GT

ally reduced. The live back axle does not betray its very simple leaf-spring location until the going gets pretty rough; otherwise, the car's cornering powers are very high on Dunlop SP41 radials. Spirited driving on a wet, twisty road reveals (surprisingly) that it is understeer, not a wayward tail, that usually sets the limit, albeit a very high one.

Although the car is quite smooth and stable at speed—except in a cross wind which induces some self-correcting weaving—the ride is choppy on poor roads, particularly at low speeds, though this sharp, staccato movement is not necessarily more uncomfortable than the bouncing you get in some more softly sprung cars. Resilient front seats, well bolstered for support, mask much of the low speed harshness but, for tall people, their range of adjustment is barely enough. Again, it is the fault of the dreadful notched arc runners that Ford persist in using on some of their cars, despite widespread criticism of them. As the seat is moved rearwards, so it tilts forward, making the squab too upright when the seat is right back. Most of us preferred to have the seat forward a little, sacrificing some leg room for a more relaxing lean-back driving position behind the small, very low-set steering wheel—so low, in fact, that it nestles in your lap and not at arm-aching shoulder height.

The GT comes as standard with more lavish trim and equip-

ment than other Escorts. A wood-grained instrument panel carries six round dials, neatly and clearly calibrated—though, depending on where you sit, the smaller quartet (oil pressure, ammeter, fuel and temperature) are partially masked by the wheel rim. In contrast, the switchgear is poor. The foot-operated washer is a good idea but too far forward to reach in comfort; and the wiper switch, low down under the scuttle, is in a dreadful position—a fact that Ford seem to acknowledge by equipping the test car with inertia reel seat belts (very good ones, too) so that the switch can be reached without un-belting. The heater is a volcanic affair which warms your legs and demists the windows very efficiently. But because the two controls also regulate the cold-air vents, the system is nothing like so versatile and controllable as, say, the Cortina's Aeroflow. Imitation wood panels decorate the door sills in an attempt to cover up the painted metal, though whether or not this actually improves the decor is debatable. No one could quibble at the standard of finish inside, though, which is high throughout. The new matt-black grille (like that of the Escort Twin-Cam) also makes the GT more easily recognisable.

At £833, the Escort seems to us a very attractive buy. Apart, perhaps, from the new twin-carb Riley/MG 1300s (which we haven't yet tested) there doesn't seem to be any other big-booted four-seater of the same price that can match the GT in all the departments at which it excels—performance, controls, handling, roadholding, smoothness and very fair comfort and quietness. And that's a formidable list.

M

The civilised cockpit has carpet on the floor, imitation wood on the facia and door cappings, and "wicker-work" upholstery on the seat pads. Note the very low-set steering wheel.

Dials on the right of a neat instrument cluster are partially masked by the steering wheel: wiper and light switches are also poorly placed, low down to the left of the steering column.

Comfortable bucket seats give quite good side support but arced runners make them too upright when fully back. The squabs are released by pressing a button at the hinge.

The only external clue to the 1300GT's high output of 75 b.h.p. (gross) is the fabricated four-branch exhaust pipe.

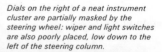

STAGE 2 1300 GT ROAD TESTS

"Gimme The Facts Man . . ."

Performance	Std 1300 GT Escort	Broadspeed stage 2 1300 GT Escort	Twin Cam. Escort
0-50	8.8 seconds	7.1 seconds	7.2 seconds
0-60	12.0 ,,	9.8 ,,	9.2 ,,
0-70	16.1 ,,	13.8 ,,	11.5 ,,
0-80	22.2 ,,	18.5 ,,	14.8 ,,
0-90	—	24.0 ,,	19.5 ,,
Top speed	93 m.p.h.	106.8 m.p.h.	114 m.p.h.
¼ mile	18.5 seconds	16.8 seconds	16.1 seconds
50-70 m.p.h.—top	11.1 ,,	9.7 ,,	9.0 ,,
70-90 m.p.h.—gear	23.6 ,,	13.0 ,,	11.5 ,,

HAVING read through the previous story on the Broadspeed/Ford kits, you'll have noticed a reference to Broad's personal transport — a very well used 1300 GT fitted with his stage 2 kit; as we said, the car has been used for shopping and practice at the Nurburgring, with the kit fitted for 7,000 of the 15,000 miles it has covered. This was the one we used to take the performance figures, and we're very pleased with our choice, because we were able to judge how well the car had worn after "7,000 miles at 7,000 r.p.m.", to quote Mr. Broad! The results of our tests show that it's much quicker than the standard 1300 GT, and damn nearly as quick as the Twin-Cam. — which we've tested, but been unable to print because of the Racing Car show.

Not only does it belt along in supercharged style, but the more mundane parts are still as good as new: the brakes are better than standard (DS11 front disc pads), steering is still completely accurate and the roadholding is still up to par. This is in spite of the shockers, which haven't been replaced since it yumped round the Nurburgring. Time has actually improved the "flickswitch" gearchange, while the transmission and clutch are still well able to cope with full-bore standing starts; we did twelve successive acceleration runs and it was still burning away with no clutch-slip or axle-tramp. Even without tramp-rods we were having no trouble in leaving dead straight black scorch-marks for the first 20 yards. We got the best acceleration figures using 7000 r.p.m. in first and second, then 6750 revs. in third: that's just over 30 in first, 53 in second and 74 m.p.h. in third.

If you're determined not to read the previous story (back a page or so, people) we'd better tell you about the stage 2 kit. The price is approx. £98 and you can only buy it outright. In the smartly-packaged box you'll find: a twin-choke downdraught 26/27 Weber (re-jetted from its standard 1600 GT settings), a polished and gas-flowed 1300 GT inlet manifold, a complete exhaust system from a two-piece, four-branch top manifold, thence into two down-pipes and a single underfloor tube which connects up to a large-bore tailpipe, which is much stronger than standard but just as quiet. On Broad's Escort the air filter had twin intake-tubes; production kits will have a single filter inlet. Digging further into the magic box will reveal a new cylinder head giving a 9.8.1 CR (standard is 9.2). The kit is complete with plugs, gaskets and destructions, though Broadspeed will fit free of charge, if you buy from them.

Now it's turn-on time, kiddies; on with the ignition, press the loud pedal twice and turn again. No doubt about it, the engine is playing our tune. It takes a few miles to warm up (all Escorts seem to run cold), so we potter round doing our flexible act: 1000 r.p.m. in fourth (15 m.p.h.) and accelerate away, there's some harshness from the transmission but the engine is quite happy. As we accelerate past 4000 r.p.m. there is an even stronger pull forwards and it feels like a steam engine has coupled up behind to send the rev.-counter round to 6500 r.p.m. and the true speed up to nearly 100 m.p.h. After this point it gets fairly easily to a true 105, while a downhill section or tailwind get it shifting along at nearly 110 m.p.h. — a pretty fair achievement for a 1300 c.c. saloon.

At high speed on motorway or exposed road, the dreaded sidewind lurch sets in, though it's only fair to point out that this feels much worse than it is, being mainly body rocking.

The suspension was unchanged, so that handling and roadholding are as the normal 1300 GT, up to a point; because you've got some more neddies it's much easier to shift the tail out, on wet or dry roads.

To make the tail hang out, you have to floor the go-pedal deliberately on the tightest part of a slowish corner; even then it may not shift unless the going is damp. The quick-action steering and your bottom make sure that no revolving goes on.

The real beauty of it is that there is nothing to tell anyone, including the driver, that the car is converted — until you depart into the distance with wheels blurring and Cinturatos chirping! This sheep's clothing bit even extends to the idling speed, which was set 250 r.p.m. slower than all the other Escort GTs we've tried.

Another point about the stage 2 kit is that it provides more flexible power throughout the speed range, being quicker than the standard car (though only by fractions) on the 20-40 and 40-60 m.p.h. range; from 60 onwards it really demolishes the standard car, knocking over 10 seconds from the 70-90 m.p.h. time!

Fuel consumption for our short test was quite good; on the road it managed 26.2 m.p.g. overall; during acceleration and maximum speed runs, this dropped to 25 m.p.g., which is about the standard 1300 GT's consumption during hard driving.

by Spencer Smith

Pirana Escort

1600 GT WITH HONOURABLE INTENTIONS

WHEN THE BUILDERS OF THE TASMAN ANGLIA DECIDE to sell a quick road car, we can't help but think that we're in for something good. A thought that proved to be true of this electric green Lumo Pirana Sprint. To start off with the Pirana was among the best finished converted cars C & CC have ever tried; with a coachwork line, 5½J Magna alloy wheels, Lumo mock leather roof, ''signwritten'' transfers in gold and that green paint job. The Americans refer to this sort of saloon as a go n'show car, a description that couldn't be bettered, for the Pirana goes well in a straight line and is even more impressive during hard cornering. We have to admit that the green machine was quicker around our steering course than Ford's very own Twin Cam and it has a remarkably high limit in the wet or grease; much of the credit for this must go to Firestone's low profile 6.20 cross-plies, which we haven't tried before.

The test car was all to 1969 specification except for the 1600 GT Cortina engine and 1300 GT transmission, which have covered many miles of development trials. This meant that the shell was trimmed inside with plastic wood and chrome, something we were prepared to bear because it also had the current front suspension which incorporates an anti-roll bar and Twin Cam type track control arms. In addition to these thicker arms Lumo Cars had lowered the suspension all round. using blocks at the back and cutting down the coils at the front. By this time we're beginning to realise that 'our' Pirana has been very thoroughly converted and there's still more work to tell you about: the shock absorbers at the front have been reset to give a firmer ride, while the back has adjustables. The engine mods aren't drastic and Lumo are planning to use different parts in the future, so we'll just give brief details. The camshaft went under the stage 2 label and gave of its best between 3-6000 r.p.m., running out of breath thereafter. The stage one head had the standard CR of 9.2 : 1. gas flow inlet and exhaust porting and equalised combustion chamber volumes—or what passes for chambers on a cross-flow Ford. The twin choke downdraught carb was re-jetted to suit the new go-bits; they seem to have got the jetting right too, because we returned close to 27 m.p.g. while on a run. As you all know (umm, well you're about to . . .) installing a Cortina engine into an Escort involves changing the sump to accept the crossmember. Lumo had fitted a prototype sump and uprated oil pump to the test car, neither of these components could stop it losing a lot of pressure on the motorway, even though the oil cooler did its best to bring it all back in cross country driving. Since our test the firm have been into this problem, changing the sump and virtually redesigning the pump, with the result that their current cars keep their pressure.

Driving it is an exciting pleasure: turn the key hot or cold and it's away first time. If it's a really cold morning the choke will be needed for half a mile or so. Once the oil is really warm you can get down to shifting along a bit sharper than next door's 1300 GT, 'cos you've got torque and plenty of ponies to move it along. With the instant gearchange and very powerful standard brakes there isn't much that'll stand in your way on crowded English roads. Pulling a very sensible 3.7 final drive we managed 0-50 in 7.2 seconds and 0-80 took just 21 seconds. With a quarter mile time of 17.5 seconds and plenty of top gear pull, we found it an ideal vehicle for fast cross-country thrashes.

Then there's the handling, what about that then? Well there are a few words that describe it, all superlatives; like it just goes round bends fella. No fuss, no lean, minimal tyre squeal and double quick. Dry or wet, it lets the driver know about any drama long before there's trouble. As you pile into a bend there's a great feeling of stability, coupled with slight understeer; the harder you press on, the more it sticks down. On a really greasy road the understeer will gradually turn to tail out, but you are unlikely to shift it more than a few degrees. On a really tight and dry corner the inside rear wheel will lift before that of a Twin Cam Escort's, all the same this doesn't lead to problems as the lifting process is easy to anticipate. We had great fun burning round our steering pad trying to make it spin by booting it through puddles and grease at 50 m.p.h. on a 100 ft. circle. Needless to say we were successful in the end. Even then, halfway through the spin, we held it travelling sideways on a dry patch, only to make it really let go forever on the grease. That experience did us well in the pub for a few days; you know the line, ''there I was looking out of the side windows when . . .''

Looking at the performance figures given we can hear you all chuntering ''where's the top speed then?'' Something we asked ourselves as we gazed horror struck at the oil pressure gauge reading less than 30 lb. sq. ins., while we were pulling 6 grand in top, which is 98 m.p.h. As the rev limit is 6500 and the car was quite prepared to make it up there, we couldn't see any point in wrecking the engine to prove it will exceed 105 m.p.h. As we sit here gazing at the festering typewriter, we can recall the Lumo man saying he'd give us a shot in his all laughing version, that's got plenty of lb. sq. ins., so if there's any doubt about that speed, you'll hear about it. What we can pass on is the word that it cruises happily at anything up to an honest 85; beyond this the noise becomes a nuisance for prolonged travel. But in bursts up to seven or eight miles the engine and wind roar just add to the fun.

With the Luton Motor Group backing Lumo Cars on this project we think it has a great future; though at present these companies are thinking about another performance car to market, there will always be room for this sort of compact, good handling, fun saloon.

PIRANA PRICES AND PERFORMANCE

M.P.H.	SECS
0-30	3.3
0-40	5.0
0-50	7.1
0-60	10.5
0-70	14.2
0-80	21.0

PRICES	£	s.	d.
Pirana Escort fitted with 1600 GT engine	919		
Extras on test car:			
Stage 1 head	25		
Stage 2 cam	15		
Oil cooler	14	10	
3.7 final drive	14	10	
Uprated front suspension	9		
Lowering blocks	4	10	
Adjustable rear shock absorbers	10	10	
Labour charge for all suspension work	5		
Uprated oil pump	5	10	
Leather rim steering wheel	7	10	
Lumo roof	21	10	
Metallic paint	6	7	10
Coach line	6	10	

Makers: Lumo Cars, London Road, Dunstable, Beds.

INSIDE INFORMATION

HOW FORD DOES IT

By David Thomas

A VISIT TO THE FORD PERFORMANCE CENTRE AT BOREHAM TO SEE THE "WORKS" RALLY ESCORTS BEING PREPARED.

SINCE the early days of competitive motoring, "works" cars have always held a great deal of fascination for the enthusiast. Not without reason, in most instances, for they often have an edge which amateur-tuned examples may lack. The top rally cars of today are no exception. One often wonders what "demon tweaks" are concealed within those standard-looking shells. How much do they differ from the basic car you and I are likely to buy? Could we buy or build ourselves an exact replica of a "works" car?

Never has the international rallying scene been as competitive as it is today. Private

This is what happens to Minilite wheels after prolonged running on a punctured tyre. A standard steel wheel would be battered to such an extent that it probably would not clear a front brake caliper.

Two of the Monte cars, with their fluorescent "colour keyed" roof panels and front skirts, nearing completion. In the background can be seen the Corsair estate cars used by the service crews. Note the circular headlamps and the re-worked wheel housings on the Escorts

Below: Despite the fact that the cars are destined to be driven under extremely arduous conditions, the Boreham mechanics take great pride in turning them out in immaculate order. The improvised wing covers were not put on for the benefit of our photographer!

A Group 2 head being fitted to the cylinder assembly. Note the tachometer drive gearbox at the bottom left of the timing cover

Photography by Ron Easton

entrants have little hope of defeating the might of the professional, factory-sponsored teams. Tremendous time, effort and money go into the running of such a team. Actual car preparation is just one aspect of their work. The gruelling pace of modern rallies is such that, despite their fantastic toughness, cars are often dependent on the backing of highly skilled service crews. Rallies differ greatly in character and the cars have to be "tailored" accordingly. This aspect demands much experience and foresight. Careful planning is also required to ensure that spares and equipment are available at the right place and at the right time.

Tyres are a classic example—on the Monte Carlo Rally, for instance, conditions can be so unpredictable that having the right tyres available for use in the special stages can be a major headache. Another aspect that can spell the difference between success and failure is how much the drivers and navigators know about the terrain over which the special stages are held. For this reason, reconnaissance trips are made where possible and detailed "pace notes" prepared. Sometimes, when patches of ice are likely to be encountered in a special stage, a spare car is used to make a last-minute recee and the presence of ice is indicated in the pace notes. Such tactics are obviously out of the question for the average private entrant. But what of the cars themselves? One of the most successful machines on the rallying scene at the moment is the Escort Twin Cam. We were invited to go along to the Ford Performance Centre at Boreham to see this year's Monte cars in the course of preparation and to talk to the man responsible for their preparation, Bill Meade.

A visitor's first impression is that of calm efficiency. In addition to the three Escorts for the Monte there was also a lone car being built for the Swedish Rally. Despite all the activity this involved, the workshop was almost uncannily tidy and clean.

The "works" rally Escorts normally compete in Group 2. In this category, only series production cars, of which at least 1,000 have been produced, are eligible. The extent to which they can be modified (this is described as an "improved category") is limited and all the parts used have to be available for sale to the general public. There are "recognition forms", approved by the Federation Internationale de l'Automobile, in which the specification of the basic car and all the available extras are defined clearly. Only the components detailed

Continued

A front suspension cross-member being brought up to heavy-duty specification. This particular example, which has extensions for mounting track-control-arm bump stops, is a Mk I Cortina component

Below : The engine being lowered into position on one of the Monte cars. Note the quick-action oil filler cap and the additional breather in the front face of the cam cover

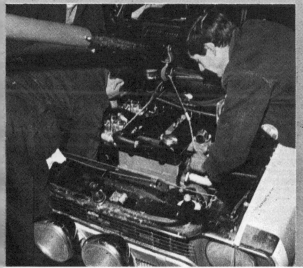

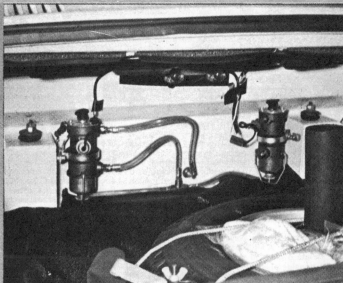

Seen in this photograph are the two Stewart-Warner electric fuel pumps, which are mounted on the special turrets which form the upper attachment points for the rear shock absorbers

This example is not destined for the Monte. Plastic guards protect the rectangular headlamps. Note that the 6in. wheels fitted to this car do not necessitate wheel housing modification. The electron sump shield, made by Tech Del, can be clearly seen

INSIDE INFORMATION...

on these forms are homologated for use in Group 2. This ensures that, theoretically at least, the cars incorporate only "over the counter" parts. Readers can probably recall that there have been some unfortunate disputes concerning the eligibility of some past rally winners. This has made the factory teams today even more careful.

At one time, a rally Ford started life as a fully-assembled standard car. Nowadays, the Performance Centre's facilities are such that it is more convenient to start with a painted and trimmed body shell, which comes complete with bonnet, boot-lid and doors. These have, in any case, to be retained on Group 2 cars, since light-weight substitutes have not been homologated. Neither had plastic side and rear windows when we visited Boreham, but the situation has apparently changed since then. Since plastics show a weight saving of over 60 per cent compared with glass, they will almost certainly be used in future events.

Front and rear wheel housings, are modified to accommodate the 7in. wide Minilite wheels now being used. A fairly extensive re-work is required at the rear but the front modification is basically a matter of trimming the aperture suitably and welding on "eyebrows". At one time these were fabricated from Transit van rear mudguards. Incidentally, the standard housings will accommodate the 6in. Minilite wheel, which until recently was the widest one homologated for Group 2.

On the rougher type of special stage, the Boreham people have found that vertically disposed rear dampers provide better axle control and such a system is used on all the works cars. A kit of parts is available to enable private owners to carry out this modification. A considerable amount of work is involved and only a really serious rally competitor would find the effort worth-while.

A side-effect of these rear-end modifications is to eliminate the steel rear bulkhead. In its place is rivetted a sheet of aluminium alloy. This is also bonded to the car's structure by means of glass fibre. In fact, the whole of the boot area is carefully sealed off from the "greenhouse". Since a petrol tank lives in both of the vulnerable rear quarters, together with the battery on the boot floor, this is a very sensible precaution.

In all other respects, the body is standard. Great care is taken, of course, to ensure that there are no faulty welds. On the rare occasion when a car is competing in Group 5, the standard spot welding is supplemented in places by gas tack-welds. This is particularly the case around the front strut housings. On the British Fords, front suspension bump travel is limited by the spring becoming coil-bound. Since spring loads are transmitted directly into the strut housing, excessive "crashing-through" can impose very severe stresses in this area.

With the exception of the revised rear damper set-up, the suspension at both ends is surprisingly standard. Spring rates, damper settings and ride-heights are tailored to suit the type of event. Heavy-duty front strut upper mountings are used. These incorporate a ball bearing and are the type that were fitted to the Mk 2 Cortina when it was introduced. Since noise insulation is of no consequence on a rally car, a harder rubber-mix is used for the majority of the suspension bushes. In fact, only the rear spring shackle bushes remain standard. More accurate handling and better rear axle control is the result. British Fords are fitted with Armstrong dampers, but we noticed that Boreham were testing Bilstein front struts, which are made in Germany.

The front cross-member is strengthened (available over the counter at Boreham, as are all the special parts mentioned). The plate which closes the bottom of the top-hat section pressing is extended at each end and gussets are welded inside the engine mounting pedestals. Gas welding supplements all the standard spot welds.

So far as the steering is concerned, only the ratio of the rack and pinion gear is changed. The higher gearing gives 2.7 turns from lock to lock, compared with the standard 3.5.

Front hubs are carefully selected and care is taken to ensure that the amount of metal machined from the wheel mounting flange is kept to a minimum.

Not only are the wide Minilite electron wheels very handsome—they also have a number of very significant advantages. The Ford rally team first adopted them on the Mk I Cortina-Lotus to combat very severe brake over-heating problems they were experiencing on the Alpine Rally. They did the trick. Bill Meade is of the opinion that the electron wheel acts as a far more effective "heat sink" than its steel counterpart, as well as significantly increasing the flow of air over the brake assembly. Other advantages of the Minilite are lightness, strength and the ability to keep a car moving should it be unfortunate enough to suffer a puncture on a special stage.

Not a great deal is done to the braking system. Hard pads (Ferodo DS 11) and linings (Ferodo VG95/1) are used. An interesting point concerning these materials is that it is generally considered necessary to fade them deliberately once before they achieve a stable state. The disc shields are modified considerably to improve cooling and racing fluid is used in the system. The servo is standard, but is moved back to the scuttle to make the alternator easier to get at. Spring steel wire spirals are used to protect the flexible hoses and the Bundy tubing is protected by taping rubber piping over it. In any case, as much as possible of the tubing is routed inside the car to minimize the risk of damage. This also applies to the fuel line and to the cable from the rear-mounted battery.

Nobody can fail to be impressed by the battery of lamps a typical rally car possesses. Add to these an electrically heated windscreen plus odd items such as windscreen wiper, a heater blower, a map reading lamp and an electric fuel pump, and it is soon evident that something very non-standard is required in the generating department. Ford use a Lucas II AC alternator, which is mounted on a robust aluminium-alloy bracket. During last year they experienced a great deal of trouble with the alternator's built-in diode pack. It was eventually found that an unfortunate vibration period was the cause of the trouble.

A new set-up using a remotely mounted diode pack seems to have overcome the problem. Cibié lamps are used exclusively, the headlamps now being round, 7in. units. The electrically heated windscreen is a Triplex laminated component. At the maximum setting, which is used for de-icing or rapid de-misting, the current flow is 18 amperes. There is an on/off switch, plus a warning light but there is also a time relay switch which prevents the driver using the full-heat setting for more than 15 minutes without re-winding the relay. At the lower setting, which can be used continuously, the flow-rate is reduced to 4.5 amperes. This provides efficient de-misting and a measure of de-icing without caning the battery. The latter, incidentally, has a capacity of 57 ampere-hours. A master switch is used (in the boot) and the electrical system is liberally fused. The fuse boxes are very accessibly mounted on an auxilliary panel. This also carries a 60-0-60 remote-shunt ammeter. The whole electrical system is meticulously installed and is provided with such refinements as multi-pin connectors to facilitate rapid servicing. To equip a car to this high standard is obviously very expensive.

Instrumentation is not as elaborate as was fashionable in rally cars at one time. Since the cars comply with Group 2 requirements, the standard instruments and panel are retained but a separate mechanical tachometer is mounted on the belt-rail. Bill Meade has little faith in the accuracy of the various electric tachometers and the results of our road test checks suggest that he may well have some justification for mistrusting them. The naviga-

tion instruments consist of a Halda and a pair of Heuer watches. An interesting point is that a very large oil-pressure warning light is fitted. The pressure switch is arranged to operate at 25 p.s.i. A steady pressure lower than this probably spells big trouble anyway. An incidental advantage of this system is that oil surge in the sump causes the light to flash if the level is allowed to drop rather low, but sufficient warning is given to enable engine damage to be avoided.

Engine specification is quite straightforward. The bore is increased to 83.5 mm, thus bringing its capacity to near the class maximum (up from 1,558 c.c. to 1,594 c.c. Special Mahle pistons are used. Connecting rods are standard "C"-type although the BRM ones have, in fact, been homologated. The crankshaft is basically standard but the oilways are re-arranged so that numbers two and three big-ends are not required to share the oil supply from the centre main bearing. This revised arrangement is standard on the Kent series bowl-in-piston engines, incidentally. The crankshaft undergoes a process called "Tufride", which in-

Above: Jim Bullough's privately prepared and entered Group 2 car which finished third in last year's RAC Rally—the first British car to finish

Far left: The Clarke and Simpson entered Escort, crewed by Makinen and Easter, competing in last year's RAC Rally. Head gasket failure, caused by a leaking top hose, caused its retirement whilst in the lead

Left: Soderstrom and Palm in their Escort on last year's Alpine rally. They finished on the end of a tow-rope with a burst engine.

creases its resistance to fatigue fractures. An increased capacity oil pump is used, in conjunction with a higher pressure release valve setting. A paper element filter is retained—Boreham make a point of using Purolator units—and the filter by-pass valve is still operative. It breathes through Weber 45 DCOE carburettors—40 DCOE are standard—and the camshafts are Cosworth L1. A Lucas competition distributor supplies the sparks to Autolite AG12 plugs.

Bonding and rivetting is used for the Ferodo RYZ clutch facings. The only other clutch change is the substitution of a heavier diaphragm spring. A weight saving of over 40 per cent is achieved by using electron for the bellhousing and extension housing castings. Electron gearbox and final drive casings are also available, but are not homologated for Group 2. The works cars use what the Boreham people refer to as the "Bullet" gear cluster. The ratios provided are 1.28 to 1, 1.697 to 1 and 2.296 to 1—close, but with a realistic first gear ratio for a rally car. Drive is through what used to be the standard *one-piece* propellor shaft,

although a two-piece shaft is sometimes used for very fast rallies. The final drive ratio for the Monte cars is 5.1 to 1. Works cars always use the Salisbury Mk II limited slip differential. Incidentally, the rear axle failure on Roger Clarke's Cortina in the London-Sydney was caused by the loosening of bolts which secure the crown wheel to the differential casing—they are normally installed using Loctite but this was omitted on this assembly, which was not screwed together at Boreham. Loctite is used extensively, throughout the car.

Another security dodge is to drill and wire together the exhaust manifold studs, outboard of the nuts. This enables the nuts to be tightened occasionally without "unwiring" but prevents studs loosening off and dropping out. It is also important to wire the radius arm front pivot bolts—they have a habit of loosening off. The gearbox cross-member securing bolts are also wired.

An additional fuel tank is fitted. This fits into the left-hand rear quarter and is coupled to the original tank. Two Stewart-Warner pumps are

installed but only one is used—the other is there as a quick changeover emergency measure.

Castrol oils are used—generally 187 in the axle and 185 in the engine, although GTX is often used in the latter. A quick-action, hinged oil filler cap is fitted at the front of the camcover to ease filling and to minimize the risk of serious loss of oil in the event of the cap being left off or falling off. This special cam cover is also provided with an additional breather.

Well, there you are. You really can buy all the parts. Although these are likely to cost a pretty penny—the special electron sump guard retails for around £18 and the 7J wheels for about £30 each—the infinite patience, care and attention to detail which goes into every works car could not be bought. Unfortunately, this is often what makes the difference between a winner and an also-ran. We were fortunate enough to sample the car in which Roger Clarke and Jim Porter won the 1968 Circuit of Ireland (see issue for 11th July 1968). To say that we were impressed is putting it mildly—apart from the too-low gearing, it made an admirable road projectile.

IT is curious that, whereas the Ford Escort is sold with 1100 cc and 1300 cc engines, the only 1600 cc unit which is standardised is the rather specialised Twin Cam. Lumo Cars Ltd, of Dunstable, therefore fit the 1600 cc Cortina GT engine to this car, which goes by the somewhat elaborate name of LuMo Pirana Sprint. Indeed, the title was emblazoned on the vehicle in such large letters that it caused me acute embarrassment.

However, I soon found that this firm had made a very good job of tuning the engine, a modified cylinder head and special camshaft being the principal ingredients. The tuning had not been carried too far and the car actually seemed smoother and more flexible than a standard model. The normal 4.125 to 1 axle ratio is retained, and the test car was able to push the rev counter into the red section on top gear, which is equivalent to 102 mph. Incidentally, the speedometer of the test car was one of the most accurate I have met.

The superb Ford gearbox was a delight as always, and I was able, aided by its quick changes, to record some most satisfactory acceleration times. The acceleration is the most impressive feature, with plenty of punch in the middle ranges, and all normal main road hills are taken at speed in top gear. The tuned engine is at least as economical on fuel as a standard one, which is by no means without interest to most prospective buyers.

The suspension of the test car had been lowered, and the machine was fitted with very wide wheels and radial ply tyres. As would be expected, the rather hard ride of the Escort therefore became distinctly choppy, and passengers knew all about the road surface. On typical British roads, though, the ride is quite acceptable.

The roadholding is really excellent and no car needs less skill in going really fast through corners. The traction of the wide tyres is so good that racing getaways can still be made on wet roads. It is evident that Lumo know all the right things to do to a Ford, and the resulting vehicle is great fun to drive, with extremely safe handling. It makes a driver feel that he is an expert and there are certainly no tricks to learn, apart from a slight tendency to dart about in side winds. The throttle return spring fell off, but otherwise the car was completely reliable.

A good deal of extra equipment was fitted to the test car, as the data panel shows. This firm specialises in supplying cars to suit the personal whims of its customers, and a very long list of optional extras is catalogued. Such things as the leatherette roof cover give some individuality to a popular model such as this.

There is no need to discuss the other features of the car, which are to standard Escort specification. This machine is just as practical a family car as are the normal production models, but much more fun.

JOHN BOLSTER tests . . .
The LuMo Pirana Sprint
A modified Ford Escort

The tuned 1600 cc GT Cortina engine has a modified head and camshaft which does not affect flexibility but considerably boosts performance.

SPECIFICATION AND PERFORMANCE DATA

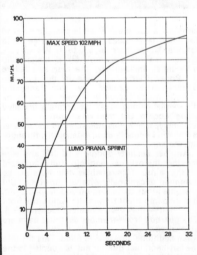

MAX SPEED 102 MPH

LUMO PIRANA SPRINT

M.P.H. / SECONDS

Car tested: LuMo Pirana Sprint 2-door saloon, price £921 including PT. Extras on test car: Modified cylinder head, £25. Camshaft, £15. Minilite 6½J wheels, £18 each, plus radial tyres. Leatherette roof covering, £21 10s. Steering wheel, £6 19s. 6d. Interior Silent Travel, £9 10s. Lowered suspension, £9.

Engine: Four cylinders, 80.97 mm x 77.62 mm (1598.8 cc). Pushrod-operated overhead valves. Compression ratio 9.2 : 1. 93 bhp at 5000 rpm. Weber twin-choke downdraught carburetter.

Transmission: Single dry plate diaphragm spring clutch. 4-speed all-synchromesh gearbox with central change and hypoid rear axle, overall ratios 4.125, 5.849, 8.229, and 13.765 : 1.

Chassis: Steel body and chassis. Independent MacPherson front suspension. Rear axle on semi-elliptic springs. Telescopic dampers all round. Rack and pinion steering. Front disc and rear drum brakes. Minilite 6½J wheels fitted Goodyear 175-12 radial ply tyres.

Equipment: 12-volt lighting and starting. Speedometer. Rev counter. Voltmeter. Oil pressure, water temperature and fuel gauges. Heating, demisting and ventilation system. Windscreen wipers and washers. Flashing direction indicators. Cigar lighter.

Dimensions: Wheelbase 7 ft 10½ ins; track (front), 4 ft 0½ ins, (rear) 4 ft 1¾ ins; overall length, 13 ft 3¾ ins; width, 5ft 1¾ ins; weight, 15½ cwt.

Performance: Maximum speed 102 mph. Speeds in gears: third, 71 mph; second, 53 mph; first, 34 mph. Standing quarter-mile, 17.1 s. Acceleration: 0-30 mph, 3.2 s; 0.50 mph, 7.2 s; 0-60 mph, 10.0 s; 0-80 mph, 18.6 s.

Fuel consumption: 26 mpg.

Crayford's 3-litre Escort Eliminator

With 175-13 radials on 5½J rims, the Eliminator had plenty of grip on a dry road. Wheel spin and a wagging tail were easy to provoke in the wet, though.

● WE ARE often tempted to use the word "silent" to describe the quietness of a motorcar but, as our editor never fails to remind us, "silence" is an absolute, not a relative, word. Nevertheless it is useful to apply it to the most outstanding characteristic of the new Crayford Escort Eliminator: not its quietness, which is unexceptional, but its quietness in relation to truly tremendous performance which enables one to squirt "silently" and safely—often without having to bother to change to a lower gear—past a long column of dawdlers into the slot at the head of the queue. No booms and howls from the exhaust, no gnashing of valves or noisy gobblings from carburetter intakes like a farmyard of indignant turkeys; just a smooth, discreet hum.

This virtue accrues from the oldest and most effective tuning expedient of all—putting a large, lazy engine into a small, light, car. The engine is the standard 2,994 c.c. Ford Zodiac V-6 unit developing 136 (net) b.h.p. at 4,750 r.p.m. with 181.5 lb. ft. of torque at 3,000 r.p.m.; the car a specially modified Escort GT, and the marriage has been brought about by Crayford Engineering Ltd. Shoehorning the beefy V-6 engine into the little Escort—or to be more exact, setting it far enough back in the chassis still to retain a fair 56/44 front/rear weight distribution—has necessitated a specially designed front bulkhead and means some loss of legroom. There is enough space for a tall driver when his seat is pushed right back, but there is then little legroom behind him. But legroom behind the passenger's seat is adequate, and the car remains capable of carrying, say, two adults and two children, or three adults and a child, which is all that small cars are generally asked to do.

The other major modifications include a pair of additional air intakes feeding a special cross-flow radiator, extensively modified front suspension to cope with the extra weight (the battery has been moved to the boot), servo brakes and a 3.5:1 final drive ratio. Like the Escort TC, the Eliminator has slightly flaired wings to accept the 13-in. wheels with 5½J rims, but the tyres fitted are larger, 175-13 instead of 165-13. The trim, instruments, etc., are basically as for the 1300GT but with comfortable rally-type front bucket seats which gave good lateral support and are fitted with headrests (reclining seats are an optional extra). Outside; the most noticeable departure from standard is the matt-black bonnet with a power bulge to accommodate various types of air cleaner for different markets; at the back the only visible change, apart from a slight lowering of the suspension, is a small "3-litre" badge. The cost is £1,495 including purchase tax, and the full Ford warranty is retained, as are normal servicing schedules. Crayford also intend to sell a Clubman Racer version of the car with a modified fuel-injected engine (put out of warranty), wider wheels, greater roll stiffness, a glass fibre bonnet and other goodies.

The simplest way of describing the Eliminator's performance is to state that it now heads the 3-litre class in our standing-start acceleration league. It gets to 60 m.p.h. in less than 8 seconds and recorded a MIRA lap speed of 113.7 m.p.h., but more important is the superb top-gear squirt provided by the torquey V-6 engine. With performance like this the overall fuel consumption of 17.8 m.p.g. is not unreasonable for a mileage which included a high proportion of testing; most owners should be able to better 20 m.p.g. All these things add up to make the Eliminator a very quick car indeed, and a car that can respond to every mood: big-car loafing or small-car pressing-on.

Here, too, the Eliminator does well, once the driver has got used to the heavy, rather dead steering commanded by an over-small wheel which obscures the instruments. With plenty of power on tap, corners can be taken in a satisfyingly neutral way, though at times there is strong understeer and on slow corners it is easy to break traction at the back. In the wet the tail slides out easily, and a sensitive throttle foot is called for. Heavy usage failed to fade the brakes, though their mushy and slightly unprogressive action made it easy to lock the front wheels on occasion.

There are few failings to balance against the virtues. The mechanically actuated clutch is sudden and very heavy (lighter hydraulic operation will be provided on production versions) although the Corsair gearbox fitted is very pleasant to use with much nicer ratios than the usual Zephyr set. The ride is hard and, on poor roads, very bouncy but these are minor defects when weighed against the good handling and roadholding and the performance of a top sports car.

Anthony Curtis

The 3-litre V-6 is a tight fit in the Escort's engine bay—but fit it does after considerable tin-snipping to get it well back in the chassis.

Performance comparison

	Escort Twin-Cam	Eliminator			
	m.p.h.	m.p.h.	40-60	9.1	5.2
			50-70	9.5	5.2
Max (banked track)	111.3	113.7	60-80	10.6	6.3
Best one-way	116.9	116.9	70-90	12.7	7.2
			80-100	16.3	9.4
Acceleration	sec.	sec.	Third		
0-30 m.p.h.	3.0	2.6	10-30	6.6	4.6
0-40	4.4	4.0	30-50	5.5	3.6
0-50	6.4	5.6	50-70	6.1	4.2
0-60	8.7	7.6	Consumption	m.p.g.	m.p.g.
0-70	11.8	10.2	30 m.p.h.	34	30.9
0-80	15.6	13.3	40	37	29.9
0-90	21.6	17.1	50	34.5	28.8
0-100	29.5	23.1	60	33	27.0
Standing ¼m.	16.9	15.8	70	25	24.4
Top gear			80	23	21.8
20-40	9.3	5.8	90	20.5	19.9
30-50	9.1	5.7	100	17.5	17.6
			overall	23.4	17.8
			touring	23.6	22.7

Special bucket seats and a tiny (too tiny) steering wheel are additional Eliminator goodies. The revised bulkhead, which encroaches on footwell legroom, can just be seen here.

DASHING ESCORT

Package deal Broadspeed conversion transforms the 1300GT

THE HORROR WITH WHICH the tuning industry regards the production of tuning equipment by the major manufacturers is matched only by the horror of the manufacturers at the thought of a league of little men wreaking untold ghastliness on their perfectly good motor cars. Not that the motor industry is really out to deprive the tuners of a living; modern production exponents abhor the idea of small numbers of non-standard parts creeping into the system. Nor is the tuning industry by any means as uniformly irresponsible as some of the manufacturers sometimes seem to think. But there has to be a halfway house, and in recent years this has taken the form of a major manufacturer taking a thoroughly respected tuning firm under its wing, farming out work on performance versions of its cars in exchange for flogging the end product through its dealers and agreeing that the work will not affect the warranty.

BMC were first in the field with their famous link-up with Coopers, after which Vauxhall surprised everybody by entering an alliance with Brabham, a move that must have taken a bit of getting past the anti-competition GM moguls.

But these were links with people who were really chassis developers and had been lured into the performance option business as much for the sake of their name. The next stage was to lay hands on the real engine wizards. Again BMC were first in the field, extending their relationship with Daniel Richmond and the Downton organisation in an agreement which promised much but seems to have got bogged down in the morass of takeover politics.

All this has left a clear field for Ford to announce a tie-up with Ralph Broad. No nonsense here about having to sell the idea to the management as a marketing exercise; and precious little doubt but that Ralph was the man for the job. Ideas developed on the remarkably successful Broadspeed 1300cc racing Escorts were developed, with the enthusiastic support of the Ford Competitions Department at Boreham (a relatively small, very well-run offshoot which must by now be worth its weight in gold to Ford) to be applied to the standard Escort GT either new or used.

The plan is simple. Stage 1, as tested for this report, consists of a new Weber 26/27 compound downdraught carburettor, inlet and exhaust manifolds, a new carburettor air filter, all the gaskets and so on required for fitting, a full flow, large bore silencer and a set of instructions. It can be ordered through your Ford dealer by its catalogue number (CD1000/54) like any replacement part, and costs £50. Stage 2 throws in a reworked cylinder head together with plugs, gaskets etc for good measure, which pushes the price up to £95. This is part number CD1000/55. And Stage 3 consists basically of a special cam to add to Stage 2 plus new jets for the carburettor, for another £20 (Part number CD1000/56).

Each stage will give you an extra seven to eight horsepower. Each shifts the peak power higher in the rev range, but the claim is that only Stage 3 lacks flexibility (it is sold for the rally specialist who is more concerned with top-end power). One word of warning; the breathing improvements which are the secret of the conversions are matched to the GT cam—so if you put Stage 1 on your 1300 Super without changing the cam as well, you are going to end up disappointed. You'll need part number 116E6250 if you want to change to the GT cam.

Results? Well, look at the table. Our test figures for the Stage 1 car are matched with Ford's claimed times for the standard car (which for some obscure reason we haven't got around to testing yet) and the Stage 2 car—which we hope to lay our hands on later in the year. There are certainly tangible improvements in acceleration all the way down the line, and this has not been achieved at the expense of flexibility or of fuel consumption. The really lazy driver may be aware of a slight unwillingness to lug along in top, but with the Escort's gearchange, who really wants to? Neither was noise any sort of problem, and in fact the free-flow exhaust system gives a pleasant boom.

The only thing which did strike us was that the car felt undergeared, to the extent where we once or twice found ourselves groping for another gear when already in top. Unfortunately Ford do not offer a higher final drive. ●

FORD GT COMPARED

	*Standard GT	†Stage 1 GT	*Stage 2 GT	*Stage 3 GT
gross power bhp	75.0	81.5	90.5	98.5
rpm	5400	6000	6500	6500
gross torque lb ft	71.0	76.5	83.0	86.0
rpm	3800	4300	4500	4500
extra cost £	—	50	95	115
acceleration 0–30	—	3.9	—	—
40	—	5.8	—	—
50	8.8	8.1	7.1	—
60	12.5	11.3	9.8	—
70	17.4	16.0	13.8	—
80	25.9	21.8	18.5	—
90	41.2	32.0	24.0	—
max speed mph	93	100	106	112
overall mpg	25.3	27	26.2	—

*Ford claimed figures
†CAR figures May 1969

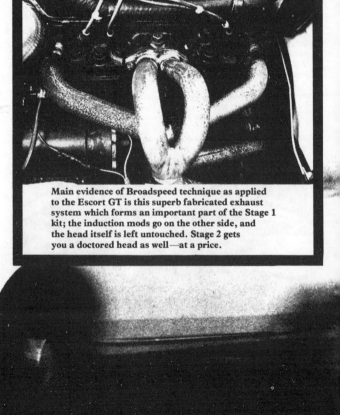

Main evidence of Broadspeed technique as applied to the Escort GT is this superb fabricated exhaust system which forms an important part of the Stage 1 kit; the induction mods go on the other side, and the head itself is left untouched. Stage 2 gets you a doctored head as well—at a price.

MOTOR TESTED

Performance potential

16-valve engine gives similar performance to
Twin Cam with better economy and greater tuning
potential; superb roadholding and handling
on corners; twitchy in straight line; poor ride

It has long been established that the combined area of four moderate-sized circles inscribed within a larger circle is significantly greater than that of two inscribed circles of the largest possible size. Many competition engines have been provided with four valves per cylinder to take advantage of this geometrical principle and give improved breathing at high rpm, the best-known of recent times being Keith Duckworth's Ford-based 16-valve four-cylinder Formula 2 unit (itself a sort of pilot build for his later V-8 Formula 1 engine) capable of producing some 220 bhp from its 1600 cc at getting on for 10,000 rpm. Now Ford's AVO (Advanced Vehicle Operations) centre is making available to the ordinary enthusiast a special version of this engine developed by the Cosworth organization and differing only from its Formula 2 brother in being substantially derated for road use and having its twin overhead camshafts driven by a toothed belt rather than gears. By analogy with the FVA designation of the racing engine (Four Valve engine type A) the new variant is known as the BDA engine (Belt Driven engine type A) but the car is to be called the RS (Rallye Sport) 1600.

The BDA is also quite closely related to the Lotus twin-cam engine in having two overhead camshafts and in using the existing camshaft to drive the auxiliaries—which means that the distributor is similarly buried under the carburetters. Unlike the twin-cam engine, however, which uses the block of the old 1500 cc series of Ford engines, the BDA is based on the Kent 1600 cc cylinder block and appropriate crankshaft with tuftrided journals and a nosepiece modified to take the sprocket for the belted camshaft drive. Development showed the BDA capable of

running on 92 octane fuel, a remarkable achievement in view of the 10:1 compression, but to allow a little margin 3-star 94 octane fuel is recommended.

If the engine gets its design rationale from the laws of nature, the car into which it fits—an Escort with "Twin Cam" chassis modifications—largely owes its existence to an FIA regulation that says 1000 examples of a car must be built for homologation in Group 2. Only a very small proportion of the development costs of this exercise, and of the expense of low-volume production, is to be passed on to the customer: although a price has not yet been decided it is expected to be around £1450 compared to the £1291 asked for the ordinary Twin Cam Escort which it closely resembles in many respects. Theoretically the buyer should get slightly improved performance for his extra £159, since the BDA engine is claimed to give 120 (net) bhp at 6500 rpm and 112 lb.ft. of torque at 4000 rpm compared to 109.5 bhp at 6000 rpm and 106.5 lb.ft. at 4500 rpm of the Lotus-Ford unit. In practice, it seems, the difference depends on the excellence of the particular twin-cam engine used for comparison: because our road test Escort Twin Cam was an extremely good one the BDA car was only marginally superior to it in certain aspects of performance. So for a little more money the buyer will have the satisfaction of owning an unusual race-bred vehicle with considerable—to say the least—tuning potential for which kits are likely to become available, though no definite plans have yet been announced. But many customers are likely to be enthusiasts with serious competition plans.

No fewer than six pumps of the accelerator were suggested as being necessary to prime the two 40 DCOE 48 Weber carburetters for a cold start, and without using the choke this technique always caused the engine to fire promptly, but the voltage drop in the long and inadequate-looking cable connecting the

PRICE: not yet decided—approximately £1450.

boot-mounted battery to the starter motor made it reluctant to turn the engine at all on a cold morning. Once running, the BDA engine pulled more promptly when cold than many cooking engines of half its specific power output. Throughout most of its rev-range the BDA engine is perhaps very slightly rougher than an ordinary twin-cam unit, though when we removed the ignition cut-out for our standing start acceleration tests it justified its breeding by running up to 7000 rpm with unperturbed smoothness. The BDA engine also makes louder and slightly less pleasant noises dominated by a whine which sounds like an overtightened timing chain—presumably generated by the toothed rubber belt of the camshaft drive.

Improved low-speed torque is a claimed advantage of the BDA unit over the Lotus engine. In fact, our figures show a slight gain in top-gear acceleration from 30 mph onwards, but the 20-40 mph time was rather worse and accentuated by considerable snatch in the transmission which made about 27 mph a sensible minimum speed for top gear. The same slight torque deficiency at very low speeds can have quite an influence

on the getaway of standing start acceleration tests for which we removed the ignition cut-out and used 7000 rpm. The engine may be safe to higher rpm, but the breathing limitations imposed by the size of carburetter fitted as well as the camshaft overlap make any higher speeds pointless; our main purpose was merely to cancel the effect created by a cut-out which on our test car sometimes started its work at around 6350 rpm during acceleration rather than at its designed 6500 rpm setting. In consequence our standing start acceleration figures were a little better than for the ordinary Escort Twin Cam.

For our top speed measurement it was merely necessary to prove that the engine would attain its maximum 6500 rpm in fourth gear (the cut-out was less capricious and more accurate for constant speed running) which it was comfortably capable of doing, so that the actual 114.4 mph figure recorded was again slightly better than for the Escort Twin Cam.

In all other respects the BDA car is identical to the Twin Cam, being essentially an ordinary Escort with a 3.78:1 final drive ratio, a close ratio Corsair gearbox, stiffened and lowered

PERFORMANCE

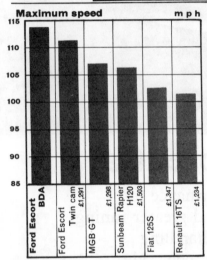

Performance tests carried out by Motor's staff at the Motor Industry Research Association proving ground, Lindley.

Test Data: World copyright reserved; no unauthorized reproduction in whole or in part.

Conditions

Weather: Dry and fine, wind 8-13 mph.
Temperature: 50-56°F.
Barometer: 29.5in Hg.
Surface: Dry concrete and tarmacadam.
Fuel: Mixture grade 94 octane (RM) 3-Star rating.

Maximum Speeds

	mph	kph
Direct top gear ⎫	114.4	184
3rd gear ⎪ at 6,500 rpm	82	132
2nd gear ⎬	57	92
1st gear ⎭	38	60

"Maximile" speed: (Timed quarter mile after 1 mile accelerating from rest)
Mean 108.3
Best 111.1

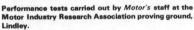

Accelerating Times

mph	sec.
0-30	3.2
0-40	4.5
0-50	6.4

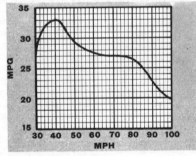

0-60	....	8.3
0-70	....	11.5
0-80	....	15.0
0-90	....	20.0
0-100	....	29.9
Standing quarter mile		16.5
Standing kilometre		30.7

	Top	3rd.
mph	sec.	sec.
10-30	—	—
20-40	10.5	5.9
30-50	8.8	5.5
40-60	8.9	5.3
50-70	9.7	5.9
60-80	10.3	6.6
70-90	11.8	—
80-100	16.2	—

Fuel Consumption

Touring (consumption midway between 30 mph and maximum less 5% allowance for acceleration) . . 25.5 mpg
Overall . . . . 25.3 mpg
(=11.1 litres/100km)
Total test distance . . . . 1,147 miles

SPECIFICATION

Engine

Block material	Cast iron
Head material	Light alloy
Cylinders	4
Cooling system	Water
Bore and stroke	80.97 mm (3.19in.) 77.60 mm (3.06in.)
Cubic capacity	1601 c.c. (97.7 cu. in.)
Main bearings	5
Valves	4 per cylinder, belt-driven & ohc operated
Compression ratio	10:1
Carburetters	Two 40 DCOE 48 Webers
Fuel pump	Mechanical
Oil filter	Full flow
Max. power (net)	120 b.h.p. at 6500 r.p.m.
Max. torque (net)	112 lb.ft. at 4000 r.p.m.

Transmission

Clutch . . . . Borg and Beck 8in. s.d.p.

Internal gear box ratios

Top gear	1.000:1
3rd gear	1.397:1
2nd gear	2.010:1
1st gear	2.972:1
Reverse	3.324:1
Synchromesh	All forward ratios
Final drive	Hypoid 3.77:1

M.P.H. at 1,000 r.p.m. in:—

Top gear	17.6
3rd gear	12.6
2nd gear	8.8
1st gear	5.9

Chassis and body

Construction . . . . Unitary

Brakes

Type	Discs/drums
Dimensions	9.6in. dia. front; 9.0in. dia. rear

Friction areas:
Front: . . . . 20.64 sq. in. of lining operating on 189.5 sq. in. of disc
Rear: . . . . . 48.0 sq. in. of lining operating on 96.1 sq. in. of drum

Suspension and steering

Front	Independent by MacPherson struts with coil springs and anti-roll bar
Rear	Live axle on leaf springs with radius arms
Shock absorbers: Front: Rear:	} Telescopic
Steering type	Rack and pinion
Tyres	165-13 India Autoband radials
Wheels	13in.
Rim size	5½in.

suspension with marked negative camber at the front and locating radius arms at the rear with $5\frac{1}{2}$J wheels accommodated within slightly flared wheel arches. As before we found the ratios first class for road use—nearly 60 mph can be attained in second gear—and the change superb in its precision and lightness, though during the really frantic changing of our acceleration tests the synchromesh was sometimes beaten.

With such strong negative camber in conjunction with the very light, rather dead and high-geared steering there is virtually no understeer at all, and this made the car a little difficult to get on with at first since such complete neutrality is rare even among race-bred performance cars. But the task of acclimatization was well worth while, for the chosen handling compromise gave truly marvellous cornering powers with very little roll, tremendous controllability and a capacity for progressive steering on the throttle found in only a handful of the cars that pass through our hands. The India Autoband tyres provided stable and progressive grip in the wet on clean roads but on the greasy surfaces near big towns they are inclined to be a little treacherous at times, and they also showed a tendency to climb up white lines and the like.

Most of these comments apply to behaviour on relatively good main road surfaces, or on a circuit, to which the car was ideally suited. For some kinds of road use it was less satisfactory, the front-end negative camber making it very twitchy and sensitive to sidewinds at anything above 80 mph. On one straight but bumpy and undulating road it became positively unstable at high speeds.

On rough roads of this sort the car pitched, bounced and floated, giving an uncomfortable ride. The front seats were potentially quite comfortable, but without reclining backrests —or much lateral support—and located too close to the pedals for a tall driver. Heeling and toeing is easy for medium drivers but less so for tall drivers and also for the latter the steering wheel obscures the instruments. As with the Ford Escort GT the minor controls such as the lights and wiper switches are very badly located. Low speed road noise is well suppressed, and there is little wind noise.

You too can have a Formula 2 engine in your car. Only the carburetters—rather than fuel-injection equipment—distinguish this BDA engine from its full-race brothers. Interior is identical with that of the Twin Cam, in turn the same as the 1300GT. Leather rimmed wheel is an extra. Squat and squirt. We liked our Escort's discreet anonymity and complete absence of boy-racer stripes

EVEN A TRIP TO IS AN

MAKE:	Escort 1600T/C	PRICE:	Approx $3500

PERFORMANCE:

SPEEDS IN GEARS: — Equivalent rpm

First	36 mph at 6500 rpm
Second	55 mph at 6500 rpm
Third	80 mph at 6500 rpm
Fourth	113.8 mph at 6500 rpm

ACCELERATION THROUGH THE GEARS:

0-30 mph	3.3 sec
0-40 mph	4.8 sec
0-50 mph	6.3 sec
0-60 mph	8.7 sec
0-70 mph	11.3 sec
0-80 mph	15.0 sec
STANDING QUARTER MILE	16.9 sec

SPECIFICATIONS:

ENGINE:

Cylinders	four
Cubic capacity	1558 cc
Compression ratio	9.5:1
Carburettors	two x 40DCOE Webers
Power	109.5 bhp at 6000 rpm
Torque	106.5 ft/lbs at 6500 rpm

DIMENSIONS:

Length	13 ft
Width	5 ft 2 in.
Height	4 ft 6 in.

TYRES:

Size	165 x 13
Make on test car	India autobands
Weight (kerb)	1832 lb

We drive a 1600 twin-cam Ford Escort soon to be released on the Australian market.

HOMOLOGATION is not only hard to say, it is one of motor sport's dirty words. Ask any car maker. But it has got a bright side.

How else could you buy racing cars off the showroom floor? Well, perhaps not the REAL thing but about as near as a car dealer would ever see to a real racing car.

That's how the Twin Car Escort got that way. There were these events in Europe which needed a car with certain attributes. So the requisite numbers were built and one was snapped up by an Australian enthusiast.

The Twin Cam bit is just the Lotus/Cortina motor with a new home. But the Escort bit suits it marvellously. The car is sold in homologated (that word again) form — round lights, wheels, seats and suspension — for the enthusiast to permit the factory to race and rally them like that.

And the road version is just a sniff away from the mickey race or rally car. Ford has just released the Escort here (by the time you read this it will be touted as Mum's ideal shopping

THE SUPERMARKET ADVENTURE

car by Ford dealers) but overseas they are rushing about jousting with Minis for supermarket space.

In Twin Cam form the Escort comes with the Lotus motor, the Lotus front end with negative camber, GT rear suspension with track rods and leaf springs with power discs for the front.

The homologated car goes further. Fat wheels, Lotus competition seats, twin fuel tanks and battery at the back, the Lotus spongy-rimmed steering wheel. Really it's enough to make a chap either bolt a sump guard and Halda into it and chase rallies—or chuck out some weight and go racing. It's delivered in a form suited to either by gearing and equipment. It's at the crossroads.

As it stands it would make a fine hillclimb car.

First identification of the homologated competition Escort Twin Cam is the round lights. Let's face it, those oblong things just don't work well. And the Ford rally team had a nice set of Cibie Biode twin bulb quartziodine things which turn the night into day and are round. So the customer's car must have round lights. (Incidentally, the round lights are fitted to the bog standard, nasty 1100 Escort in Britain.)

Together with the round lights, fatties 6 in. with India Autoband radials and the comfortable

First identification of the homologated twin-cam competition Escort is the round headlights. The car is delivered in a form which makes it suitable for racing or rally work. It's virtually at the crossroads.

gear inside, we suspect there is a certain amount of fiddling with the motor. Certainly the oblong-lighted Twin Cams didn't go as hard as the round-light ones.

The familiar motor is a 1558 cc, four-cylinder Cortina with the twin-chained, twin-cam Lotus head and a pair of 40 DCOE Webers. Two stabs on the accelerator and its burst to life with the usual Weber chortling sound and the chain thrash of the camshaft drives.

Behind the spongy steering wheel the dials are those of the 1300 GT Escort, the rather vague "she's right" or "watch it" variety, and these flickered to life.

Biggest surprise was the smooth and light close-ratio gearbox. And the motor's flexibility. With 109 hp (net) at 6000 rpm, the motor whams the lighter Escort along much faster than the Cortina Lotus. Gearing is the same and the Escort saves 1.5 cwt on the Cortina so it just has to go.

The ratios of the gearbox give intermediate speeds of 36, 55, 80 mph and the gearshift is smooth as suntan lotion. But the motor with only 1832 lb to pull along is quite happy to snuffle about at under 2000 rpm.

With 1500 miles on the motor the car hit 50 mph in 6.3 sec, the sort of acceleration which had the tail skewed to the right off the line and saw off all the big noise, stripey stuff.

But if there were enough wiggles in the road, the big iron just wouldn't see which way the Escort went. The 165 section tyres on 13 in. wheels (note that diameter, Escort buyers, it's up an inch on standard cars!) gripped as they should, and rack and pinion steering gear gave the car an almost nervously sensitive steering.

For the first dozen or so bends we were still finding out how far you could go with this car. With the fat tyres, negative camber front suspension, sensitive steering and a weight distribution of 53/47 front/rear it clung on well.

It understeered into bends and through them if it wasn't hurried. A flick on the steering, a second's backing off on the throttle or a stab on the throttle would have the nose coming in and the tail going out delightfully. Result—the corner could be tightened either speeding up or slowing down, a nice balance when either the corner opened unexpectedly or a sand truck rumbled out of a concealed drive.

Just as it was, that car could have been rallied or hillclimbed and given a good account of itself.

One of the Escort's big advantages is that it can put the full 110 bhp of the motor on to the ground more easily than the Cortina. The shorter wheelbase is the secret. The weight transfer backwards produces more tyre adhesion.

Once the car got wound up, it sang along at a most relaxed 80 mph. It seemed carburetted and geared for this speed since it just didn't want to run any slower in top. At 17.6 per 1000 rpm in top that's about 4800 rpm. Once you get over that, there's a lot of commotion going on in front, although the surge forward continues.

There is plenty of engine vibration, an increased sensitivity to side wind and the rev counter will shoot around to 6500 rpm.

Few owners will ever fully extend this car unless they compete with it. And it's built with competition in mind. But if they do decide to explore its limits, they'll need concentration since things occur awfully fast at the Escort GT's limits, well beyond the usual sports car stuff.

Once the driver has sufficient bravery in store to take the car to its limits the Escort Twin-Cam really zooms along with the sort of swoopy, rev, twitch, tweak, opposite lock desperation which brings delight to the wringers-out of cars. The car's predictable response for power, torque, handling, roadholding, even stopping is rather abnormal.

For a family wagon it doesn't make it. The back seat is rather small and tall front occupants take most of the rear legroom. In the boot, the bags fit around the spare on the floor, the battery beside the back seat and the fuel tanks in each back mudguard.

Further, this is a machine which simply would not rank when slotted into the club car park, the line-up at church or even the line at the pay station. It looks very plain. After all the pretty jazz does up the weight. Further, the types likely to appreciate the belled mudguards, the black grille and the weightless austerity wouldn't want the status stripes.   #

The Homologated car comes complete with Lotus competition seats and leather bound steering wheel. But the gauges are the same as used in the 1300 GT.

The twin-cam motor comes straight from the Lotus Elan and is the same used in the successful Lotus Cortinas. Escort body suits engine well.

From the rear there is nothing to give the homologated Twin-Cam Escort away. In fact the whole appearance of the high performance car is plain.

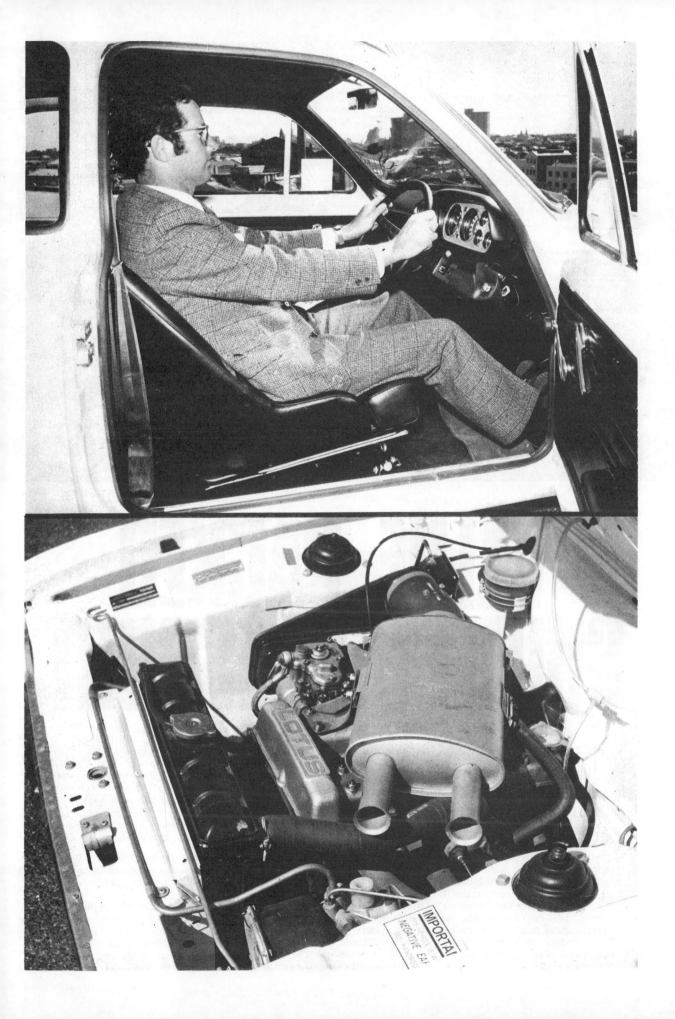

FOR A BABY SUPER ROO THIS JOEY HAS SOME REAL KICK....

VALUE-PACKED SUPER ROO ESCORT

The Escort 1300 GT leaps the value-for-money hurdle right into Japanese territory. When this baby Super Roo starts hopping both on the road and in the showroom, the competition will only see its tail.

STAND the Ford Escort on its merits and you have a truly captivating small car. Back it with Ford's marketing and local involvement — which will have to make it "go" — and you have one enormous headache for the competition — GM-H's Torana four and six range, Toyota's Corolla, Datsun's 1000 and British Leyland's Mini and 1500.

The Escort range as a whole is the first product of Ford's Anglo-European design co-operation. Paradoxically it has been released in Australia after the second co-operative design effort, the Capri. The Capri hit Australia merely three months after its UK release. With strikes (and parts coming from both the UK and Germany) assembly was a nightmare. The evidence was a brilliantly designed car which

Three quarter rear shows up the small back window on this 1300 Super model. Backdrop is Chateau Tahbilk vineyards near Mangalore. Dash of 1300 Super is neater than GT (shown in background). Super gets carpeting throughout and fan boosted heater/demister.

fell down in its execution. We are happy to say this has been much improved, as the Capri V6 has shown.

The Escort has benefited magnificently by the Capri's assembly teething problems. It is a brilliant small car which we found taut in suspension and body and well finished in trim and paintwork.

VALUE-PACKED SUPER ROO ESCORT

Above: The Escort GT is skittish on dirt despite its radial tyres and well tied-down back axle. Over rough work there are no rattles.

Below: Minor dials on GT dash are hard to see around wheel rim. Radio is almost impossible to reach with belt done-up tightly.

Like Capri and Cortina, engine has little presentation—but it really works. Note brake power booster for this GT to far left of bay. ▶▶

The range as a whole is a gem — no single model could be singled out as particularly outstanding value-for-money. In their own particular price classes, all the Escort models are excellent value, from the $1770 basic car to the ultimate GT which swallows most of $2500.

We drove all the models briefly at their release in the picturesque surrounds of Chateau Tahbilk, near Mangalore in Victoria. Our 1300 GT was singled out and driven back to Sydney to be paced out in our normal road test procedures.

In the space of a few days it gave us a condensed view of the whole range, plus nearly 1000 miles in the GT. Undoubtedly the sensation is the Twin Cam 1600 which will sell for $3000. This and other models WHEELS will cover in later tests and comparisons.

The Escort success story (as most enthusiasts will know it is a top seller and devastates competition overseas) lies in its brilliant design. The Escort you buy is low priced, not cheap. By defraying cost over volume, Ford is able to buy the best in design research. And by using already well-proven components, it can reap the benefits of parts interchangeability in servicing and spares.

In Australia, the Escort uses only one engine-transmission package common to its big sister, the Cortina, and that is the optional 1300. The 1600 which really makes the Escort a flier conflicts with the Government's requirement for small volume production (the 1600

being used both in the Capri and Escort) and thus will not be seen in the Australian Escort in the forseeable future. Government restrictions are primarily responsible for the Escort's belated arrival here.

Under Plan A in early 1968, when they were released overseas, the local content requirement was 95 percent for unlimited production. In the fierce competition of the light car market, the required sales for reasonable economic gain was an unsolvable equation. Small volume assembly was out — due to insufficient difference between Escort, Capri, Cortina models.

The requirements, however, were relaxed in December, 1968, and Ford has played its hand shrewdly to put the Escort out with unlimited production and a need to gain an 85 percent local content in five years — which it should be able to achieve equitably without the Escort suffering any loss of quality. So Ford is committed — and the Escort is going to go.

And it does. Despite its bluff front, we saw 7000 rpm consistently in top gear, and in fact had to back off to stop the needle rising. That's around 103 mph, according to our maths.

But even the 1100 Escort has the lively feeling that Continental and English engineering inspires in a car. The 1100 engine is an orphan. The original Cortina engine, being 1200 cc, was uprated to 1300 cc for the new Mk Two Cortina, then uprated again with cross-flow head and bowl-in-pistons only months

after the Mk Two's release. This is the Escort's optional engine and in tweaked form is standard in the GT.

The 1100, however, had to be developed specially for the Escort. It is an extension of the Anglia 105E oversquare design which has had wide success in small-bore Formula racing, producing incredible horsepower. It has a strong five-bearing crank and is assembled — as are all current Ford engines — by computer control.

Out of a batch of pistons, the computer control will choose the four best suited to the individual block as it is founded. Incrementally the tolerances are miniscule but this control puts an engine under your bonnet which is far closer to a "blueprint" engine than mass-production has allowed to date. With matched pistons and bores, running-in is virtually eliminated.

All the Escort range bar the GT and Twin Cam uses the same gearbox and rear axle. The differential ratio is the optional UK 3.9 to 1 rear end. The UK 1100s and 1300s use the 4.125 diff, standard in our GT. To us it should be the other way around, or all models committed to the 3.9 diff. Touring at speed in the GT keeps the little 1300 very busy. The GT gears are slightly closer ratios than the 1300 and 1100. The Twin Cam uses even closer ratios with a 3.778 diff.

CONTINUED ON PAGE 42

TECHNICAL DETAILS

MAKE: .... Ford	COLOR: .... hot orange
BODY TYPE: .. 2-dr sedan	MILEAGE START:
OPTIONS: .. GS pack $95	.... (2260 kilos) 1210
WEIGHT: .... 15.5 cwt	MILEAGE FINISH:
MODEL: ... Escort 1300 GT	.... (3460 kilos) 2185
PRICE: $2350	DISTRIBUTION F to R:
($2445 optioned)	.... 53.5/46.5

FUEL CONSUMPTION:
Overall .... (11.1 kl) 25.1 mpg
Cruising .... (11.1-13.2kl) 25-31 mpg

TEST CONDITIONS:
Weather .... fine, cool
Load .... two persons
Surface .... hot mix bitumen
Fuel .... premium grade

SPEEDOMETER ERROR:

Indicated mph:	30	40	50	60	70	80	90
Actual mph:	29	38	47	56	66	76	86

PERFORMANCE

Piston speed at max bhp .. (6750 m/min) 2210 ft/min
Top gear mhp per 1000 rpm ...... (38.2 kph) 14.8
Lbs (laden) per gross bhp (power-to-weight)
.... (10.3 kgm/bhp) 23.8

MAXIMUM SPEEDS:
Fastest run .... (165 kph) 103 mph
Average of all runs .... (154 kph) 96.4 mph
Speedometer indication, fastest run (162 kph) 101 mph

IN GEARS:
Drive
1st .... (48 kph) 30 mph (6500 rpm)
2nd .... (80 kph) 50 mph (6500 rpm)
3rd .... (112 kph) 70 mph (6500 rpm)
4th .... (154 kph) 96.4 mph (6500 rpm)

ACCELERATION (through gears):
0-30 mph .... 4.0 secs
0-40 mph .... 6.1 secs
0-50 mph .... 8.5 secs
0-60 mph .... 12.0 secs
0-70 mph .... 17.2 secs
0-80 mph .... 24.5 secs
0-90 mph .... 40.1 secs

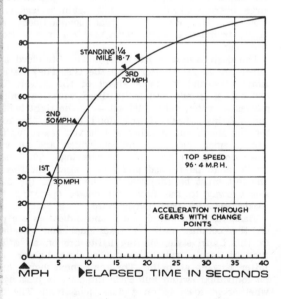

STANDING 1/4 MILE 18·7
3RD 70 MPH
2ND 50 MPH
TOP SPEED 96·4 M.P.H.
1ST 30 MPH
ACCELERATION THROUGH GEARS WITH CHANGE POINTS

MPH   ELAPSED TIME IN SECONDS

	3rd gear	4th gear
20-40 mph	6.4 secs	10.4 secs
30-50 mph	6.2 secs	10.0 secs
40-60 mph	6.5 secs	10.2 secs
50-70 mph	8.0 secs	11.6 secs

STANDING QUARTER MILE:
Fastest run .... 18.6 secs
Average all runs .... 18.7 secs

SPECIFICATIONS

ENGINE:
Cylinders .... four in line
Bore and stroke .... 80.98 mm by 62.99 mm
Cubic capacity .... 1298 cc
Compression ratio .... 9.2 to 1
Valves .... ohv pushrod
Carburettor .... Weber compound
Power at rpm .... 75 bhp at 5400 rpm
Torque at rpm .... 91 lb/ft at 2500 rpm
(12 kg-m at 2500 rpm)

TRANSMISSION:
Type .... four-speed all syncro
Clutch .... (18 cm) 7.5 in. sdp
Gear lever location .... central console
Direct ratio: mph/1000 rpm
   1st .... 3.337   4.5 (7.4 kph)
   2nd .... 1.995   7.7 (12.3 kph)
   3rd .... 1.418   10.7 (17.1 kph)
   4th .... 1.000   14.8 (23.7 kph)
   Final drive .... 4.125 to 1

CHASSIS and RUNNING GEAR:
Construction .... integral
Suspension, front .... Macpherson struts, anti roll bar
Suspension rear .... radius rods, leaf springs
Shock absorbers .... telescopic
Steering type .... rack and pinion
Turns 1 to 1 .... 3½
Turning circle .... (885 cm) 29 ft
Steering wheel diameter .... (38.1 cm) 15 in.
Brakes, type .... power assisted disc/drum
Dimensions: 8.6 in. (22.2 cm) dia disc/8.0 in. (21.5 cm)
dia drum
Friction area .... (141 sq cm) 218 sq in.

DIMENSIONS:
Wheelbase .... (244 cm) 94.5 in.
Track, front .... (126.5 cm) 49.0 in.
Track, rear .... (127 cm) 50.0 in.
Length .... (396 cm) 13 ft 0.6 in.
Height .... (134.5 cm) 4 ft 5 in.
Width .... (159 cm) 5 ft 1.8 in.
Fuel tank capacity .... (33 litres) 9 gals

TYRES:
Size .... (5.50-12) 155-12
Make on test car .... Olympic GT radial

GROUND CLEARANCE:
Registered .... (17 cm) 6.3 in.

We're not entirely convinced the 75 horses of the GT are quite the well-fed brutes found in, say, the Cooper S. The 1300 GT revs freely but needs all the rpm to keep power up. Alternately at highway speeds in the 6000 rpm band, nothing will stop the little flier as it storms highway hills at 90 mph — and maintains it. If only it had the higher rear axle ratio (lower numerically) it would make touring more relaxed. At speed the engine and Aeroflow vents make the most noise.

The gearbox has ideally-spaced ratios for a small car giving 30, 50, 70 mph through the gears. It seems just no sweat for the well tied-down engine to spin to 7000 rpm. Sitting in the redline sector for mile after mile on our quick trip back to Sydney after the Victorian Press release, we found the little engine seemingly unburstable. It uses a little less than a quart of oil for 1000 miles, a healthy sign for an engine run hard while new.

Although high rpm torque for maintaining near top speed is a feature, the GT doesn't lack low speed pull either. From 1500 rpm (22 mph in top) the GT pulls strongly and turns in good times for plugging holes in traffic without downchange — that's if you can resist using the beaut gear change.

We felt cheated in highway touring that you just can't get three up-changes and three downchanges in the space of every city block. The shift is the ultimate in the legendary knife-through-butter change. It is quite unbaulked and for all the world could be connected to nothing, except moving does get another gear. The only slight criticism is the definite gate which is a bit wide and must be followed.

Using the shift so often takes toll on the fuel consumption which touring hard averages around 25 mpg. That should go up to 31 easily, if you stop playing boy-Fangios with the console shift.

To match the willingness and smoothness of engine and gearbox, are brakes and handling which are obvious products of Ford's competition involvement. Light and progressive, the brakes give the Escort bags of reserve stopping power.

Even stamping on the brakes in a corner brought just an instant stop with no drama. The same disc front-drum rear set-up as the GTs is carried throughout the Escort range except for the basic 1100. This has drums which stop well but the re-assuring power-assisted discs are a happy option for the 1100. Like the Cortina, the Escort has a soft front suspension which shows up brake dive.

The brake pedal is beautifully aligned so full braking to the point of lock-up is available with sufficient shoe-over lap to blip the throttle. This ball-of-the-foot swivel is easy for even small feet, gives perfect, safe throttle-brake co-ordination and makes heel-and-toeing seem old fashioned. The clutch is an equally well placed and sensitive control with a wide gap to the drive tunnel, allowing space for the left foot to rest.

It has taken a long time for any company to produce a car whose handling can be improved sufficiently to out-handle the Mini — in whatever form. We found there were very few highway corners the Escort even considered corners. In tight work it develops some degree of understeer, but back off and the little car comes back on line precisely. And it has already proven a match for the Mini, both in stock and improved forms.

On dirt or in the wet we could recommend discretion. On dry bitumen we found the tail almost impossible to break away. The back axle is so well located. But in the suet it breaks at will.

It can be corrected easily with the direct rack and pinion steering but, like the Capri, needs quick reactions if it's not being flung around deliberately.

On dirt, the Escort gets caught up on ridges of gravel or ruts and feels mildly unstable. Wider tyres would possibly help here as we thought the car rather under-shod on its 4½ in. rims and 155 by 12 radials (Olympic GTs on the test car). Five inches on the GT and 5½ on the Twin Cam would improve the already excellent roadholding and directional stability.

In the wet, a tail slide is easily caught by stepping off the throttle, at which the car snaps back into line. Drive through on power, and it comes straight more progressively. Backing-off on dirt or gravel roads in a tail slide will end you in a spin, and the point where you can power out comes too soon — so just take care!

The steering is both light and direct but lacks feel and could do with stronger self-centring action. The wheel (all the test cars are fitted with the optional sports wheel — $25) is just where a steering wheel should be, although some tall drivers will find it snags their knees. Vinyl bound, it has a good firm feeling of great control over the car. We presume the stock wheel is the three-spoke, heavily dished affair used on the UK cars. A heavily padded boss sits atop the collapsible column with the ignition switch set on a moulded cowl around the column near the dash. This is not designed to take a steering lock — only a safety measure.

Interior fittings make the Escort 1300 GT a comfortable and enjoyable touring or commuter car. The seats are slightly uprated beside the Standard and Super's. The GT seats are better contoured, softer and have a perforated weave centre section. The cost-cutting over-centre mounting — similar to the Cortina's — is less obvious in the Escort. It means that as the seat goes back the squab straightens as the seat flattens, which is not entirely comfortable for those who relish the semi-reclined position apparently fashionable among the checkered flag set.

There is carpeting throughout the fluffy, loop-over haircord variety used in Capris. It is soft and looks good but collects dirt easily, rubs and needs a vacuum cleaner to clean properly. A token gesture at crash padding tops the dash while the surrounds are black matt painted, which numbs the shock of large untrimmed areas — once again a legacy of economy. The doors and rear compartment are neatly trimmed through, with usable armrests front and rear.

The dash layout is less happy. The Standard and Super are in fact better than the GT. They have a simple two-dial binnacle ahead of the driver. The GT puts a speedo and tacho there, with four minor gauges — water, volts, fuel, oil — to the right behind the steering wheel. If you don't run off the road reading them, you possibly will as you reach for the lights, wipers or radio controls which are set way down low either side of the steering. The radio cradle is to be revised and those minor controls to the left must be changed. To rub salt in, the dash slopes away to the floor and makes operating the rocker switches particularly hard.

Flashers, beam switch, horn and indicators are put on the column stalk in traditional and excellent Cortina/Capri style. Driving lights are on an afterthought toggle switch near the cigar lighter, the latter ring-lit at night. The instrument lights have no individual switch but their intensity is just right, whether in town or on a dark, long road. The GT gets a centre console which doesn't carry a clock like the overseas GT, but it does have useful odds 'n ends bins with slides to anchor the seat belt buckles when not in use. CONTINUED ON PAGE 100

The World Cup rally winner is no road-rocket in basic trim...

TWIN CAM-ESCORT WITHOUT GAS

wheels ROAD TEST

Ford fires off a fizzer... the Lotus-engined Escort "prowl growler." It stops magnificently and is one of the safest small high performance cars you can buy, but it won't win races.   **BY ROB LUCK.**

IT is hard to believe Ford Australia was running 5000 mile durability tests on the Escort Twin Cam at its You Yangs (Geelong) proving grounds as far back as December, 1969. The car eventually popped unobtrusively onto the Australian

Roll bar reduces front end kneel, and twin trailing links keep the back happily tied in place for controlled oversteer. Understeer is evident in this shot on Oran Park's tight CC turn, but car is a basic oversteerer — and a safe one.

market about June 1, 1970 (it was released in the UK early in 1968) and WHEELS acquired a road test car in mid-July. Our test lasted little more than 12 hours — for reasons explained later.

Ford's NSW Public Relations Manager, Max Ward, probably runs the most efficient test car fleet of any NSW manufacturer base. His preparation workshops at Road and Track Automotive Services, headed by Len Dunne and Fred Gibson, usually turn out the best-prepared

cars we get for test. But their combined efforts in providing an immediate test of the Escort Twin Cam couldn't gloss-over basic manufacturer shortcomings that rate the Escort Twin Cam as the worst road test of 1970 in my experience.

The Twin Cam was more than two years old at the point of its market introduction in Australia — and it seems inconceivable that Ford Australia hasn't had English cars

PHOTOS BY ROB LUCK

Interior is disappointing for the money. Seats are uncomfortable, switchgear is poorly placed and that sports wheel hides the auxiliary instrumentation.

Front end negative camber, flared wheel arches and a well-tied-down rear end are evident in this rear cornering shot. Muffler has fallen out of its O-rings.

here for that full two years and fully evaluated and sorted the car for local conditions.

The Escort Twin Cam is a raw, unimproved import — nothing more. In the glamorous tone drop-out color brochures it reads as a go-machine offering value for money. The test car I drove certainly didn't offer value for money, and its go-potential was confined to brute acceleration. Its stamina and durability for Australian conditions were negligible.

We have already criticised Ford for its manufacture and assembly of Capris and Escorts — and we have noted the considerable improvements in many fields. Our road test car didn't reflect any of them. It was very loose in the body, the doors didn't fit properly and were hard to close, there were obvious rattles from most areas of the car, trim didn't fit properly, some of the equipment didn't work at all, paint quality was poor, and there were break-downs in major mechanical points — the engine broke loose from its stay and successfully destroyed the starter solenoid, the muffler dropped out of its retaining thongs at least a dozen times, the cam cover leaked oil continuously, the heavy duty battery fitted in the boot lacked a proper manufacturer-originated cover and the body paintwork and boot showed the obvious scars of a fire prior to our test.

Why — when the basic Escorts are

so good? The Twin Cam is built on a small separate production line which matches local bodies with fully imported CBU engine transmission units. The assembly side-line simply isn't up to standard.

Apart from the manufacturing deficiencies, the Twin Cam didn't perform well in all the fields it should have, and the equipment is well below par for the money. The Twin Cam shows up on the price lists at $3000 and looks very attractive at that. Our test car showed just how unattractive the basic car is. It was optioned to the extent of tinted, laminated windshield ($50), quartz iodine lamps ($30), slotted road wheel covers ($26), sports steering wheel ($25), exterior racing mirror ($4), push-button radio ($93), rear seat lap-belts ($10). Heavy duty battery ($6) — adding $234 to the basic price. The test unit wasn't fitted with the entire GS pack — which apart from QI lights, wheel covers, side mirror, sports steering wheel, and tuned muffler also includes side stripes and Super-roo decals, and wood-stick gearlever knob — total value $95.

Broken down to basics, the prospective Twin Cam owner would have to spend an average additional $150 to get the car he would like to drive on the road — and that doesn't stack up as good high performance motoring value in an ultra-compact economy size car. It still stands as reasonable value

Stopping power is magnificent — our test car always pulled up straight in brutally short distances with perfect control, but noticeable weight transfer. It is one of the safest of high performance cars.

when compared with an Escort GT or Cortina GT but that's only comparing it with other Fords, not its competitors.

The Australian Twin Cam has virtually the identical specification of the English cars — engine performance, suspension engineering, gearbox ratio and final drive, clutch and road gear. The WHEELS test Twin Cam produced identical or better figures in all acceleration ranges compared with English test car averages — but failed to produce a top end comparable and broke down before we could get it to the track. At 6000 rpm in top (indicated) the car timed out at 105 mph — consistent with the mph per 1000 gearing figure of 17.6 in top. English testers amazingly produced 110-116 mph top speed averages, although they admitted their cars have distributors governed to 6500 rpm, and 6500 rpm is only 113.4 mph!

In any case the local test car would not run beyond 6000 in top with very long wind-ups and was very noisy and hard-running at that speed.

ESCORT WITHOUT GAS *Continued*

Conversely it could be screwed up through the gears to produce gear maximums of 38, 58 and 85 at 6500 rpm or 42, 65 and 90 at 7000 rpm, and turn in 8.5 second 0-60 squirts and 16.7 second 1320s (indicating 90 mph going through the traps).

The Escort's performance is not sufficient to give it a class rating at Bathurst against six-cylinder Torana GTR XU1s, and it will have a battle to beat off the new Valiant Pacers (an indication of value for money at that price level) — so where is it good?

The answer is, of course, rallies. The Escort Twin Cam, totally rebuilt with many components replaced, would make an unbeatable rally car since it shatters every other car in performance up to 100 mph, and handles like an express train. Brakes are also totally above reproach, and performance on the dirt is unbelievable — or would you believe victory in the World Cup rally for proof.

Terminal approach speeds to corners in the Escort Twin Cam would probably be the highest of any series production rally car in the world, and actual corner negotiation speeds have never been achieved on our test course by any other car. Control is also way above general standard — and the Escort Twin Cam would have to rate as one of the safest high performance machines in the hands of an expert driver. On top of that, it is sheer fun to drive — for anyone.

Its built-in safety limits are extraordinary. The car can be driven at corners on left-foot brake, handbrake slide or sheer full-bore oversteer slide at incredible speeds with little drama.

The car thrives on oversteer, and due to a combination of completely re-engineered and relocated suspension (lowered too), bigger wheels, more power and better steering shows no sign of the usual Escort understeer, and in fact uses a stabilised tyre-pressure system — unified pressures in all four corners instead of a heavy bias in favor of the front tyres.

The secret is negative camber on the front wheels, 13 in. wheels with 5JJ rims, front stabiliser bar and rear trailing links (radius rods), stiffer shocks and springs, lower overall height (1 in. lowering on front coils). The overall effect is complete stability in all conditions — except a straight line, where the steering-wander and sticky feel at the wheel persists.

There are ample signs of the fact the Escort wasn't originally designed to accept the Twin Cam. Under the bonnet the area is crowded, hard to work on and poorly laid out. The engine had token stiffening from a slotted, open-ended stabiliser bar that broke out of its bulkhead mount at the first hard corner and proceeded to beat the bakelite starter solenoid into a pulp.

Placement of cables, electricals and piping is bad, and the lack of retaining clips on the joiner hoses for the brake fluid reservoir was alarming. The Twin Cam with its leaky alloy gear cover (racing drivers usually bond the whole business down semi-permanently) and big twin 40 DCOE Webers doesn't leave room for the battery which uses up the left well of the boot and displaces the spare on to the floor — effectively halving usable boot space, and providing a drop-current power supply to the engine that virtually demands a heavy duty battery.

As already explained the H/D battery has no protective cover and any metal object bouncing around in the boot readily shorts the terminals and starts a fire. The other disappointing performance note to be found

Heavy duty battery in side well has no cover, caused a fire in our test car. It also displaces spare on to boot floor to absorb much of the useable space, and petrol tank is still a measly nine gallons.

in the back compartment is the same stock tiny 9 gallon fuel tank, which with hard use will take the Twin Cammer less than 190 miles — in other words useless in this country for interstate tripping, racing or rallying.

Torque is reasonable — the engine will pull from 20 mph in top with a stretch and fuel consumption can be boosted to 28 mpg with a gentle right foot.

The cockpit is also an anti-climax. The optional extra sports rally wheel and standard expanded instrument cluster adds an impressive air to the dashboard area, but most of the little auxiliary gauges are obscured by the little wheel, the seats are unbearably uncomfortable over any distance (due chiefly to the former ride), and the switchgear is poorly placed.

The gearlever is perfectly positioned, reflecting the new gearbox internals (heavy components, close ratios) in the same casing, with a beautiful short, sharp shift in a tight gate that can't be beaten to any slot. It stirs the car up the performance scale with confidence and ease.

Features you notice with time in the cockpit are the poor ventilation, two-speed wire non-lift wipers (excellent), highly usable exterior racing mirrors, vibration-prone interior rear vision mirror, pathetic horn, slipping seat belts, and excellent driver visibility (lights are quite good at night with optional spots).

The clutch is very heavy to use (quite beyond women drivers for sustained city use), the engine loads up frequently, providing lumpy, fluffy city running (cold starts are chokeless — two squirts on the throttle) and the "prowlgrowl" muffler sounds great (only one restrictor on the straight-through pipes), but keeps falling from its rubber thong retaining clips.

The Twin Cam is most definitely a second car for the enthusiast with lots of cash and a workhorse for general transport. It's not the young enthusiast's ideal GT car since it doesn't provide general all-round transport in the way a Torana GTR, Valiant Pacer or even Morris Cooper S does.

It's the most specialised freely-available GT car ever released on the Australian market. It won't win its class at Bathurst, it certainly won't win races in this country, and it would make easily the top rally car for Australian Championship events and major rallies — given proper preparation and team presentation. Unlike the Torana GTR XU1 it's not restricted to specialist sales but by virtue of its concept it will reach only a highly specialised market.

With improved development for local conditions and uprated manufacturing techniques it could provide exceptional performance value on our market. At the moment it is just mediocre.　　　　　#

TECHNICAL DETAILS

MAKE: .... Ford
MODEL: .... Escort twin cam
BODY TYPE: .... 2-door sedan
OPTIONS: .... Radio, driving lamps, sports steering and
road wheels, external mirror, special screen, 4/D
battery, rear belts.
WEIGHT: .... 1820 lb (830 kg)
COLOR: .... Mustard
PRICE: $3000
DISTRIBUTION F to R: 53/47
FUEL CONSUMPTION:
Overall .... (9.7 kpl) 23 mpg
Cruising .... (11.8 kpl) 28.1 mpg

TEST CONDITIONS:
Weather .... cool, dry
Surface .... dry hot mix
Load .... two persons
Fuel .... premium

SPEEDOMETER ERROR:

Indicated mph:	30	40	50	60	70	80	90
Actual mph:	30.5	39	48.5	58	67	76	85

PERFORMANCE

Piston speed at max bhp .... (475 m/min) 1400 ft/min
Top gear mph per 100 rpm 17.6
Engine rpm at max speed 6500
Lbs (laden) per gross bhp (power-to-weight) (7.3 kg)
16 lb

MAXIMUM SPEEDS:
Fastest run .... (168 kph) 105.1 mph
Average of all runs .... (160 kph) 100 mph
Speedometer indication, fastest run (176 kph) 110 mph

IN GEARS:
Drive
1st .... (61 kph) 38 mph 6500 rpm
2nd .... (93 kph) 58 mph 6500 rpm
3rd .... (136 kph) 85 mph 6500 rpm
4th .... (168 kph) 105 mph 6500 rpm

ACCELERATION (through gears):
0-30 mph .... 3.1 secs

0-40 mph	....	5.2 secs
0-50 mph		6.4 secs
0-60 mph		8.5 secs
0-70 mph		11.5 secs
0-80 mph		15.2 secs
0-90 mph		21.5 secs

	2nd gear	3rd gear	4th gear
20-40 mph	3.3 secs	4.9 secs	9.0 secs
30-50 mph	3.2 secs	5.0 secs	7.5 secs
40-60 mph	3.5 secs	4.9 secs	6.7 secs
50-70 mph		5.0 secs	7.1 secs

STANDING QUARTER MILE:
Fastest run .... 16.7 secs
Average all runs .... 16.8 secs

BRAKING:
From 30 mph to 0 .... 1.8 secs
From 60 mph to 0 .... 3.2 secs

SPECIFICATIONS

ENGINE:
Cylinders .... four in-line
Bore and stroke .... 82.55 mm (3.25 in.) x 72.75 mm
(2.87 in.)
Cubic capacity .... 1558 cc (95.2 cu in.)
Compression ratio .... 9.5 to 1
Valves .... dohc
Carburettors .... 2 twin-choke Weber 40 dcoe
Fuel pump .... AC mechanical
Oil filter .... full flow
Power at rpm .... 115 bhp at 6000 rpm
Torque at rpm .... 116.5 lb/ft (16.1 kg/m) at 4500 rpm

TRANSMISSION:
Type .... four speed, close ratio, all syncro
Clutch .... Borg & Beck SDP 8 in.
Gear lever location ....
Ratios:

		Direct	Overall
1st		2.972	11.225
2nd		2.010	7.592
3rd		1.397	5.276
4th		1.000	3.778
Final drive		3.778	

CHASSIS and RUNNING GEAR:
Construction .... unitary
Suspension, front .. McPherson strut, coils, roll bar
Suspension, rear .... leaf springs, twin trailing lines
Shock absorbers .... double acting
Steering type .... rack and pinion 16.63 to 1
Turns 1 to 1 .... 3½
Turning circle .... 29 ft (.8 m)
Steering wheel diameter .... 15 in. (38.1 cm)
Brakes, type .... disc front, drum rear
Dimensions .... (24.6 cm) 9¾ in. disc; (22.8 cm) 9 in.
drums
Friction area .... (1840 sq cm) 28.5 sq in.

DIMENSIONS:
Wheelbase .... (244 cm) 94.5 in.
Track, front .... (126 cm) 49.5 in.
Track, rear .... (123 cm) 50.5 in.
Length .... (395 cm) 13 ft 0.6 in.
Height .... (139 cm) 4 ft 6.8 in.
Width .... (159 cm) 5 ft 1.8 in.
Fuel tank capacity .... (40.5 litres) 9 galls

TYRES:
Size .... 165 x 13; 5JJ rims
Pressures .... 26 all round
Make on test car .... Dunlop SP 41

GROUND CLEARANCE:
Registered .... (12.3 cm) 4.85 in.

MEXICO

On The Tijuana Trail
With The Escort
By David Briggs

WHEN THEY DEPARTED from the competition scene last year, British Leyland's farewell was accompanied by a half-hearted promise to come back some time to continue the battle with Ford, the only British manufacturer of importance to still be involved in racing and rallying.

Rather than lay down their polished conrods in sympathy, Ford have urged themselves into greater participation, to the point where they now have the International rally scene fairly well under control. Of course, Ford were unlucky not to win the London–Sydney Marathon, but they got their revenge in the London–Mexico, although half the battle is winning the event and the other half is capitalising on it. Ford have now done both, for they have heavily advertised the victory and followed it up with an Escort Mexico—a car for commuters who like to make something special of their journey.

The birth of the Mexico means that the Escort is now available with six different engines, which makes it a comprehensive range by any standards. When the car was first unveiled there were just four options—the 1100, the 1300, the 1300GT and the 1600 TwinCam. Then came the complex RS1600 BDA engine and now, finally, the Escort has got a plain old 1600cc GT unit, which we thought Ford

The latest powerplant to go into an Escort is the 1600 GT engine as used in the Cortina GT (above). The already well-proven engine fits nicely in the hole under the Escort bonnet and accessibility is reasonably good once you have removed the air cleaner. The unit produces 98bhp which is enough to take this Escort up over the ton

the same as the all-up price of an RS1600. Although the Mexico represents nothing very new or exciting, it has the advantage of using a well tried engine from a proven performance car.

Apart from the optional and very efficient cloth-covered seats, the interior is mostly standard, being finished in matt black throughout and with the instrumentation of a GT Escort. Worth noting is the 14in steering wheel,

RS1600 came out the idea seemed to be to make the identifying motif as small as possible, but now the thinking has swung the other way and the word Mexico is plastered down the sides. We were assured that these stripes are optional, but no doubt the market that Ford are trying to reach—the younger swinging set—will lap up an extra decoration, specially as it does not add to the price.

Having been fairly devoted fans

The conventional layout of the Escort GT remains unchanged in the Mexico (above). Those exceptionally good looking seats are really the nicest we've ever tried in a Ford product, being very comfortable and offering good support all round. They are extras, the standard ones not being nearly as good. The rear of the Mexico (left) shows the extra paintwork that distinguishes the Mexico from any other Escort

standard Mexicos in which to thrash, Ford Advanced Vehicle Operations (which produce the car), provided an assortment of Escorts so that we could compare the Mexico alongside its AVO sisters. There was a tuned Mexico, a standard RS1600 and an RS1600 with the full treatment (producing about 140bhp) and, of course, there was the standard Mexico.

Even compared to the three other cars, the standard Mexico

pronounced. While the engine of the Mexico is quiet—up to 4500rpm, the old Ford problem of wind noise was still evident. Even in the confines of the test track, where 80 and 90mph were just about the limit, the continual hissing around the door seals was annoying. On a later and longer journey we completed in the car the noise was quite shameful.

The only other real criticism we can level at this car concerns the clutch. A 7.5in clutch mates the larger engine to the very nice gearbox, but on both the Mexicos we have driven the clutch was heavy to the point that driving in town made one's left foot become almost numb with the effort.

The Mexico handles as impeccably as any of the Escorts. It has the power to allow more adventurous things. It clings to the very last—rolling slightly in the process —and then finally breaks away at the rear. Correction is easy and quick with the small wheel and rarely does one have to make a battle out of getting straight.

Other extras offered for the car include Minilite wheels, spot lights, extra-wide flared wheel arches, heavy-duty disc pads (we found the standard ones quite adequate), as well as several bits for the handling. The suspension is quite adequate but when there are four up the car does tend to hop around on corners.

Regardless of what Ford would have you believe, the new Mexico

TwinCam. The latest powerplant —one of the Kent series of engines as used in the 1600cc Cortina GT —has been mated to the running gear used in the RS1600 and the TwinCam and has been tuned to give 98bhp, as opposed to the TwinCam's 115bhp and the RS1600's 125bhp. With some costly tinkering, the Mexico could be made to churn out about 125bhp but the work needed to gain this type of power, along with the cost of a new Mexico, would be about

The lack of seat adjustment prevents some tall drivers taking up a straight-arm driving position. For the majority, however, it is quite satisfactory.

Externally, the Mexico is substantially different from all other Escorts. Broad stick-on stripes down both sides of the car and along the roof distinguish this from the common Escort, and also sets a new trend in Ford design. When the

approached the Mexico with glee. We did not expect it to be up to the standard of the RS1600 but thought that the 1600GT engine should turn in an exciting performance compared with the 1300GT. We were not disappointed.

The motoring press were given their first look at the car at the Ford test track in Essex. Rather than just turn on a batch of

Mexico and found that even this machine was hot enough not to be overshadowed by the more powerful cars. The most striking thing about the Mexico is that while it has ample punch, it is more refined and quiet than either of the double overhead camshaft cars. The RS1600 sounded dreadful next to the Mexico, and when you get out on the road and start pushing up the revs the difference is even more

cannot be achieved with a starting new model since it uses bits from the rest of the range. It is an interesting car, though, since it is a bold attempt to produce a model for one market only, rather than one for the masses. Total price is £1150, which is a lot for a small saloon, but it is still a good goer for the money. ●

Fuel Consumption **28** mpg

MOTORING PLUS

FORD ESCORT MEXICO

We are never sure whether products from A.V.O. should be treated as Motoring Plus or road test cars. We gave the RS1600 *Motor's* brief test treatment, justifying A.V.O.'s role as a manufacturing plant (even though the BDA, as we call the RS1600 in the office, was being assembled at Halewood at the time), but we decided to cover the Mexico in Motoring Plus for two reasons. Firstly we have tried the components that make up this package in other Ford cars; and secondly we think few buyers will keep the car in standard trim.

The Mexico fits perfectly into a ready-made slot in the performance car market. Take an RS1600, replace the BDA engine with a cooking pushrod 1600 GT unit and you have the basic recipe for an ideal club rally car which can be flavoured to suit your particular requirements and pocket.

After driving the car for nearly 2000 miles over a five day period while covering the RAC Rally we reckon its appeal will go a lot further since it represents an excellent compromise between the rather ·frenzied performance and cruising capabilities of the Escort GT and the nervous boy racer style of the RS1600 (and to a slightly lesser extent the Twin-Cam).

As eagle-eyed readers who use the A5 will have noticed, the bodyshells for the Mexico are shipped from Halewood to South Ockendon ready painted bar the stripes. Fortunately these are what Ford term a delete option— you need not have them. They certainly attract a lot of attention to an otherwise standard-looking Escort (unless you spot the 1600 GT badges on the flanks and the flared wheel arches to take the 5½J section 13 in. wheels), but we prefer an inconspicuous 'Q' car.

Our Mexico was fitted with several Rallye Sport performance parts including a pair of superb front seats, a sumpguard (thoughtfully provided so we could take the car on to stages to find the best photographic locations), a battery of four Cibie Oscar quartz halogen driving lights, and a set of Minilite wheels. The addition of these goodies raises the price from a basic £1150 4s. (including purchase tax) to a grand total of £1412. For road use the seats, though expensive, are certainly a worthwhile addition. The driver's was of the small non-reclining bucket type which gave outstanding support and remained comfortable after the inevitably long driving spells entailed in covering a five day event. The passenger seat reclined to give a comfortable bed for the navigator. Both were cloth-covered so they were pleasantly warm to sit on after the car had been left standing in the freezing cold. The lights were not so useful as we could find no means of adjusting the beam height since the lamp backs came into contact with the radiator grille before they gave any useful forward spread of light —this could of course be rectified with modi-fied brackets. Minilites, which are stronger and lighter than the standard steel wheels, probably only reveal their true benefits in competition, but on the road certainly contribute to the car's outstanding handling. A leather rimmed steering wheel is now part of the standard specification on the RS1600 and Mexico and the facia surround is painted matt black.

We have been very impressed with previous 1600 cc-engined conversions based on the GT Escort, but starting with the RS gives several significant advantages and makes the Mexico a very well balanced car. The 1600 GT engine fits snugly under the bonnet and in its latest form gives 86 bhp DIN at 5500 rpm and 92 lb. ft. torque at 4000 rpm. The standard 1300 GT Escort gives 72 bhp DIN at 6000 rpm and 68 lb. ft. torque at 4000 rpm. At 16¾ cwt. the Mexico's kerb weight is slightly greater than the GT's 15.5 cwt (much of the extra weight being accounted for by the Mexico's streng-thened bodyshell), and this and higher gearing and larger tyres all combine to reduce the Mexico's acceleration potential. Even so

SPECIFICATION

Block material	Cast iron
Head material	Cast iron
Cylinders	4 in line
Cooling system	Water: pump, fan and thermostat
Bore and stroke	80.98mm. (3.19in.) x 77.62mm. (3.06in.)
Cubic capacity	1600 cc (97.51 cu.in.)
Main bearings	5
Valves	Pushrod ohv
Compression ratio	9:1
Carburetter	Weber compound
Fuel pump	Mechanical
Oil Filter	Full flow
Max. power (DIN)	86 bhp at 5500 rpm
Max. torque (net)	92 lb.ft. at 4000 rpm

Transmission

Clutch	7.5 in dia. s.d.p. diaphragm spring

Internal gearbox ratios

Top gear	1.000
3rd gear	1.397
2nd gear	2.010
1st gear	2.972
Reverse	3.324
Synchromesh	On all forward gears
Final drive (type and ratio)	3.77:1 hypoid bevel

Mph at 1000 rpm in:

Top gear	17.6
3rd gear	12.6
2nd gear	8.8
1st gear	5.9

Chassis and Body

Construction	Unitary

Brakes

Type	Disc/drum: servo assisted
Dimensions	9.6in. dia. disc 9.0in. dia. drum

Friction areas:

Front	20.64sq.in. of lining operating on 189.5sq.in. of disc/drum
Rear	48.0sq.in. of lining operating on 96.1sq.in. of disc/drum

Suspension and steering

Front	Independent by MacPherson struts with coil springs and anti-roll bar.
Rear	Live axle located by radius arms: leaf spring suspension

Shock absorbers:

Front	Telescopic
Rear	Telescopic
Steering type	Rack and pinion
Tyres	165-13 Goodyear G800
Wheels	Pressed steel
Rim size	5½J.

Weather: Dry and fine wind 10-16 mph
Fuel: Premium 98 octane 4 star

	Mexico Escort	Escort GT	Escort RS 1600
Maximum speed	mph	mph	mph
Lap	101.0	93.4	114.4*
Best ¼ mile	104.7	95.8	—
Mean Maximile	100.0	91.9	108.3
Best Maximile	102.3	92.8	111.1
* Rev limited			

Acceleration

mph	sec.	sec.	sec.
0-30	3.9	4.0	3.2
0-40	5.9	6.2	4.5
0-50	8.3	8.8	6.4
0-60	11.5	12.5	8.3
0-70	15.8	17.4	11.5
0.80	21.5	25.9	15.0
0-90	30.9	41.2	20.0
0-100	—	—	29.9
Standing ¼ mile	18.4	18.9	16.5
Standing Km	34.3	—	30.7

In Top

mph	sec.	sec.	sec.
20-40	9.7	10.6	10.5
30-50	9.3	10.1	8.8
40-60	9.7	10.2	8.9
50-70	10.3	11.6	9.7
60-80	11.6	14.2	10.3
70-90	15.4	24.0	11.8
80-100	—	—	16.2

In third

mph	sec.	sec.	sec.
10-30	7.1	7.2	—
20-40	6.3	6.6	5.9
30-50	6.1	6.5	5.5
40-60	6.3	6.8	5.3
50-70	7.3	8.5	5.9
60-80	—	—	6.6

Fuel consumption

Steady mph	mpg	mpg	mpg
30	47.0	39.0	28.0
40	46.5	36.5	33.0
50	41.6	32.5	29.3
60	36.4	27.7	27.5
70	31.8	23.9	27.0
80	26.5	21.0	26.5
90	21.0	—	22.8
100	17.2	—	20.0
Overall	27.8	25.3	25.3
Touring	32.3	25.8	25.5

Mexico with
goodies (right)
and in standard
trim (left)

KWC 434J

it steps off the line fairly well to reach 50 and 60 mph in 8.3 and 11.5 sec. respectively. Ford claim a 0-60 mph time of under 11 sec. but we couldn't achieve this. The car is difficult to start quickly as it proved impossible to promote more than just an initial squeal from the 165 x 13 Goodyear G800 tyres. So we had to resort to the clutch slip technique to maintain engine rpm.

The gear ratios are well spaced, and the change is outstanding; however quickly you flick the lever through the gate the synchromesh is unbeatable. With the Corsair 2000E gearbox, as used in the RS1600 and the Twin-Cam, first is good for 35 mph, second 53 mph and third 75 mph at the 1600 GT's usable rev ceiling of 5000 rpm. The tachometer is red-lined at 6500 rpm but the engine note gets frenzied at such speeds. The poor engine insulation is one feature that spoils the Mexico since at various engine speeds there are unpleasant periods which promote sympathetic resonances in the body. But we suspect these faults may have been a feature of our car and will not be present in production vehicles. For instance they were not so apparent in the RS1600 but the BDA engine revs more freely and smoothly than the pushrod 1600.

Reference to the tables show that the

Prices

Mexico Escort			
(incl. purchase tax)	1150	4	0
4 Cibie Oscars at £7 15s. each	31	0	0
4 Light brackets at			
10s. 6d. each	2	2	0
Sump guard	36	0	0
5 (no.) 5½J Minilite wheels			
at £26 12s. each	133	0	0
Set of wheel nuts	8	0	0
Set of wheel caps	2	8	0
Driver's seat			
(non-reclining)	18	10	0
Passenger's seat			
(reclining)	31	10	0
Total	**£1412**	**14**	**0**

performance of the Mexico falls neatly between that of the RS and the GT and our figures are predictably accurate. Assuming the BDA gives a comparable 120 bhp the 0-60 mph time for the Mexico should be $\frac{120}{86} \times 8.3 = 11.6$ sec.; we recorded 11.5 sec. Performance comparisons with the GT do not bear such analysis since the GT has different gearing.

Maximum speed, too, is predictable; using a cube root relationship and a lap speed for the RS1600 of 114 mph the Mexico should reach $114 \times \sqrt{\frac{86}{101}} = 101.1$; we did 101 mph.

The Mexico scores over coverted GTs on cruising performance more than any other single factor since at a steady 70 mph the engine is turning at just under 4000 rpm. With a 1600 cc-engined GT the corresponding engine speed is 4650 rpm. And on a long run that 650 rpm makes a lot of difference to driver fatigue. And it reaps benefits on fuel consumption too since over 2000 miles we regularly recorded 27.8 mpg—the GT Escort could only manage 25.3 mpg. From 70 mph there is a lot of punch to accelerate past other cars reflecting the benefit of a large engine in a light bodyshell. On the road the Mexico pulls impressively smoothly from low speed, so in spite of the stripes you don't have to drive it in boy racer style.

Other mechanical features are unchanged since we tested the RS1600. The roadholding and handling are superb with razor sharp responses to the light and precise steering. In many respects we preferred the Mexico's behaviour to that of the RS since with less power it shows less tendency to tail slide on wet and greasy surfaces; so you don't have to work quite so hard to drive fast. As one member of the staff put it you could let your wife loose in a Mexico on a frosty day, but you'd think twice before giving her an RS1600.

The ride is still very firm; a penalty you have to pay to combine good road manners with a light body on a leaf-sprung rear axle, but the seats do much to cushion the worst bumps.

The heating and ventilation is still a class leader and Ford have made things even better by providing for volume control on the windscreen demist and fresh air outlets. In addition you now get a floor-mounted wash/wipe button and we understand the lighting switch has been moved from its much criticised location beside the wiper switch to the right of the steering column on 1971 Escorts—our Mexico had the 1970 switch layout. At £1150 it is very competitively priced and we wonder whether A.V.O. will be able to satisfy the demand. ∎

WIDE MINI TYRE

Goodyear have announced a 165/70SRx10 Rally Special tyre for Minis. Before this announcement the widest Mini road tyres were of 145 section.

The 165/70SRx10 radial has the same tread pattern (but a smaller version) as the existing 195/70HRx13 tyre which Ford used on their victorious World Cup Rally Escorts. The tyre will not be available until the new year when it will cost £9 7s. 0d. without tube.

Technical data
Goodyear 165SRx10 Rally Special
Rim size: 4½-5½ J
Radial tube recommended: 145x10
Section width: 6.5in.
Tread width: 4.75in.
Overall diameter: 19.2in.
Revs per mile: 1084
(Revs per mile for a Goodyear G800 145Rx10 tyre: 1090)

Comparison of the revs per mile figures shows that fitting the 70 series tyre will have little effect on gearing, which for a 1275GT (3.65:1 final drive) will be raised from 15.1 to 15.16 mph per 1000 rpm in top.

ESCORT SUPER SPEED 2000 GT

"THE most enjoyable road-going Escort to date" is how one *Autocar* tester summed up this latest high-performance model from Super Speed Conversions Ltd, of Ley Street, Ilford, Essex. Seldom, in fact, has a radically modified saloon received such enthusiastic praise from all who drove it.

Its sparkling performance is only part of the story, albeit an important one in a car of this type. Much of the model's appeal stems from its excellent road manners and that undefinable feeling of harmony which characterizes competently executed conversions.

Specification. Based on a brand-new Escort GT (two- or four-door, according to customer requirements), the 2000 GT is powered by a Cortina 2-litre overhead-camshaft unit. This requires very little modification, there being sufficient room for Cortina manifolds, carburettor and air-cleaner in standard form. The Corti-

na's pre-engaged starter is also used, but the original Escort dc dynamo is retained. A special large-bore exhaust system is mated to the Cortina cast-iron manifold. Other than the addition of an overflow reservoir, the cooling system remains unchanged.

Despite the 63 per cent increase in peak torque (111 lb.ft., compared with the 1300 GT unit's 68 lb. ft.), the Escort GT gearbox is retained. In its recently uprated form, it is claimed to be entirely adequate for all but the most severe competition use. The fact that the test car gave no hint of trouble suggests that this is probably so.

Basically a Cortina diaphragm-spring unit, the 8.5in. diameter clutch incorporates a special driven plate. This is necessary for correct mating of Cortina engine and Escort gearbox. Cable actuation is retained.

The remainder of the drive-line is standard Escort GT, although a 3.54-to-1 final drive ratio

(instead of the standard 3.9-to-1) is listed as an extra.

Turning to the chassis, the most obvious change is the adoption of larger wheels and tyres. Rim size is 5½J and standard tyre equipment 165-13in. radials (usually Pirelli Cinturato or Michelin ZX). Front wheel apertures are slightly modified to accommodate these, but appearance remains unchanged. Goodyear Grand Prix low-profile tyres (175 HR 70) can be specified at extra cost, as can Rostyle wheels.

Less conspicuous, but no less important, are the changes made to the suspension. Front springs are special and the rears are modified to improve axle control. Koni adjustable dampers are used on all four corners.

Brakes are basically Escort GT, but fade-resistant pads are used at the front. The slight increase in weight and the harder pads have meant a redistribution of braking effort, achieved by the use of smaller rear slave cylinders.

"Super Speed" and "2000 GT" decals explain the decidedly non-standard performance to casual observers, while front quarter bumpers (with over-riders) impart a distinctive and business-like appearance. A leather-rimmed steering wheel is standard, as is chromium plating of cam and cam-belt covers.

Prices. In basic two-door form, the Super Speed 2000 GT costs a total of £1,299. An equivalent four-door model is priced at £1,329.

Higher gearing (almost essential) costs another £25 fitted. Rostyle wheels up the price by £38, while Goodyear Grand Prix tyres add another £25 to the bill. Special front seats (Microcell) cost an additional £29 each. This by no means exhausts the list of extras, which includes such items as additional sound insulation, air horns, etc.

Our test car, a two-door model, was equipped with higher gearing, Rostyle wheels and a Microcell driver's seat. In this form, the price totals £1,391.

Performance. The 2000 GT returned the remarkable 0-30 mph time of 2.9sec, beating the Mexico (3.9sec), Twin-Cam (3.8sec) and RS 1600 (3.4sec) by a significant margin. Despite the punishment meted, the transmission behaved faultlessly and there was never a trace of axle tramp. This underlines Super Speed's views that a correctly designed leaf-spring layout requires no additional radius arms.

This excellent step-off stands the car in good stead further up the speed range, 60 mph being reached in only 8.6sec. Again, this betters the Mexico (10.7sec), Twin Cam (9.9sec) and RS 1600 (8.9sec). The standing quarter time of 16.7sec equals that of the RS 1600 and is significantly better than those returned by the Mexico (18.0sec) and Twin Cam (17.2sec). At this stage, however, both the twin-cam cars are travelling faster—a fact reflected in their better times to 90 and 100 mph. For example, the 2000 GT takes 37.8sec to 100 mph, compared with the Twin Cam's 33.6sec and RS 1600's 32.3sec. Top speed is also slightly down (106 mph, compared with the 113 mph recorded by both twin-cam models). However, the 2-litre model's superior low-speed performance more than compensates for this. Despite higher gearing, the 2000 GT's 20-40 mph time in top gear (7.9sec) is head-and-shoulders better than that of the Twin Cam (10.6sec), the RS 1600 being reluctant to pull at all from such a speed. Not until the 70 mph mark is passed does the Twin Cam begin to turn the tables on the Super Speed car, which still has a 3.8sec advantage at 80 mph.

Fuel Consumption. Over the 1,200-mile test period, petrol consumption averaged 24.4

mpg—a highly creditable figure for such a vivid performance. This compares with 21.5 mpg for both twin-cam models and 25.4 mpg for the standard-engined Escort GT (Autocar, 11 February 1971). The Mexico, on the other hand, returned on average of 27.5 mpg—a figure which reflects a particularly frugal trip to Cornwall.

Oil consumption averaged 400 miles per pint. Although quite acceptable, this is appreciably worse than the 1,000 miles per pint returned by the Cortina 2000 GXL with identical power unit (Autocar, 8 October, 1970).

Ride, handling and braking. Although the ride is no harsher than that of the standard Escort GT, the suspension modifications effectively cope with the increased weight. There is, perhaps, a trace more understeer—a factor which helps combat the Escort's notorious sensitivity to side winds. The Super Speed car, in fact, is significantly better than most in this respect.

With such an abundance of power, it is possible to spin the wheels on most surfaces. Nevertheless, traction is surprisingly good, even in tight turns.

We must confess to some misgiving when told that standard-sized brakes had been retained. Nevertheless, despite some very hard usage, they gave no cause for concern, and Super Speed seem to have got the distribution just right.

Noise. The 2000 GT is much quieter than either of the twin-cam models, being a rival to the Mexico in this respect. While the latter is the sweeter and quieter at low and medium speeds, the 2000 GT's overhead-camshaft unit sounds less "thrashy" at high revs. In fact, we

used an indicated 6,500 rpm during performance testing—just under 6,300 rpm in fact. Unlike the Escort GT tachometer of the 2000 GT that fitted to the Cortina is red-lined at 6,000 rpm.

Summary. Potential 2000 GT buyers will want to know how it compares with its "production" rivals, the Mexico and RS 1600 (the Twin Cam no longer being in production). Much, of course, will depend on what the car is to be used for. Some people may well plump for the 2000 GT simply because of the availability of a four-door version, while competition-minded clubmen will naturally favour a Mexico or RS 1600.

Price is likely to be an important factor. Least expensive of the trio is the Mexico, selling at £1,219. An equivalent 2000 GT will cost an additional £80, making it a reasonable alternative. The RS 1600, on the other hand, is listed at a formidable £1,585. Few will consider paying such a premium for its questionable advantages as a road car.

The most likely choice, therefore, is between a Mexico and a 2000 GT. Those who habitually drive *very* hard may find the Mexico's larger brakes, stronger transmission and heavy-duty body and suspension components worth while. The Mexico also has the advantage of an alternator and more efficient (round) headlamps. On the other hand, its battery lives in the boot, which means that the relocated spare wheel occupies much valuable luggage space.

Although likely to be less tolerant of abuse (or extremely severe use), the 2000 GT has a substantial performance advantage. It is also more flexible, less fussy and has a rather better ride. Spares are unlikely to be a problem, the majority being volume-produced Ford parts. □

PERFORMANCE CHECK

Maximum speeds	mph		kph		rpm	
Gear	Super Speed	Twin Cam	Super Speed	Twin Cam	Super Speed	Twin Cam
Top (mean)	106	113	171	182	5,580	6,300
(best)	110	113	177	182	5,800	6,300
3rd	84	81	135	130	6,300	6,300
2nd	60	56	97	90	6,300	6,300
1st	36	38	58	61	6,300	6,300

Standing ¼-mile, **Super Speed**: 16.7 sec 80 mph
Twin Cam: 17.2 sec 81 mph
Standing kilometre, **Super Speed**: 31.7 sec 97 mph
Twin Cam: 31.9 sec 98 mph

Acceleration, **Super Speed**:	2.9	4.5	6.4	8.6	12.0	16.7	24.2	37.8
Twin Cam:	3.8	5.2	7.2	9.9	13.0	16.8	24.2	33.6
Time in seconds 0—								
True speed MPH:	30	40	50	60	70	80	90	100
Indicated speed \ Super Speed:	29	39	49	60	69	79	88	98
MPH / Twin Cam:	28	37	47	57	66	76	86	96

Spead range, Gear Ratios and Time in seconds

Mph	Top		3rd		2nd		1st	
	Super Speed	Twin Cam	Super Speed	Twin Cam	Super Speed	Twin Cam	Super Speed	Twin Cam
	(3.54)	(3.78)	(5.02)	(5.27)	(7.06)	(7.59)	(11.81)	(11.22)
10-30	—	—	5.9	7.7	3.9	4.7	2.2	3.6
20-40	7.9	10.6	5.1	6.2	3.6	3.8	—	—
30-50	7.8	9.8	5.2	6.0	3.5	3.6	—	—
40-60	8.6	9.7	5.3	6.2	4.3	—	—	—
50-70	9.4	9.9	6.0	6.5	—	—	—	—
60-80	10.6	10.6	7.6	7.1	—	—	—	—
70-90	13.2	12.4	—	—	—	—	—	—
80-100	21.6	16.5	—	—	—	—	—	—

Fuel Consumption
Overall mpg. **Super Speed**: 24.4 mpg (11.6 litres/100km)
Twin Cam: 21.5 mpg (13.1 litres/100km)

NOTE: Comparison figures for Escort Twin Cam tested in AUTOCAR of 6 June 1968.

THE INSTANT MOTOR RACER

The Assistant Editor tries his hand in an Escort Mexico

THE FLAG dropped, the revs screamed and there I was fighting to get to the first corner ahead of the other chaps. After ten years of weekly motor racing spectating, reporting and team managing I was out there having a go myself and, by some strange quirk of nature, feeling a lot less nervous than I usually do when at the start of a race in which I am only on the sidelines.

One should not get the impression that MOTOR SPORT'S Assistant Editor has gone out and blued all his savings into becoming a full-time racing driver—that is an ambition I passed over some good few years ago—but due to a culmination of circumstances I found my way into the hot seat of a Ford Escort Mexico at Thruxton. This was obviously a cue, not only for an article on Group 1 racing, of which the Editor has already written enthusiastically earlier in the year, but also an ideal opportunity to go through the well-trodden path of the actual mechanics of finding oneself on the grid. This is one of the most regular posers we receive from readers and, though there have been a great number of previous articles on the subject, the letters continue to flood in.

The story really starts with MOTOR SPORT'S conversions and tuning contributor Jeremy Walton, whose tasks at Standard House also include writing for the weekly motor-racing paper *Motoring News*. J.W. has long been a racer at heart and enjoyed considerable success in Autocross with an Imp. So when the first Group 1 saloon car racer was scheduled for last May he saw this as an ideal opportunity to have a go on the race track. Not surprisingly the management were not at all keen on the Editorial Capri taking to the circuits and so J.W. hustled up a Hillman Avenger from Janspeed. He thoroughly enjoyed the experience and when news came of two more Group 1 races in late August he was seen rushing around trying to find a suitable car.

The enthusiastic management at Ford's Advanced Vehicles Operations came up with an offer of a machine they call "the purple passion", which was, in fact, the first-ever production Ford Escort Mexico which had already seen some active racing service. This was duly entered for the race at Brands Hatch and a week later at Thruxton. Then Janspeed phoned up and announced they had entered J.W. at Thruxton in the Hillman Avenger. Our man just could not see a way he could drive both cars at once, so he offered me the Mexico drive. Somewhat taken aback that the chance to race had actually come, I forestalled a decision until over a weekend but naturally I was mad keen.

The race was to be the last on the programme at the Chevron Oils 100 km. race meeting at Thruxton on August Bank Holiday Sunday and was scheduled as a seven-lap handicap. First we dropped a line to the organisers to inform them of the change of driver and I reimbursed J.W. with the £4 he had paid the organisers as an entry fee. This covers the paper work and so on and is an average figure, although, of course, at higher level they pay you to race. Normally an entry for a meeting would have to be made something like a month beforehand and at that stage the driver would have to be in possession of certain documents.

The most important is a racing licence issued by the RAC from their Motorsport division which nestles amongst the embassies at 31, Belgrave Square, just off Hyde Park Corner. We called in (although you can write) to find that there are various categories of licence and the one we wanted was obviously the Restricted Track, which in effect is a provisional licence which only allows you to take part in club racing. As the season is now tailing off, this only takes four days to come through (even quicker if a special 50p extra rush fee is paid) and at £1.50 seemed excellent value. As well as the licence, which is thoughtfully provided with a plastic cover, came a copy of the RAC Blue Book, which is a mine of racing information and rules plus the regular motor-racing bulletins issued by the RAC. Further, the licence entitles one to discounts with various companies. On the back of the licence is a space to be filled in, each time one races, by the stewards of the meeting and if one behaves in six meetings (*i.e.*, doesn't spin dangerously or crash) one receives a signature from the steward of the meeting which leads to upgrading from restricted to national status. After a further probationary period one can then obtain a full international licence.

The idea of all this is to stop a chap who has just won the pools rushing out and buying the spare Tyrrell Formula One car and entering it in the British Grand Prix for his debut race. Personally I think the system with regard to novices could be tightened up further, particularly in respect to single-seaters, but that is another subject.

With the Competition Licence comes a medical certificate which has to be filled in by a doctor. The RAC would prefer one's regular medico to do this as he knows a patient's history, and the form draws special attention to the prospective racer's cardiac condition as well as eyesight. Also one is expected to have full movement of all limbs. If there is any doubt a special medical panel sits every so often to discuss border-line cases. The fee for the doctor's inspection depends entirely on the man himself, although don't expect it to be done on the National Health.

Thus with a licence to race, and a medical card duly signed, the final paper work to overcome is club membership. Many prospective racers may already be members of a motoring club but, of course, only some of them organise race meetings. The Thruxton meeting was being run by the British Automobile Racing Club of Sutherland House, 5-6 Argyll Street, London, W1 (next door to the London Palladium). Although I used to be a member I let it lapse and I had to join up again. With an entry fee, and the addition of competition membership, this came to a total of £6, for which, of course, one receives various other benefits. The BRSCC also organises a great number of meetings and is also worth joining. Membership of these two will enable one to enter the great majority of race meetings in Britain.

With the paper work complete I was obviously well on my way to becoming a racing driver, but there was still the problem of the special clothing and crash helmet. There has been a great deal of progress in recent years, particularly with regard to fire protection, so I decided to go along and investigate the prices of the equipment. The firms run by Gordon Spice (such as the City Speed Shop) or Les Leston's Racekit firm are probably the best known and have the largest selection. It has long been a desire of mine to own one of those spaceman-like Bell Star helmets, although obviously this is not necessary for a saloon car but I rashly parted with £30 of hard-earned cash. In fact, one can obtain a good open helmet for half that price.

Having been so extravagant I decided against any special fireproof clothing, knowing that I could borrow some for the day. Racing regulations in Britain only oblige you to roll your sleeves down and do not insist on racing overalls but for anyone who intends to race regularly I feel these are essential. Apart from the protection they offer, they are tailored for the job, look smart and give one an air of professionalism. If one has real talent and starts to do well prospective team managers will start to take note, and if it comes to the choice of one driver who wears a beat-up old helmet, dirty jeans and a pullover and another chap who very much looks the part in freshly-laundered racing gear and his Bell Star, the choice is fairly plain.

At the moment there are various firms claiming to produce overalls that offer the greatest protection against fire. Having investigated these my personal opinion is that overalls made from the new TT wool is the best. I found that Racekit did not have any readily available but will have soon and the price, at around £40 for the full garb, is cheaper than some of the synthetic fibre overalls from America presently on the market. One last point on the subject of race wear and that is that a pair of specially-made driving shoes without welts are a worthwhile investment, not just for the track but also for day-to-day driving. The Edward Lewis ones have a particularly good name, although, in fact, I raced in some thirty bob cord shoes from "Marks and Sparks".

Race day seemed to approach with considerable speed and the week-end was decidedly busy for the Thruxton meeting was sandwiched between reporting assignments at Oulton Park on the Saturday and Castle Combe on the Monday. J.W. had raced the Escort the previous weekend and, although he spun it wildly at one stage, it was delivered to me a couple of days later without a scratch. It was pretty well a standard Mexico apart from some Koni inserts in the McPherson strut front suspension which stiffened it up (these are allowed in Escort Mexico racing) and mods to keep the scrutineers happy. Racing tyres are not allowed in Group 1 and the Mexico was fitted up with some low-profile Dunlop SP radials.

Motor racing is a sport in which one seems to have to get up half-way through the night, spend hours waiting around and return cold and hungry after all the pubs are shut.

I decided to get to Thruxton as early as possible in case there were any problems but thanks to the new M3 arrived even earlier than expected. The Mexico seemed in fine tune and once at the circuit I was allocated a spot in the paddock where I taped up the lights and checked the car over. Obviously the Escort was basically a road car and needed little attention but a full racing saloon can take nights of preparation.

Then I joined the long scrutineering queue, in which RAC-appointed officials check the safety (and sometimes eligibility) of the competitors' cars. It seemed hours before it was my car's turn and by then I had numbers painted on the side and had the appropriate licences, etc., checked. I told "the scroot" that I was writing this article about how to start racing and rather laconically he replied that my time would be better put to use writing an article on how to stop motor racing rather than start! However, he was very thorough with his check, paying particular attention to fire walls between the engine and passenger compartments which had been added by Ford, the fact the car had laminated windscreen, an oil catch tank for the rocker cover filler and breather, an external throttle return spring, and so on. I hadn't taken the hub caps off so their removal was requested, while I think he was somewhat staggered to find the boot packed with cases when he investigated the fixing of the battery.

This ordeal over, and a ticket to prove the check had been done dangling from the heater control, it was just a matter of clearing all the rubbish out of the car and waiting for the 30-minute practice session. In fact, on J.W.'s advice, I added some more oil and thanks to the generosity of Chevron, who were sponsoring the meeting, put in the least amount of petrol necessary.

I lined up in the marshalling area in plenty of time and I was soon to be joined by a strange collection of Group 1 cars—in fact, the rules were not too strictly applied. There were three other Mexicos, four Porsche 911s, several Cooper Minis, a Triumph 2.5 PI, two BMW 2002s, a Jaguar 3.8, the Janspeed Hillman Avenger, a Vauxhall Firenze and even a Fiat 500. The great majority of the drivers were regular racers, including some with quite impressive records, although there were others, like me, with the novice X on their boots to indicate their lack of experience.

I was trying to remember where the circuit went, for I did about five laps of Thruxton at a Press day before it was reopened, when suddenly a man started to wave me out, and along with 22 others I accelerated on to the circuit. I was a racing driver!

Soon I was rushing round trying to sort out the right lines through corners, pick braking points and generally hustle round as quick as I could and I was pleased to notice that my lap times, shown to me from the pits by grinning friends, started to fall. I had intended to follow J.W. but never saw him, but when Brian Cutting came by in his Escort Mexico he was obviously a good man to follow as he is one of the instructors at the Thruxton saloon car school. After two corners he had disappeared into the distance so I contented myself with lapping on my own. I found that Allard Corner after the pits was flat out but the right-left-right at the Campbell, Cobb, Segrave complex was very difficult indeed and, in fact, I am sure that this is where I lost most of my time. After that Kimpton Bend is flat out and, once one plucks up courage, so is the long Village Curve and Church Corner which has a nasty bump on the apex, and I probably lost a little time by lifting off occasionally when the excessive understeer of the Escort looked as if it was getting the better of me. After Church came the long haul down to Club—that Armco chicane—and before braking the Mexico was showing about 105 m.p.h. Braking for the chicane is difficult for it is on a curve and one then flicks right, left and right and past the pits once more. Thruxton is a good beginners' circuit and very enjoyable to drive on and I was undoubtedly pleased that my first race was not going to be at Brands Hatch, which would give me the shivers. After about 12 laps I was getting very hot and sweaty and pulled in for a rest only to find the session about to finish.

The practice times were duly issued on a duplicated sheet and I noted I had lapped in 1 min. 57.2 sec., an average speed of 72 m.p.h., which made me about 14th fastest out of the 22 who practised. However, because this was a handicap event, some competitors had obviously been playing it canny and not going full speed while I reckoned I did not have much in reserve.

To put my time in perspective Bill Tuckett, who normally drives a Chevron B16 in long-distance events, had lapped his Porsche 911S in 1 min. 47.4 sec. to head the list, Brian Cutting was the quickest Mexico at 1 min. 50.8 sec. and Gerry Marshall, who usually drives the Blydenstein-prepared racing Viva GTs, lapped his Vauxhall Firenze at 1 min. 51.8 sec.

My heart sank when the handicaps were announced. Naturally Tuckett was scratch man and the three other Porsche 911s were either with him or 5 sec. ahead. Then off 20 sec. came myself and three other Escort Mexicos (one which had lapped in a similar time to mine), while people like Marshall and another Mexico (illegally on racing tyres) which had practised quicker than me were to start before me. The handicapper explained afterwards that the whole thing had to be done in a huge rush during the lunch hour and as Cutting had lapped his Escort Mexico quickly we were reckoned to be about the same. Previous experience was just not taken into account at all and obviously this gives very little incentive to the novice. With only the four Porsche 911s behind and great chunks of time to catch up on the rest I had no chance of a decent placing. Perhaps this was one reason why I sat on the grid quite impassionately when the time came.

The meeting had run off smoothly when it came round to Event 6— The Adlards-Contour Saloon Car Handicap race. I lined up in the marshalling area in car number 212 in plenty of time, strapped myself in and waited. After what seemed hours we were all waved out on our warming-up lap to find the rain starting to spot down—something I just dreaded. Fortunately the threat relented and once on the grid the sun peeped out from behind the clouds and there were sighs of relief. In handicap events the cars are flagged off in groups and, of course, our group of four Escorts were almost last to go. In fact, I made the best start of the four (it's all those 0-60 m.p.h. road-test runs) but decided discretion was the better part of valour and let Brian Cutting take Allard ahead of me thinking I might be able to hang on to him and pull away from the other two. In fact, I was so intent on this that I almost went straight on at Campbell and a youngster called Ian Deevin, who was racing his own Escort Mexico, overtook me. By now I was well out of my stride and it wasn't until two laps later that a chap in a Mini-Cooper caught me up and I started to drive half-properly again. All the Porsches had gone by at this stage while the Mini man had started 10 sec. behind but with a lap credit. For the rest of the race we had a really enjoyable dice and he passed me into the chicane on one lap when I so nearly had an accident. The next lap I re-passed him when he went wide coming out of the chicane while all the time we had another Escort hot on our tails. Finally the Mini man got the better of me and I was tucked

Continued on page **100**

AUTO TEST

FORD ESCORT SPORT

VALUE FOR MONEY GT

AT-A-GLANCE:
Basic version of Escort GT with less trim and bigger wheels. Good performance, excellent handling, sticky steering, light brakes. Ride tends to be choppy. Bad deflection in side winds. Good basis for a rally car.

IT is pretty common knowledge that a Ford Escort makes a good basis for a rally or competition car, and the sight of the works machines doing well is familiar enough. Although the cars prepared at the Boreham Competition Centre bear only a superficial resemblance to the kind of Escort most customers buy, the model identity is clear for all to see.

For a keen young driver to cut his teeth on, therefore, one of the several larger-engined Escorts offered by the factory is ideal. The 1300 GT with either two or four doors is rightly popular among the ranks of motoring clubs and it is long established as a reliable and entertaining model. More serious enthusiasts with fatter wallets can buy a 1600 GT Mexico or a 1600 RS from Ford Rally Sport dealers, the latter being in many ways the ultimate in fun cars.

Aware though of a more basic need, Ford introduced another Escort derivative in time for the Earls Court Show called the Escort Sport. This is available from any Ford dealer and is in effect a cut-price Escort GT, stripped of luxuries like sound deadening and carpet, but coming as standard on bigger wheels and tyres with flared wheel arches to suit.

Mechanically the specification is identical with the two-door Escort 1300 GT (apart from the wheels and a change of axle ratio to restore reasonable gearing) but the list price is £47.50 less. The body looks the same as the heavy-duty Mexico and RS shell, but in fact it is purely standard, without the extra strengthening welds applied to these other two versions which are built by the Advanced Vehicle

Operation at Aveley. Escort Sports go down the normal production line at Hailwood and are trimmed to the same standard as the basic 1100 versions.

The engine for the Sport and 1300 GT Escort is the latest five-bearing cross-flow unit which was uprated to produce 72 bhp (DIN) at 6,000 rpm in October 1970. Gearbox ratios are unchanged, but instead of a 3.9-to-1 final drive, a 4.125 assembly is fitted to offset the larger rolling radius of the 165-13in. tyres; Escort GTs have 155-12in. tyres on 4.5in. rims. Comparative mph per 1,000 rpm figures in top are 15.9 for the GT with 3.9 axle and 16.3 for the Sport with 4.1. Acceleration differences between the two versions should therefore be negligible.

With the Escort GT though, the 4.1 axle was an option and the car we tested in February this year was fitted with it. In fact every Escort GT we have tested since the beginning of 1969 has had this ratio; a production change to the 3.9 was made about two years ago although there seem to be a lot of newer GTs around with the 4.1.

As a performance reference standard our 1971 GT test is therefore not quite typical. No GT has actually managed to beat the standing-start acceleration times measured on the long-term car we bought in 1969, and the performance range seems to span a 0 to 60 mph time between 12.2 and 14.8sec. Although the Sport's time of 13.8sec looks slow compared with the 12.4sec measured on the GT in February, it is explained by the gearing difference and the very windy weather prevailing during this latest test.

Top speed, too, was affected by the weather, and on the MIRA banked circuit we could not average more than 92 mph on a flat-out lap. This corresponds with a point about 300 rpm short of the power peak and we have little doubt that the Sport would record a mean maximum of 97 or 98 mph in better conditions.

The engine is always a willing starter and it warms up evenly within a very short time. There is a manual choke slightly buried to the right of the steering column, alongside twin rocker switches for the heater fan and wipers. At the lower end of its rev range the unit is crisp and punchy and towards maximum revs it still sounds smooth and eager. There is much more mechanical noise and induction hiss transmitted through the bulkhead than on the GT, a direct result of less sound deadening. At high speed it* is this engine noise which becomes the predominant sound, actually drowning out the radio above 80 mph. As a cruising speed, around 85 mph feels within bounds, despite rather too much fussiness for the gait to be relaxed.

Something must have been wrong with the speedometer gearing fitted to the test car as there was a consistent 10 per cent of optimism built in, which has not been our experience with other Escort GTs. The rev counter had a 200 rpm zero error, its linear increments being accurate up to a point around 6,000 rpm when needle swing prevented us reading it.

Unlike the Escort GT the Sport has only a two-dial instrument binnacle and there is an additional rev counter bolted through the right-hand end of the facia capping. Fuel gauge and coolant thermometer are combined in the right-hand dial, which is an arrangement much easier to read than the four tiny dials fitted to the Escort GT. There is no oil pressure gauge nor is there a battery condition voltmeter, both these being standard on the GT. The Sport has a Capri GT type of padded steering wheel with leather covered rim as standard, in place of the all-plastic affair fitted to all other Escort except the Mexico and 1600 RS.

Steering on this test car was sticky and dead, a fairly general fault to be found on most Ford rack and pinion systems. It is the result of too much friction in the mechanism and too little castor in the front suspension geometry. There is plenty of precision and the steering effort required is always light, but we found we had consciously to unwind the lock, after a turn, more than we felt was right.

Handling, if anything, is improved by the fatter tyres, which are on 5in. instead of 4½in. rims, and the neutral balance of the car is as good as ever. The feeling of security when cornering fast is excellent and we had no adhesion problems on greasy wet London streets.

The higher unsprung weight of the larger

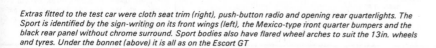

Extras fitted to the test car were cloth seat trim (right), push-button radio and opening rear quarterlights. The Sport is identified by the sign-writing on its front wings (left), the Mexico-type front quarter bumpers and the black rear panel without chrome surround. Sport bodies also have flared wheel arches to suit the 13in. wheels and tyres. Under the bonnet (above) it is all as on the Escort GT

FORD ESCORT SPORT (1,297 c.c.)

ACCELERATION

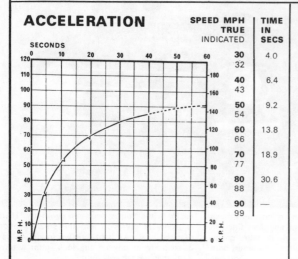

SPEED MPH TRUE INDICATED	TIME IN SECS
30 / 32	4.0
40 / 43	6.4
50 / 54	9.2
60 / 66	13.8
70 / 77	18.9
80 / 88	30.6
90 / 99	—

GEAR RATIOS AND TIME IN SEC

mph	Top (4.12)	3rd (5.85)	2nd (8.23)
10-30	—	8.2	5.2
20-40	12.3	7.3	4.8
30-50	11.9	7.2	5.3
40-60	12.8	7.8	—
50-70	15.9	10.1	—
60-80	20.2	—	—

STANDING ¼-mile
18.9 sec 70 mph
Standing Kilometre
35.8 sec 84 mph
Test distance
1,215 miles
Mileage recorder
8.3 per cent over-reading

PERFORMANCE

MAXIMUM SPEEDS

Gear	mph	kph	rpm
Top (mean)	92	148	5,650
(best)	96	154	5,900
3rd	75	121	6,500
2nd	53	85	6,500
1st	32	51	6,500

BRAKES

FADE
(from 70 mph in neutral)
Pedal load for 0.5g stops in lb

1	25	6	35-45
2	25	7	35-45
3	25	8	35-45
4	25	9	45
5	35-45	10	45

RESPONSE (from 30 mph in neutral)

Load	g	Distance
20lb	0.30	100ft
40lb	0.72	42ft
60lb	1.02	29.6ft
Handbrake	0.34	89ft
Max. Gradient	1 in 3	

CLUTCH

Pedal 20lb and 5in.

COMPARISONS

MAXIMUM SPEED MPH

Simca 1100 Special	(£1,039)	9
Austin 1300 GT	(£1,034)	9
Toyota 1200 SL	(£1,164)	9
Ford Escort Sport	**(£940)**	**9**
Mini 1275 GT	(£898)	9

0-60 MPH, SEC

Simca 1100 Special	13.
Mini 1275 GT	13.
Ford Escort Sport	**13.**
Toyota 1200 SL	14.
Austin 1300 GT	14.

STANDING ¼-MILE, SEC

Ford Escort Sport	**18.**
Simca 1100 Special	18.
Mini 1275 GT	19.
Toyota 1200 SL	19.
Austin 1300 GT	19.

OVERALL MPG

Mini 1275 GT	30.
Toyota 1200 SL	30.
Austin 1300 GT	25.
Ford Escort Sport	**25.**
Simca 1100 Special	24.

GEARING

(with 165—13in. tyres)

Top	16.3 mph per 1,000 rpm
3rd	11.5 mph per 1,000 rpm
2nd	8.15 mph per 1,000 rpm
1st	4.9 mph per 1,000 rpm

CONSUMPTION

FUEL
(At constant speed—mpg)

30 mph	47.0
40 mph	43.
50 mph	37.8
60 mph	32.8
70 mph	28.0
80 mph	22.8

Typical mpg 26 (10.9 litres/100km
Calculated (DIN) mpg 25.3 (11.2 litres/100km
Overall mpg 25.0 (11.3 litrs/100km
Grade of fuel Premium, 4-star (min. 97 RM

OIL
Consumption (SAE 20W/50) Negligible

TEST CONDITIONS
Weather: Fine Wind: 22-30 mph.
Temperature: 1 deg. C. (34 deg. F).
Barometer: 29.5in.hg. Humidity: 61 per cent.
Surfaces: Dry concrete and asphalt.

WEIGHT:
Kerb Weight 15.8 cwt (1,764lb-800kg)
(with oil, water and half-full fuel tank).
Distribution, per cent F, 52.8; R, 47.2
Laden as tested: 19.0 cwt (2,134lb-968kg).

TURNING CIRCLES:
Between kerbs L, 32 ft 0 in.; R, 30 ft 2 in.
Between walls L, 33 ft 10 in.; R, 32 ft 1 in.
Steering wheel turns, lock to lock 3.5.
Figures taken at 3,350 miles by our own
staff at the Motor Industry Research
Association proving ground at Nuneaton,
and on the Continent.

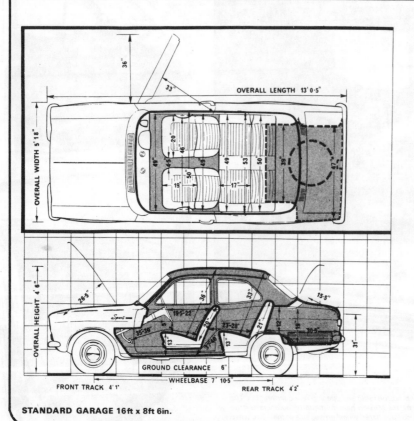

OVERALL LENGTH 13' 0·5"
OVERALL WIDTH 5'18"
OVERALL HEIGHT 4' 6"
GROUND CLEARANCE 6"
WHEELBASE 7' 10·5"
FRONT TRACK 4' 1"
REAR TRACK 4' 2"

STANDARD GARAGE 16ft x 8ft 6in.

SPECIFICATION

FRONT ENGINE, REAR-WHEEL DRIVE

ENGINE
Cylinders	4 in-line
Main bearings	5
Cooling system	Water: pump, fan and thermostat
Bore	80.97mm (3.19in.)
Stroke	62.99mm (2.48in.)
Displacement	1,297 c.c. (79.2 cu.in.)
Valve gear	Overhead: pushrods and rockers
Compression ratio	9.0-to-1 Min. octane rating: 97RM
Carburettor	One progressive twin-choke Weber downdraught
Fuel pump	AC Mechanical
Oil filter	Full flow, renewable element
Max. power	72 bhp (DIN) at 6,000 rpm
Max. Torque	68 lb.ft (DIN) at 4,000 rpm

TRANSMISSION
Clutch	Borg and Beck diaphragm spring 6.5in. dia.
Gearbox	4-speed, all-synchromesh
Gear ratios	Top 1.0
	Third 1.42
	Second 2.0
	First 3.34
	Reverse 4.23
Final drive	Hypoid bevel 4.12-to-1

CHASSIS and BODY
Construction	Integral, with steel body

SUSPENSION
Front	Independent coil springs. MacPherson struts, bottom links, anti-roll bar, telescopic dampers
Rear	Live axle, half-elliptic leaf springs, telescopic dampers

STEERING
Type	Rack and pinion
Wheel dia.	15in.

BRAKES
Make and type	Discs front, drums rear
Servo	Vacuum
Dimensions	F 8.6in. dia.
	R 8.0in. dia. 1.5in. wide shoes
Swept area	F 143.5 sq. in., R 75.4 sq. in.
	Total 218.9 sq. in. (232 sq. in./ton laden)

WHEELS
Type	Pressed steel disc, 4-stud fixing 4.5in. wide rim
Tyres — make	Goodyear (on test car)
type	G800 radial ply tubeless
size	165-13in.

EQUIPMENT
Battery	12 Volt 38 Ah.
Generator/ Alternator	Lucas C40/1 22 amp a.c./d.c.
Headlamps	Lucas 120/90 watt (total)
Reversing lamp	Standard
Electric fuses	6
Screen wipers	2-speed, self-parking
Screen washer	Standard, foot-operated
Interior heater	Standard, air-blending
Heated backlight	Extra
Safety belts	Extra, anchorage built-in
Interior trim	Cloth seats, PVC headlining
Floor covering	Rubber
Jack	Screw scissors
Jacking points	4, under body
Windscreen	Toughened
Underbody protection	Phosphate treatment prior to painting

MAINTENANCE
Fuel tank	9 Imp. gallons (41 litres) (no reserve)
Cooling system	9 pints (including heater)
Engine sump	6.4 pints (3.6 litres) SAE 20W/50
	Change oil every 5,000 miles.
	Change filter element every 5,000 miles.
Gearbox	1.6 pints SAE 80EP. No change needed
Final drive	2 pints SAE 90EP. No change needed
Grease	No points
Tyre pressures	F 24; R 24 psi (normal driving)
	F 28; R 28 psi (fast driving)
Max. payload	815 lb (370 kg)

PERFORMANCE DATA
Top gear mph per 1,000 rpm	16.3
Mean piston speed at max. power	2,480 ft/min.
Bhp per ton laden	74.9

AUTOTEST FORD ESCORT SPORT

A two-dial binnacle is fitted to the Sport, with a separate rev counter up on the right. A Capri GT type sports wheel is standard. There are rubber mats on the floor

wheels and tyres (the Sport weighed some 56lb. more than the GT, a lot of which must be from this source) tends to make the ride slightly more choppy than on the GT and once or twice we heard a front strut reaching the limit of its rebound travel noisily on rough surfaces.

During the gusty weather of the test we suffered badly from instability at speed, and for resistance to side-wind deflection the Escort rates poorly.

FITTINGS AND FURNITURE

You do not get a mock-wood instrument panel on the Sport like you do on the GT, nor the matching strips across the facia and along the window sills. The alternative black paint looks functional rather than frugal and it seems to blend better with the padded facia capping. There are no carpets, just rubber floor mats which fit well but lack padding under them. The test car had charcoal cloth facing (£16.56 extra) on its seats, which was luxurious to sit on and made the padding feel softer. The shaping of the seat is basically good but a swinging link adjustment instead of runners does not seem to suit either very tall or very short people. There is not enough rearwards travel on the driver's seat for anyone over 6ft.

Room in the back is quite generous for a small car, recesses in the side trim pads adding a lot to the elbow room. Leg and knee room is restricted, but no more than usual in this size of car. The test car was fitted with opening rear quarterlights, which cost £7.50 extra and improve the throughput of air considerably without adding a great deal to the wind roar at speed.

On the outside the Sport is easily identified by sign-writing on the front wings and its Mexico-type quarter bumpers at the front. The badges say "1300" instead of "GT" and there is a black tail panel as on the Escort GT. Side windows do not have bright metal surrounds, but there is chrome moulding attached to the roof gutter. Over-riders are not fitted, and there are no wheel trims for the plain, silver-painted road wheels.

Circular headlamps will be much preferred by keen drivers and the Sport has these in place of

the GT's rectangular ones. They are Lucas sealed units with 60/45 watt filaments. They are adequate without being impressive and can be converted easily to halogen use. One deficiency carried over from the basic Escort specification is the fitting of only single-speed wipers. The Escort GT has a two-speed motor.

Because the 13in. tyres are larger in diameter than the normal Escort's 12in. ones, the spare must lie flat on the floor of the boot instead of standing up in the left-hand wheelarch. This cuts the luggage space height from 19 to only 12in. and means that cases must be selected carefully to fit the irregular shape left.

Under the bonnet the accessibility is generally good, with battery, brake reservoir, washer bottle and oil filler all easy to get at. The distributor is a little buried, but most routine attention presented few problems.

With the extras as tested the Sport could be delivered for just a little over £1,000 and for £955 with inertia-reel seat belts only. In these times when there is precious little costing under four figures other than real economy cars, the Sport is remarkably good value and within reach of many a young blood who wants to have a go now and again. □

MANUFACTURER:
Ford Motor Co. Ltd., Warley, Essex.

PRICES
Basic	£752.00
Purchase Tax	£188.00
Seat belts (inertia-reel)	£15.00
Total (in G.B.)	£955.00

EXTRAS (inc. P.T.)
Push-button radio	£33.44
Cloth seat trim	£16.56
Opening rear quarterlights	£7.50

PRICE AS TESTED £1,012.50

TAKING STOCK No. 20

What it means to own a Ford Escort Mexico

By Edward Eves

Introduced:	December 1970
Price:	£1211.96
Seat Belts:	£9.69
Plates:	£6.50
Year's Tax:	£25.00
	£1253.15

THERE is a restricted choice for the buyer who is looking for a full four-seat 1,600cc fun saloon with pretensions to being a serious competition car, homologated and ready-to-rally. The Ford Escort Mexico is just about the only off-the-shelf car within the price range of ordinary people which does not have to be extensively modified to get it on a competition footing. It is now homologated in groups 1 and 2. Possible alternatives are the Avenger GT or the Marina. But neither of these cars are readily available in the same state of ready-to-go. In other words the Mexico is in a unique spot in the market.

What it costs

In basic form the recommended price of the Mexico is now £1,211.96. As the heading figure shows, the on-the-road price mounts to £1,253.15 by the time seat belts, index plates and Road Fund Tax are paid for. There is no delivery charge. "Our" car came fitted with the Clubman's Pack costing £148.88 which gives you four quartz-halogen spotlights, uprated suspension, Bilstein shock absorbers, bucket seats, a roll-over bar and a map-light. It also had what used to be called off-road equipment consisting of open-tread tyres, an oil cooler and a magnesium sump-shield. These last named items now feature in the Ford Advanced Vehicles Special Group programme and can be had individually. Incidentally, RS light-alloy wheels cost a further £65.97. Add to this a factory-fitted radio (£34.55) and one finds oneself motoring around in a rather stark £1,584 motor car. And the typical purchaser, if he is 30 years old and living in the Midlands, will have a bill for £110 (Group 5) for comprehensive insurance.

As an alternative, for those who prefer to combine the sturdiness and performance of the Mexico with a little luxury, there is a Custom Pack. It offers sound insulation, cut-pile carpets, fabric-trimmed seats, a heated rear window, map-reading light and coach striping for a price of £111.58. If you were living with the car all day the sound insulation and heated rear window would be well worth while.

Living with the Ford Escort Mexico

One cannot apply ordinary standards of comparison to a car which has been adapted for a special purpose. The Mexico's new reclining rally-type bucket seats are not easy to get into because of the relative closeness of the roof to the edge of the seat. Once in the seat, you have really positive location. You can bounce over mountain roads and dice round fast corners with no fear of coming unseated. In a tough, Austrian one-day rally in the Corinthina mountains, we covered the road section without penalty, after driving down from England via Hanover in a couple of days. On the return journey we covered 720 miles in exactly 12 hours including meal stops and two sets of customs. We were glad of the oil cooler when cruising in the nineties on the *autobahn*. Fears that the open-tread tyres would heat up were unfounded; the excellent Dunlop tyres fitted became barely warm after 100 miles of non-stop flat-out driving.

This is not to say that the car is perfect. The driving position is a compromise. One needs to sit "arms-stretched" to see the important bit of the instrument dials through the tiny steering wheel. In this position the pedal pads are at the wrong angle. Also, with static seat-belts one cannot reach the lighting switches without slipping out of the shoulder strap.

Internal stowage is restricted to a small parcels shelf immediately in front of the passenger. Rally types need a lot of spill-free stowage for their maps, calculators and small spares. Boot space was somewhat inhibited by the presence of the large, naked spare wheel with a metal valve cap sticking up all set to pierce one's favourite soft case. Nevertheless, two large suitcases and a host of oddments could be stowed in it and still leave room for a Continental touring kit. Wheel changing equipment is stowed in a bag behind the spare wheel. A wheel change when touring entails unloading the boot to get at the spare and tools. A good type of triangulated jack is provided, operated by a ratchet spanner.

Keeping the car clean and ship-shape presents no problems. It is smooth and rounded to wash and the paint seems to need only an occasional touch of polish to stay shiny. There are certainly no snagging points on the body but the wheels require more than a casual wipe over if you want them to look clean in the recesses of the spokes. A mop is the best instrument for cleaning the inside.

Fits and Finish

The finish of the Escort Mexico submitted for assessment was well up to Ford standards of paint quality, bearing in mind that this is basically the cheap model of the range. Patches of "orange peel' were not difficult to find but the coating was sound throughout, thick and well baked. I think I prefer this type of finish to one that has been cut down and is full of microscopic scratches.

Panel fits could be adequately described as rough and ready but honest. Neither of the two doors would shut flush — this could be adjusted — and the boot lid wore a rather wicked leer. But in the heaviest rain not a drop of water entered the car.

The interior is spartan but practical. All the trim is in black leathercloth and moulded rubber mats cover the floor, unless you specify the Custom Kit. At first glance the floor mats appeared to be detachable but on closer inspection they prove to be coming away from their permanent moorings. This was easily rectified. Being firmly fixed to the floor there is no danger of the Escort mats "ruckling up" under the pedals during hard driving.

All chromium parts are to the full BSS 1224 standard, the window frames are stainless steel and the well engineered spotlight brackets are welded up from $1\frac{1}{2}$ x $\frac{1}{4}$ in steel bar and cadmium plated. Unfortunately, the lights proved a little too detachable. Some German rally enthusiast in the Hanover area is now sporting a pair of Cibie iodine vapour spotlights which are not his own.

On the Forecourt

In common with most modern cars the Escort is designed not to be a nuisance on the garage forecourt. Water, oil and hydraulics filler apertures are level with the top of the engine bay and are readily accessible. The engine oil aperture could with advantage be a little bigger. One tends to spill oil if filling from a can. And one has to search for the dipstick until one discovers that it is simply a piece of curly wire. You might have to help a forecourt attendant to find it. Topping up the battery is less simple. It is located in the boot where it helps to redress the front to rear weight ratio but is less accessible than one located under the bonnet. Some batteries are fitted with vent tubes and extra care must be taken when removing the filler plugs.

Doing it yourself

Although the instruction book supplied with the car restricts itself to minor maintenance and operating instructions, the Mexico lends itself to owner maintenance, and typical owners will most likely want to do their own work — especially if they are taking part in competition work of one kind or another. There are no problems of accessibility in the engine bay. Valve adjustment or cylinder head removal are straightforward in the wide "engine room". Routine jobs like changing fan belts or adjusting tension are equally simple. It is also quite easy to drop the gearbox from beneath the car simply by disconnecting the propeller shaft and clutch operating gear and undoing the bellhousing bolts. The axle comes out equally easily for changes of ratio. There are plenty of these to choose from ranging from the standard 3.7 through to 6.1 to one in nine steps. Along with other performance-inducing aids they are available from Ford Rallye Sport dealers.

All the service checks are listed in the instruction book. None of them is beyond the capability of a good amateur. The most expensive tool you are likely to need is a torque spanner to check-tighten the cylinder head nuts. If you obtain a service manual it is a useful tool for a host of jobs such as re-assembling the final drive after a ratio change, as one example.

There are no grease points on the car. The

GOOD POINTS

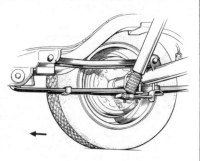

Above: Anti-tramp bars control rear axle movement and help to keep handling predictable

Left: Roomy engine compartment with all major service items readily accessible

BAD POINTS

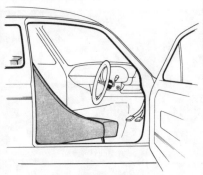

Above: The roll-over bar is a comforting thing to have in any car

Above: The car is difficult to get into because of the high sides to the seat

Below: The steering wheel rim hides important sectors of the instruments

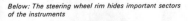

Above: Pedal angle is shallow for arms-length driving

A worthwhile annual job would be to clean the car underneath and give it a spray of Tectyl or similar wax spray. It is particularly important if you are in the habit of bouncing around on rocky roads. Flying stones will remove the thickest paint.

Electrics

Rather a lot of electricity is required when the Clubman Mexico has all its lamps on. It is provided by a 28 amp. alternator and a larger-than-standard battery. A seven-fuse box is mounted on the rear bulkhead where it is accessible to anyone who can prise the bonnet open. It is surprising to find the side-lamps and tail-lamps of each side of the car on separate circuits. Failure of a fuse can douse all the "position" lamps on one side of the car. However the dipped and main beam circuits are on separate fuses so that failure of either of them at night would be immediately obvious.

For headlamp changes or adjustment the whole grille must be removed. It is retained by nine screws. Access to the rear lamp bulbs is from inside the boot by removing a nut holding a protecting cover on either side. Other bulbs can be replaced by the usual procedure of removing the screws retaining the lenses.

Mention has been made of the sturdy mounting brackets for the Cibie spotlamps. Some form of thiefproof locking device on the lines of thiefproof wheelnuts would be a useful addition. They are very easy to remove using a single spanner. Incidentally the switches are located on the left of the panel right out of reach of the driver. One does not always carry an experienced navigator to work them.

Summing Up

It was rather like a cold shower to step out of the Silver Shadow and straight into the spartan Mexico. However, it soon impressed its very definite personality on me. It feels so sturdy and indestructible, and examination of the structure revealed a good deal of strengthening. It is true to say that an amateur cannot make a Mexico out of an ordinary Escort. I also liked the sports car ride imparted by the uprated suspension. If I lived out in the wilds with lots of rough tracks to cover, I reckon a Mexico would be competition for a Land-Rover. It's an ideal countryman's car with its big "boots" and easy-to-clean interior.

It would be cheap to maintain too because of Ford's service policy. And fuel consumption worked out at 30.5 mpg under hard driving. □

only tools you need for lubrication are an oil can, a ⅜in. AF spanner for the sump plug and an AC filter cartridge spanner. Brake pads are changed in the usual manner using a screwdriver to lever back the pistons. A proper tool is available and saves damage if the job is done frequently. The same screwdriver can be used to remove the screws retaining the rear brake drums with the object of either blowing out the dust — they work better when clean — or changing linings. Fully tuned the Escort will go very quickly indeed and it is a wise precaution regularly to inspect the suspension and steering joints. If the car is rallied frequently you are likely to do this in the course of changing shock absorbers or brake pads. Even if the car never strays away from the boulevards it is a good idea to have the wheels off every 6,000 miles or so.

Anti-freeze should be changed every two years. It has a two-way benefit, depressing the freezing point of the coolant at the bottom end of the scale, and raising the boiling point at the other.

Service Interval	Standard	Extended	Major
	6,000	18,000	36,000
Time Allowed	3.10 hours	3.30 hours	4.20 hours
Cost @ £2 per hour	£6.20	£6.60	£8.40
Oil	£1.25	£1.25	£1.25
Oil Filter	66p	66p	66p
Breather Filter	—	—	—
Air Filter	—	90p	—
Contact breaker points	—	41p	41p
Sparking plugs	88p	88p	88p
Total cost:	£8.99	£10.70	£11.60

Routine Replacements:	Time	Cost	Spares	Total:
Brake Pads	0.55 hours	£1.10	£3.04	£4.14
Brake Shoes	0.85	£1.70	£3.04	£4.74
Exhaust System	0.70	£1.40	£7.90	£9.30
Clutch	4.05	£8.10	£11.14	£19.24
Replacement front strut	1.65	£3.30	£10.90	£14.20
Shock Absorbers —rear	0.75	£1.50	£7.88	£9.38
Replace Drive Shaft, each	—	—	—	—
Alternator	0.35	.70p	£28.60	£29.30
Starter	0.55	£1.10	£13.28	£14.38

MOTORING PLUS

NAVAJO,
emigré from Mexico

The Navajo is a very gentle North American Indian, largely content to get on with tin-smithing and weaving when he's not busy reproducing. This must be one of his favourite pastimes as over the last century he has contrived to increase in numbers by something in the order of 1000 per cent, which can't be bad. His only major fault is that he appears to be rather accident prone: death from accidents amongst Navajo—or Navaho as most people spell it—are several times higher per capita than the United States average. Which has got absolutely nothing to do with the fact that Jeff Uren, the man behind Raceproved of the Uxbridge Road, has taken the name Navajo (pronounced Navaho despite the "j") for one of his Ford Escort conversions.

What he does is to take an Escort Sport bodyshell, lower the suspension and install stiffer dampers, fit 5J x 13 wheels and 185 Uniroyal radial ply tyres, replace the 4.1:1 rear axle with a 3.77:1 ratio, fit a shortened three-litre Capri prop shaft—wait for it, we'll get to the good bit soon. Then there's the Kenlowe fan, the modified transmission tunnel and, heart of the conversion, the two litre ohc engine and gearbox currently starring in the Cortina. The engine conversion costs £297 above list price, making a total of £1329. Perhaps it's a mere coincidence that many Navajo Indians live in New Mexico (fact), but the better informed among you can hardly have failed to notice that the Uren Navajo makes an interesting comparison with Ford AVO's own Escort Mexico, which uses the 1600GT engine and costs £1274. If you're thinking of trucking off to the Uxbridge Road with a pocketful of used notes for Mr Uren, just hang about a minute. The gearbox and propshaft on our test car cost £78.50, the wheels and tyres about £115, the suspension conversion £46 and the replacement cwp £30. This makes a total with VAT of £1604.55 still some £150 cheaper than the 113.9 mph RS1600.

Although the Navajo is quicker than a Mexico, we cannot pretend that we have not heard rumours of interesting developments in the South Ockendon area. Enough, or perha too much, said for the moment—just ke reading the ole Motoring Plus thing for couple of weeks and we'll let you know m when we know for sure what the rumou mean.

Meanwhile, back at the horizontals—tha what MIRA call their parallel, one-mile ho zontal straights which are provided for acce ration testing—there we were with t Navajo, all set to rip the spokes out of o fifth wheel with some vicious acceleratic Unfortunately all that happened was viol axle tramp which led to a broken eng mounting. Remember that the Mexico sh as well as being more rigid than that of t Sport anyway, is fitted with rear radius ar which keep the back axle in its place such occasions. No such advantages abou beneath the Sport's back end and Mr Ur did his nut, so to speak, when he found o that we had not set the rear dampers full hard before the standing starts. Pity, h he didn't happen to mention this problem us in advance.

A few days later, we were back on t old horizontals with our dampers as tight an undersize jock strap. This time we got couple of tramp-free runs in, which prov

Above: tight fit as the 2-litre engine squeezes into the Sport space. Right: there's little exterior sign of the changes. Below right: standard interior—but note the Kenlowe fan switch

Jeff's point, but on the third run the gearbo went for a Burton (derivation of this sayir from some knowledgeable reader, please). still worked in second, third, and top, but had as many teeth as my poor old gran first gear, so we had to abandon the te again. To be fair, it must be pointed th this car has been used for standing star by all and sundry and the stress reversa which the transmission had experienced often with frequent axle tramping was ve likely to weaken the gearbox. In other word we feel that the gearbox is more tha adequate for the job provided that it is n forced to try and leap out of the car wit axle tramp too often.

The same goes for the engine mounting which on the Navajo are normal two-lit components modified slightly to meet up wit the right points in the Sport's engine ba It's a bit of a squeeze to get this engine anyway: there's no room for the standa engine fan, hence the Kenlowe device whi is better anyway, and the engine is so hi at the front that the top of the cam be

Car: Ford Escort Sport
Conversion by: Raceproved Ltd, 177 Uxbridge Road, Hanwell, London, W7
Tel: 01-579 0991/2
Conversion: Two-litre ohc engine into Escort Sport bodyshell £297; 3.77:1 axle ratio £30; modified propshaft and new two-litre type gearbox £78.50; suspension lowered with uprated front struts and adjustable rear dampers £46; 5J wheels and 185 radial-ply tyres approx £115. With Escort Sport at £1032, and conversion at £520.50 plus 10 per cent VAT, total cost of car as tested £1604.55

	Escort Navajo	Escort Mexico	Escort Sport				
MAXIMUM SPEED				60-80	8.6	11.6	17.6
	mph	mph	mph	70-90	11.9	15.4	—
Lap	105.6	101.0	93.7	90-100	22.1	—	—
Best ¼ Mile	107.1	104.7	100.0	**In Third**			
ACCELERATION				mph			
mph	sec	sec	sec	10-30	5.3	7.1	7.3
0-30	2.9	3.9	4.1	20-40	5.3	6.3	6.8
0-40	4.5	5.9	6.4	30-50	4.8	6.1	6.7
0-50	6.5	8.3	9.2	40-60	4.5	6.3	7.3
0-60	8.9	11.5	13.1	50-70	5.7	7.3	10.0
0-70	12.5	15.8	19.2	60-80	8.3	—	—
0-80	17.1	21.5	28.7				
0-90	24.8	30.9	—	**FUEL CONSUMPTION**			
0-100	40.8	—	—	Steady mph	mpg	mpg	mpg
Standing ¼ Mile	16.9	18.4	19.2	30	44.3	47.0	39.0
Standing Km	31.6	34.3	36.0	40	41.0	46.5	36.5
In Top				50	37.0	41.6	32.5
mph				60	32.1	36.4	27.7
20-40	7.1	9.7	11.2	70	27.0	31.8	23.9
30-50	6.8	9.3	11.3	80	23.3	26.5	21.0
40-60	6.8	9.7	12.0	90	20.2	21.0	—
50-70	7.3	10.3	12.8	100	17.8	17.2	—
				Overall	approx 25*	27.8	25.3
				*See text			

cover actually touches the bonnet sound-proofing material.

If there are detail points to quibble over, the performance of the Navajo is effortless and very enjoyable. Despite the problems with standing starts, we managed to get from 0-60 mph in a mean of 8.9 sec, which compares well with the standard Sport's 13.1 sec and the Mexico's 11.5 sec. The Navajo lapped MIRA at 105.6 mph against 101.0 mph for the Mexico and 93.7 mph for the Sport. But most impressive was the low speed torque of the two litre engine: the Mexico is not lacking in this respect itself, as its 20-40 mph in top gear time of 9.7 sec proves —even the RS1600 takes 10.5 sec here and the Sport trickles from 20-40 mph in 11.2 sec. Even that is quite good for a 1300 but nothing to compare with the Navajo's commendable 7.1 sec.

With the interruptions to our road tests the fuel check was spoilt at one point, but a short run of almost 100 miles produced an overall figure of 25 mpg. Steady speed fuel consumption figures are shown in the tables.

The Navajo is an easy car to drive neatly and quickly round town, changing gear all the time, and it certainly isn't lacking in poke when you get it out into the country. The snag is that the engine seemed harsh, much more so than similar engines in Mk 3 Cortinas of our experience. Perhaps a bit more work on engine mountings might help to reduce the feeling of harshness. Trouble is that this impression is only exaggerated by the very noticeable induction roar which greets your ears when both chokes are wide open and the engine is nearing full revs. The non-standard air filter must be the culprit here: it's needed because there is no room

for the normal device under the Escort bonnet. At cruising speeds, though, noise levels were quite low all round, particularly for a somewhat hairy Q-car.

To obtain an acceptable ride the rear dampers had to be let down many "clicks" to a medium setting as with them set hard for the standing starts, it was almost like driving a car with no suspension at all. Even then, we can only describe the ride as passable. If it is too hard it obviously upsets the road-holding and handling to, so the dampers have to be softened enough to make the ride acceptable but not so much that the road-holding is adversely affected. We could not achieve an ideal compromise of damper stiffness for both ride and handling and wherever the dampers were set the car lacked the delightful agility and sensitivity of the Mexico and the RS1600. While the cornering limits

were high the car wanted to understeer too much and the steering felt rather dead. Lifting off on the limit could produce alarming lift-off tuck-in that was not sufficiently predictable to be employed as a rule for fast road driving. We also noticed a degree of rear wheel steer from time to time.

As the rear wheels tended to lock first under braking, the brakes could be used to set the car up for corners if necessary but it was too easy to overdo it and end up completely sideways with this little trick. For hard use, the brakes needed high pedal pressures and tended to judder slightly, though fade was not a problem. These comments apply to the car's behaviour on the limit of adhesion, of course, and we should point out that up to fairly high cornering forces it simply understeers gently and controllably.

Our overall verdict is that the Navajo is a very quick and effortless machine, ideal for slipping unobtrusively about town with great efficiency and little hard work. Perhaps it's a little expensive when all the suspension and transmission goodies are installed and it definitely needs better rear axle location. Keep your ears to the tarmac though.

Tony Dron

Top: all the trappings of something a bit more expensive, though the absence of side levers betrays fixed seat squabs. Above: GT engine with banana-bunch exhaust gives 93 mph. Above right: the lower part of the facia is finished in polished wood veneer. So too is the instrument panel, though small dials on the right are badly masked by wheel. Left: carpeted boot takes 8.5 cu ft of suit cases—quite fair for a small car. Lower left: hard-to-reach ignition/starter when you're strapped in. Right: sumptuous cloth covered seats marred by penny-pinched adjusters

BRIEF TEST

FORD ESCORT 1300 E

FOR : well equipped and finished ; fingerlight gearchange ; excellent roadholding and responsive handling ; quite smooth and lively

AGAINST : poor driving position for some ; rather cramped accommodation ; brakes pull ; ride sometimes jerky

Ford's 1600E version of the Mk II Cortina became something of a modern classic. Well equipped and appointed, it was a highly successful car and 60,000 of them were sold. You have only to look at the model's current resale value to see how much they are still in demand.

The Escort 1300E is cast in exactly the same mould. Introduced just three months ago, it boosted the best-selling Escort range to 19 models. Priced at £1180 the E offers a distinctively painted (two-door) Sport bodyshell with flared wheel arches, luxurious interior appointment and trim and, of course, the lively yet economical 1300GT power-plant. Not that the 1300E is unrivalled. The Austin 1300GT costs £1111, the Avenger 2-door GT £1126 and the 1.8 Marina £1008 are also good buys, even if none but the Austin offer the same

high standard of trim and appointment, though the Escort does lack reclining seats.

What the E buyer gets is an otherwise comprehensive specification that includes one of three exclusive metallic paint finishes (purple, amber gold and venetian gold), a black vinyl roof and triple coachlines. An exterior door mirror is fitted along with bright metal trim on the roof rails, side repeater flashers, reversing lights and chromium plated 5J wheels.

Inside, both front and rear seats are upholstered in brushed nylon and the floor is covered in deep pile carpet. There is a full set of instruments with a speedometer and matching tachometer and separate gauges monitoring fuel contents, water temperature, oil pressure and battery voltage. There are wood cappings to the doors and facia, a roomy glovebox, a centre console, a heated

rear window, hazard flashers and a leather rim wheel.

There's a lively performance to go with the cosmetics, too. Ford's 1297 cc ohv four-cylinder Weberfed GT engine develops a respectable 72 bhp (DIN) at 6000 rpm and a fairly healthy 60 lb ft of torque at 4000 rpm. With the bigger 13in wheels and tyres fitted to the E, Sport, Mexico and RS1600 (the similarly engined GT sits on 12in wheels) the gearing has been raised from 15 mph to 16.4 mph per 1000 rpm, though top speed and acceleration times remain the same as those for the GT we tested back in 1971. It still does a genuine 93 mph (at 5670 rpm) but the higher gearing means higher intermediate maxima. Given favourable conditions, the car will also pull a higher top speed (witness our best quarter time of 97 mph). A full-blooded wheelspin start sees 60 mph reached in 13.1 s— a creditable performance.

Drivers won't have any qualms about using the 6500 rpm on hand, either, for the five-main-bearing engine is beautifully smooth and revvable, and not too noisy when extended. Under-bonnet insulation is part of the standard package, making this the quietest Escort yet.

For a lively car which encourages brisk driving we were well satisfied with 27.3 mpg overall ; this gives a range of almost 240 miles from the nine-gallon tank on four-star fuel. Our computed touring figure of 33 mpg is quite good too, so most owners ought to break the 30 mpg mark without much effort.

Insulation from underbonnet thrashings highlights the slight whine from the otherwise outstanding gearbox. The change is superbly precise and fingerlight and the ratios, giving 32, 53 and

75 mph at 6500 rpm, are well chosen. The axle tramps violently when stepping off the line quickly, though.

The Escort's roadholding with its 5in rims and 165 section tyres (Michelin ZJs) is excellent and the handling nicely responsive. At a brisk pace the cornering is fairly neutral. Press it hard and the front runs a little wide. Press it harder still on tight bends and the inside rear wheel begins to spin signalling an imminent change to easily controlled over-steer. In fact the car's combination of roadholding and handling make it extremely safe and agile. But its inherent tendency to twitch in side-winds is a long-standing fault and the steering, otherwise extremely direct and precise, seems a bit dead about the straight ahead position, though it has plenty of feel on corners and in the wet.

The self-adjusting servo-assisted disc/drum brakes provide excellent stopping power but even after Ford had had the car back for remedial treatment, it still pulled slightly to the left under light braking, a trait we've noticed on other Escorts.

An otherwise pleasant ride is sometimes spoilt by jerkiness, especially at low speeds, and when pressing on through corners the body rocks quite sharply. To an extent the nylon-covered seats mask the less refined aspects of the ride, though several testers complained of discomfort. Why, in a car bristling with extras, Ford don't fit reclining backrests we don't know. Their absence, plus the continued use of the unsatisfactory "rocker" type fore-and-aft runners, makes it difficult (impossible for some) to tailor a comfortable driving position. You either sit too near the steering wheel or farther

MOTOR ROAD TEST No. 35/73 • FORD ESCORT 1300E

PERFORMANCE

CONDITIONS
Weather .... Drizzly
Temperature .... 52-56° F
Barometer .... 29.3 in. Hg
Surface .... Damp

MAXIMUM SPEEDS
	mph	kph
Banked circuit	93.0	150
Best ¼ mile	97	156
Terminal speeds:		
at ¼ mile	72	116
at kilometre	85	137
at mile	89	143
Speeds in gears (at 6500 rpm):		
1st	32	51
2nd	53	85
3rd	75	120

ACCELERATION FROM REST
mph	sec	kph	sec
0-30	4.3	0-40	3.5
0-40	6.4	0-60	5.7
0-50	9.2	0-80	9.1
0-60	13.1	0-100	14.4
0-70	18.5	0-120	18.2
0-80	27.3		
Stand'g ¼	19.4	Stand'g km	36.3

ACCELERATION IN TOP
mph	sec	kph	sec
20-40	12.3	40-60	6.1
30-50	11.8	60-80	7.2
40-60	12.4	80-100	8.2
50-70	14.8	100-120	9.0

ACCELERATION IN 3RD
mph	sec	kph	sec
20-40	7.5	40-60	3.3
30-50	7.1	60-80	4.7
40-60	7.0	80-100	4.2
50-70	9.0	100-120	5.1

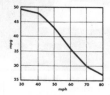

FUEL CONSUMPTION
Touring* .... 33.0 mpg
8.56 litres/100 km

Overall	27.3 mpg
	10.35 litres/100 km
Fuel grade	97 octane (RM)
	4 star rating
Tank capacity	9.0 galls
	41.0 litres
Max Range	297 miles
	476 km
Test distance	813 miles
	1308 km

* Consumption midway between 30 mph and maximum less 5 per cent for acceleration.

SPEEDOMETER (mph)
Speedo	30	40	50	60	70	80
True	30.5	40	49.5	58.5	67	77

Distance recorder: accurate.

WEIGHT
	cwt	kg
Unladen weight*	16.3	826.6
Weight as tested	20.8	1014.5
Front/rear distribution	54/46	

* with fuel for approx 50 miles.
Performance tests carried out by Motor's staff at the Motor Industry Research Association proving ground, Lindley.

GENERAL SPECIFICATION

ENGINE
Cylinders	4 in line
Capacity	1297 cc (79.15 cu in)
Bore/stroke	80.98/62.99 mm
	(3.19/2.48 in)
Cooling	Water
Block	Cast iron
Head	Cast iron
Valves	ohv
Compression	9.2:1
Carburettor	Weber twin choke, downdraught
Bearings	5 main
Fuel pump	Mechanical
Max power	72 bhp (DIN) at 6000 rpm
Max torque	68 lb ft (DIN) at 4000 rpm

TRANSMISSION
Type	4-speed all synchromesh
Clutch	Cable-operated 7.5 in dia diaphragm

Internal ratios and mph/1000 rpm
4th	1.000:1	16.4
3rd	1.418:1	11.57
2nd	1.995:1	8.22
1st	3.337:1	4.91
Rev	3.867	
Final drive	Hypoid 4.125:1	

BODY/CHASSIS
Construction	Integral chassis with steel body
Protection	1 coat phosphate, 1 coat primer, 1 coat electropaint and bitumen based protection to wheel arches

SUSPENSION
Front	Ind MacPherson strut with anti-roll bar
Rear	Live axle on semi-elliptic leaf springs, telescopic dampers

STEERING
Type	Rack and pinion
Power Assistance	None

BRAKES
Type	Disc front/drum rear
Servo	Yes
Circuit	No
Rear limit	No
Self adjusting	Yes

WHEELS
Type	Pressed steel 13/5in
Tyres	165 SR x 13 Michelin 2Xs
Pressures	20 F; 23 R

ELECTRICAL
Battery	12 Volt 38 ah
Polarity	Positive earth
Generator	Alternator
Fuses	7
Headlamps	2 rectangular 45/40w

COMPARISONS

	Capacity cc	Price £	Max mph	0-60 sec	30-50* sec	Overall mpg	Touring mpg	Length ft in	Width ft in	Weight cwt	Boot cu ft
Ford Escort 1300E	1298	1180	93.0	13.1	11.8	27.3	33.0	13 3.75	5 1.75	16.27	8.0†
Austin 1300 GT	1275	1111	95.4	13.5	11.0	30.3	38.0	12 1.75	4 11.5	16.1	6.4
Datsun 1200 Coupe	1171	1186	91.8	14.1	9.9	37.2	38.8	12 7	4 11.25	14.0	7.6
Fiat 128 Rally	1290	1280	91.0	12.9	10.8	29.1	34.2	12 7.75	5 2.5	16.45	9.5†
Hillman Avenger GT	1498	1126	96.0	11.6	10.3	23.5	30.6	13 6.25	5 2.5	16.36	10.3†
Morris Marina 1.8	1798	1008	95.1	12.2	8.6	22.5	32.1	13 10.5	5 5	18.3	12.4
Simca 1301S	1294	1226	91.8	16.8	13.3	28.3	31.4	14 7	5 3	19.4	12.3†
Toyota Corolla 1200 Coupe	1166	1239	94.8	13.6	10.2	32.0	34.8	13 0	4 11.5	14.7	7.6

*in top   †measurements take as boxes

Make : Ford
Model : Escort 1300E
Makers : Ford Motor Co, Dagenham, Essex.
Price : £1180 inc car tax and VAT. Radio, £32.38 inc tax.

back and too upright. A smaller diameter wheel such as that fitted to the RS would help for tall drivers tend to catch their hands on their thighs as they shuffled the wheel.

Access to the rear is limited, especially from the driver's side, as the forward-tipping seat fouls the steering wheel. In fact, the car is strictly a small four-seater and for passenger accommodation doesn't begin to compare with, say, the Austin 1300GT, Marina, Renault 12TS or Viva 1800 four-door—although we've yet to test these last two, they seem likely to offer a better performance/accommodation combination.

The switchgear isn't as good as in some rivals, either. The rocker switches are spread across the facia and are difficult to find without a bit of groping, especially at night. Sensibly, though, Ford have placed the lights switch entirely separate from the others and there is a wash/wipe pedal on the floor which some people like and others don't. But we wish Ford would resite the ignition switch, since it is very difficult to reach when belted in.

Visibility is good but the door-mounted exterior mirror is partially obscured by the upright window runner and the shiny wooden facia is distracting. Twin 9in rectangular headlamps are supplemented by two halogen long-range driving lamps so night visibility is excellent. It's not so good if it happens to be raining, though, for the driver's wiper lifts off at anything above 50 mph.

As we tested the E during a freakishly warm spell we couldn't test the heater, only the through-flow ventilation. This we found disappointing. The small passenger compartment and the deep windscreen combine to make the interior very warm if the sun is out. Under these conditions the only way to get a sufficiently cooling blast of air from the vents at below 50 mph was to open a window. The Escort's air extractor vents need enlarging, we feel.

The instrumentation is straight from the GT with a pleasantly styled speedometer and a rev counter (strangely not red-lined) set in front of the driver. The quartet of small instruments to the right continue to remain partially obscured by the steering wheel.

Under the bonnet the presence of the servo, a massive frying pan air filter and banana-bunch exhaust system make DIY access a bit cramped, and similarly the boot location of the spare wheel impinges on luggage space quite considerably.

Despite some detail short-comings we found the Escort 1300E is a very pleasant car. Its package deal marketing philosophy is obviously going to earn it lots of sales. But remember when casting your eyes over all those goodies that you can get bigger and quicker cars for less money.

The latest quick one from Ford—the RS2000.

FAVO's Escort RS2000

Following closely on the heels of the Dolomite Sprint announcement two weeks ago comes Ford Advanced Vehicle Operations' answer to the prospected Group 1 2-litre battle next year, their RS2000. With the single overhead camshaft four-in-line engine from the Pinto/Cortina, and the heavy duty type 49 two-door bodyshell which is already used on the Mexico and RS1600, this car is obviously aimed at competition and the competition minded.

The Ford 2-litre single overhead camshaft engine has been specially tailored for installation in the RS2000, adopting an electrically operated and thermostatically controlled fan enabling the engine to deliver 100 bhp. This is 2 bhp more than the normal Cortina, where a mechanically operated fan is employed. The engine is also equipped with a specially baffled alloy sump to prevent oil surge when racing or rallying, and a central oil pump pick-up.

Transmission of the RS2000 is through the Cortina 2000 gearbox and has a raised pivot point for the single selectro rail shift mechanism to reduce gear-lever movement between ratios. An alloy bell-housing and a single-piece tube-in-tube rubber insulated propeller shaft provide drive-line smoothness for high-speed cruising. The high rear axle

ratio of 3.54 :1 affords 18.7 mph per 1000 rpm in top gear, making the RS2000 an economical long striding motorway car.

The brakes, suspension, steering and balance have been paid particular attention, with Ford works drivers helping out considerably—particularly the late Gerry Birrell. Servo-assisted front wheel discs and rear drums on separate circuits provide braking in keeping with the performance of the new Escort. There is a 30 per cent increase in the front spring rates on the RS2000 over the Mexico and RS1600 models, while at the rear, shock absorber settings are reduced. The ride height at the rear has been lowered by the use of de-cambered leaf springs. Rack and pinion steering and 5½ in wheels shod with radial ply tyres are standard equipment.

The type 49 body shell incorporates flared wheel arches for the 5½ in wheels, and the front suspension mounting points are specially reinforced. There is a choice of six external paint schemes each with distinctive coach lines in a contrasting colour. Fully reclining black cloth seats, tachometer, gauges for oil pressure, water temperature and battery condition are standard. Quartz-halogen headlamps and hazard warning flashers are standard illumination.

There is only one word of gloom about the car, explained by Stuart Turner: "The response of our German dealers following their evaluation of the car in Britain earlier this year, has been quite overwhelming." This has resulted in them taking four times the projected number of 500, taking the whole of the first four months' production from the Advanced Vehicle Operations plant at Aveley in Essex. Consequently, the first right-hand-drive models will not be available until October 11, when customers in France and Switzerland will also be able to buy the RS2000. Meanwhile, the Escort Mexico and the 16-valve twin overhead camshaft RS1600 models will continue in production.

BOB CONSTANDUROS

First Impressions

At an ex works cost in the region of £1500 the FAVO produced Escort RS2000 will slot into place between the cheaper Mexico and the more expensive, more exciting alloy-engined sixteen valve RS1600. A brief drive in a pre-production car showed what the Cortina 2000 engine does installed in the type 49 Escort shell.

Unfortunately heavy rain falling on blind, high hedged, Essex lanes prevented finding out how the RS2000 handled with its altered spring rates (30 per cent increase at the front over the RS1600 and Mexico). Intuitively it felt as if it would be very grippy on the dry. As it turned out in the soaking wet the RS2000 felt like any other well shod and powerful Escort. Left on its own with understeer, or driven as it should, oversteering quickly, easily and very controllably.

Apart from the RS2000's very swish base specification, good seats and instrumentation etc, the first inkling that this Escort is different comes when the key is turned. It doesn't sound like it should—give the throttle a blip and it's even stranger. Put it into gear and set off along the rain soaked lanes and it's not just strange—it's now quite peculiar. Foot down and it is, definitely, all-Escort with its quick steering and pattering rear wheels twitching the car down between the hedges in fine adrenalin producing style. But that noise from the engine would take a little longer to fathom. Not that it's noisy, it is, for an Escort, quite quiet actually. A few cautious corners and straights later it comes clear.

The RS2000 has found something and lost something else. It has found an engine which feels just right for the open road and long drives. For all normal road driving it is smooth and flexible, in fact quite torquey. It has lost its rally breeding in the form of engine response. The RS2000 accelerates smoothly from low revolutions to a rather stifled and strained sounding top end without faltering, but it seems to lack immediate get-up-and-go. As the rally possiblity the RS2000 gave me the impression I could be a little quicker in a Mexico. Coming to the occasional glimpse of open road to come, it lacked what can only be called a quick, necessary "zap" squirt forward to keep it in the groove. By the time the driver should have been sizing up what to do for the approaching bend I found that I was still accelerating the 2000.

With hindsight, I feel sure that if there is any fault, it was the driver's and nothing to do with the car. The car is inanimate—the driver just couldn't get in step with the car in the time available. In defence, well, there has never before been an Escort quite like this one. It is very desirable just as it is but I would really like to see the engine awakened from its 50 bhp per litre slumber.

IAN SADLER

The RS2000's smart interior with fully reclining seats.

DOLOMITE OUT OF THE DOLDRUMS

Sixteen-valve heads are in! Here's how Triumph and Ford do their performance thing

By Ian Fraser

MEMBERSHIP OF THE 16 VALVE CLUB is so exclusive in four-cylinder society that there are still only three names on the list. Founder-member was Ford's RS1600 Escort, followed by the Lotus two-litre in the Jensen Healey with the Triumph joining up only a matter of days ago by nominating the Dolomite Sprint.

But the reasons for their existence are varied. The Lotus engine has 16 valves and two overhead cams because of the need for reasonable performance at the same time as meeting America's exhaust-emission laws. The RS1600, on the other hand, is far more pretentious; its 1.6litre engine is intended primarily for further development as a race and rally unit in the specially beefed-up Escort body that is also common to the Mexico. No doubt Triumph hope that buyers will take the Dolomite Sprint to (club) races and that other sporty types will see fit to run it in rallies, although its major role is that of a fast road car and a flag-waver for Triumph's recently-declared policy of leaving the big saloons for Jaguar and Rover and concentrating instead on performance orientated two- and four-seaters.

The standard Dolomite is hardly a flag-waver. It has performance that is easily bettered by others in its price and size class, and since is also lacks modern styling and real suspension it is hardly in the position to bolster the Triumph image.

Conversely, the Escort's image needs little help. It is a very successful small car and its performance aura has been continually held up by competition successes, albeit in versions bearing little resemblance to the ones people actually buy.

For one thing, few people are prepared to spend RS1600 money on something that looks like any old Escort, and would have a hard job convincing themselves that they really needed such a costly and superb engine. This latest version of the RS1600 engine is all-alloy, whereas the older model had an iron block capped with an alloy head, but the cylinder dimensions remain the same: 80.99mm bore by 77.72mm stroke to give a displacement of 1601cc. The compression ratio is 10 to one and the fuel is distributed by a pair of either Dellorto 40DHLAE or Weber 40 DCOE 48 double choke, horizontal carburettors. The camshafts are driven by toothed belt, but the valves have shim adjustment for the tappets which means the cams have to be removed to do it. Best done by your Ford Rallye Sport dealer, says the handbook. As an engine it would be hard to imagine anything neater; it looks just like a large alloy container with carburettors on one side and an exhaust system on the other, fitting with precious little length to spare under the Escort's short bonnet. As you buy it off the showroom floor, the RS1600 engine develops 114bhp(nett) at 6500-rpm with 105lb/ft of torque at 4000rpm, and comes complete with an ignition cutout at 6500 to make sure you don't

Photographs: by John Stewart

Escort RS 1600

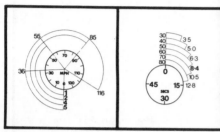

VEV 480L

rev it more or less indefinitely.

It must, of course, be said that the RS engine is primarily a racing unit capable of being developed to produce around 220bhp without much trouble, so as it stands on the showroom floor with an Escort wrapped around it, it's really only a beginning.

The Dolomite Sprint engine, however, is already quite heavily developed over the standard model. To start. with, the engine capacity has been. increased from 1854cc (87mm bore, 78mm stroke) to 1998cc by enlarging the bore to 90.3mm. Incidentally, Saab who use the same block, have a slightly smaller bore with a resultant reduction in capacity of an inconsequential 13cc.

But the real trick with this half-a-Stag engine has been to equip it with a 16-valve head. Up until the Sprint, the umpteen variations of this engine have all had a single overhead camshaft working directly onto the tappets to give nothing more interesting than inclined valves with conventional enough combustion chambers and could give no better than 91bhp at 5200rpm with 105lb/ft of torque at 3500rpm—barely enough to provide a somewhat laboured 100mph. The two-litre Saab manages 95bhp and 116lb/ft, also at 3500rpm. Hardly a worthwhile basis on which to build a performance engine.

British Leyland—and more particularly CAR's old friend Spen King—applied the gentle hand of ingenuity rather than the mailed fist of ample money, and came up with a solution that is 80percent of the way to a twin-cam configuration but considerably less than that in cost. What happens is that the single overhead (and chain-driven) camshaft remains in virtually the same position as it does on the regular Dolomite and the Saab 99, with the cam lobes pushing directly down onto the valve stems. In the normal engine these lobes work both the exhaust and inlets, but in this unit they open only the inlets. The eight exhaust valves are worked by rocker arms, the shaft of which is located on its centre line between the vee formed by the inlet and the exhaust valves. This means, of course, that the exhaust timing is the exact reciprocal of the inlet, for the camshaft carries only eight lobes. The spark plugs enter the combustion chambers from a central position, just as they do in the RS1600.

The Triumph's engine is tilted at 45degrees to the nearside leaving the exhaust beneath the engine and the induction system on the top side. A pair of long induction manifolds carry two 1.75in SU HS6 carburettors; at 9.5 to one, the compression ratio is lower than it is in the Escort. Power output, however, is higher at 127bhp(nett) at a modest 5700rpm with 122.5lb/ft at 4500rpm and, like the RS1600, peak revs are limited to a healthy enough 6500.

Both cars have four-speed gearboxes. The Ford's overall ratios of 11.25(first) 8.23(second) 5.85(third) and 3.78(top) whilst the Sprint has ratios of 10.31, 7.25, 4.78 and 3.45. The little Escort gives 17.8mph per 1000rpm on 165-13 tyres while the Sprint does 18.9mph per 1000rpm on 175/70 HR-13s. Ford's heavy involvement in motor racing has meant that RS1600 buyers can have different final drive as well as gearbox ratios, but the Sprint is so far restricted to that which is standard equipment.

As a touring car, the Dolomite scores with its 12.5gallon petrol tank (four star) but the Escort has only nine gallons (larger tankage is available) and runs best on five star, although the handbook suggests four-star as a minimum. So when you are dealing with consumption figures of about 24mpg for the Triumph and 26mpg for the RS1600, you can draw your own conclusions.

The Sprint has a total oil capacity of 7.5pints whereas the RS1600 has 8.9 pints including the 1.2pints in the oil cooler which is standard. Engine cooling arrangements are handled by a permanently engaged fan with thin, feathering blades in the Escort; the Triumph replies on a visco-coupled fan.

Both cars have servo-assisted disc front/drum rear braking systems, the RS1600 wearing 9.75in discs and 9.0 by 1.75in drums whereas the Sprint is equipped with 8.75in discs and 9.0 by 1.75in drums, giving the former 288sq in of swept area and the latter 264sq in. At 3.5turns lock-to-lock for a 29ft turning circle, the Escort's steering is higher geared than the Sprint's which needs 3.75turns (lower geared than the normal Dolomite, but more responsive) and has a turning circle of 30.9in. On the quoted manufacturer's figures for kerb weights,

Dolomite Sprint

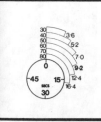

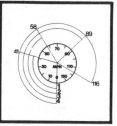

the RS1600 tips the scales at 1730lb against the Sprint's 2228lb.

Suspension systems are basically conventional in both cars, but have been dressed up to iron out inherent difficulties. The Sprint employs coil springs and dampers operating on the upper wishbones, with the single lower links located fore-and-aft by trailing radius arms. There is an anti-roll bar fitted. At the rear, the live axle is suspended on coils and held with a four-link system, the lower links carrying not only the springs and dampers, but also the anti-roll bar attachment points.

The RS1600 has Macpherson struts at the front with a roll bar and at the rear the semi-elliptic sprung live axle is located with trailing arms. Of the two, the Ford's is the simplest but not entirely as effective as the Sprint's in terms of comfort.

The Sprint is well equipped, has more space than the Escort, two extra doors, a more lavish interior, a softer ride, more luggage space and is a lot quieter on the road. That it has a good perform-

ance is evidenced by the figures, but they don't show the responsiveness of the engine has that nice, hard feeling and a willingness to get up and really run. The cruising speed is around 100mph or a little faster, although wind noise can be irksome but not totally offensive. If all this performance had been applied to a standard Dolomite with no chassis modifications it would have been a total disaster, but what has happened is that the spring rates have been altered and the suspension generally tied down to a considerably greater degree than the standard car. The high-speed stability has been assisted by a spoiler under the front bumper—and it really works. When we first drove the car in motorway conditions we were assailed by violent crosswinds that tried to take hold of the car and hurl it about. Since we were doing 100-plus at the time the situation had the makings of an uncomfortable and busy drive, but to the credit of the Sprint it tended to stabilise itself very quickly after initial deflection.

Handling and roadholding felt pretty good, particularly if the driver was prepared to use the throttle to overcome the understeer which still threatens to take over on downhill corners. Generally though, the Sprint points well, body roll is moderate and it feels safe. On poor surfaces there is some bump steer but not enough to warrant any special condemnation on that score.

The RS1600 feels tighter and rides harder than the Sprint, as you would reasonably expect in a lighter car with its suspension settings prejudiced in favour of ultimate roadholding rather than comfort. And that's exactly what you get. The RS1600 asks a lot of the driver and gives a lot in return. It tends

to oversteer more than anything else but is not as upset by uneven corners as initial impressions suggest. Above all it's a driver's car, for the passengers are not catered for in the real sense— nice cloth-trimmed front seats with a cloth-trimmed bench in the back, carpets on the floor and that sort of thing—a tremendous amount of mechanical noise when hurrying and quite a lot of exhaust din as well.

Its performance is outstandingly good, but if you live in a big city and are basically a built-up area runner, forget it. Buy a Mexico instead. Unlike the Dolomite, which is tractable and fairly polite around town, the RS gets crumpy when it's asked to run slow and tends to dirty its plugs until you can find a patch to clear them. But don't mistake the RS for being totally impractical in town; its mainly frustrating. On the open road the RS1600 is quick, being able to run to ignition cutout in top (116mph) in all the unlikely places. The high noise level is wearing, so maybe it's just as well that the tank holds so little fuel. It makes petrol stops something of a happy hour in which to collect one's senses again.

As an everyday car, the Dolomite Sprint wins hands down over the RS1600, for it has decent performance, fair comfort, satisfactorily low noise level and some of the worthwhile attributes of proper performance motoring.

On the other hand, the RS1600 is a pre-breakfast car in which to have enormous fun for short distances, before scurrying back to the garage while the law looks for you. It can, of course, be civilised but then the cost rises out of proportion again. As a sort of hairy, four-wheeled motorcycle the Escort is tremendous, but as an everyday car can prove to be too testy. ●

FORD ESCORT RS 2000

Addition to sporting Escort range puts refinement and better manners into the competition models

The RS 2000 is identified by its distinctive two-tone paintwork and small badges on the front wings. New rally seats give excellent location with built-in head-rests and reclining backrests. The ohc engine is the same as that fitted to the Cortina 2000 apart from the substitution of an electric cooling fan

SPORTING and competition-minded buyers of small saloons have more choice in the Ford Escort range than with any other model. Starting at £1,032 there is the Escort Sport with 1300GT engine and at the top end for £1,761 is the 16-valve aluminium-block twin-cam RS 1600, upon which the successful race and rally Escorts are based. In between are the regular GT for £1,082 and the 1600GT Mexico with heavy-duty RS 1600 bodyshell for £1,274.

As a high-performance road car the RS 1600 is tremendous fun but considerably lacking in refinement and slightly too highly-strung for general family use. The Mexico is much more reliable but still suffers from the same harshness and high noise levels. Conscious of these deficiencies for road use and doubtless aware of the market research which led Triumph to launch the Dolomite Sprint, Ford's Advanced Vehicles Operations have been working hard on a new derivative which is announced this week. Owing to an unexpected demand from Germany, where the first 2,000 built will be exported, the new RS 2000 will not be available here until October. We will be publishing a full *Autotest* to coincide with deliveries in the UK on 11 October.

The RS 2000 is much more than just an Escort fitted with 2-litre Cortina ohc engine. Simple engine swaps have been done before now by some of the conversion specialists (we published a test of the Superspeed Escort 2000 24 June 1971). Ford's AVO version is a fully-engineered package with all the noise, vibration and harshness taken out of the working rev range and some changes to the suspension which considerably improve the handling. No UK price has been fixed yet, but it is expected to be about halfway between the price of the Mexico and that of the RS 1600, at about £1,500 including tax.

The engine is basically identical with that of the Cortina 2000, which is an advanced single overhead cam design developing 98 bhp (DIN) at 5,500 rpm. In the Escort an electric cooling fan replaces the fixed drive of the Cortina version which puts the peak power up to 100 bhp (DIN) at 5,700 rpm. A new sump and oil pick-up were needed to clear the Escort front cross-member so an aluminium casting was made to help reduce the noise level. This, together with an aluminium bell-housing puts the natural boom resonance of the engine up from 5,400 rpm to over 6,000 rpm where it is seldom encountered. A standard 2-litre Cortina gearbox is used with remote control revised to reduce lever movements.

At the bottom end of the range the Cortina engine develops more torque than the 120-bhp RS 1600, even though the peak torque of 112 lb ft (DIN) is the same. The Cortina gearbox has a much lower bottom (3.65 to 1) than the RS 1600 (2.98 to 1), so a 3.54-to-1 final drive is used for the RS 2000. This compares with 3.77 on the RS 1600 and Mexico and gives 18.7 mph per 1,000 rpm in top on the standard 165-13in. radial tyres. Low-profile 70-series tyres do not give sufficient snow chain clearance as required by German regulations.

To give more inboard clearance as well the size of the rear brake drums has been reduced from 9 x 1.75in. to 8 x 1.5in. as fitted to the Escort GT. This improves the braking balance and prevents premature rear wheel lock into the bargain, the general feeling being that the RS 1600 and Mexico are overbraked at the rear.

With assistance from international racing driver Gerry Birrell the suspension for the RS 2000 has been completely revised with front spring rates 30 per cent stiffer and the rear about 10 per cent softer. New damper rates to suit and a slight lowering of the rear ride height have worked wonders for the comfort and made the RS 2000 a much more progressive car when driven to the limits of adhesion. Quite strong initial understeer leading eventually to power or roll oversteer has now been tempered to a much more consistently neutral characteristic, although a brief run around the Essex lanes revealed that there was still the ability to kick the tail out under power when required.

As well as attending to the fundamental vibration frequencies in the engine and transmission, the Ford AVO engineers have done a lot of work on sound deadening and a new sandwich material is applied to the underbonnet area, engine bulkhead and complete floor. The result is a dramatic reduction in noise level throughout the range and especially at high speed.

The new Escort complies with all the existing noise standards and the European emission standard (ECE 15) which comes into effect in the UK on 31 July this year. At a future date it is expected that performance equipment for this model will be added to the Ford Sport range. □

TWO-LITRE TIGER
Escort RS 2000

FORD have introduced yet another luxury **hot** version of their very successful Escort range.

Just when we thought they had used every possible combination of power-packs, they planted the 2-litre OHC four-cylinder Cortina engine in the Escort's ubiquitous engine bay. Pricewise the new car, called the RS-2000, fits between the Mexico "boy-racer" version and the sophisticated, alloy-engined, 16-valve top of the range RS-1600.

The result is a lively 100bhp model with a top speed of 110mph, a 0-60mph time of just under 9secs and priced around $A2300 ex-factory, but without Britain's value tax.

The idea originated from Ford Germany who wanted a high-speed luxury-performance version to go with the Escort Mexico ($A1950, ex-factory) and the 16-valve twin OHC RS-1600 ($A2700 ex-factory). The bigger engine unit makes the RS-2000 quieter and the finish is much more luxurious — just what the Germans wanted as a high-speed autobahn cruiser.

The Germans have collared the first four months' production of 2000 units which they say, have already been sold. The British market and other right (and left-hand) drive markets,

won't see the new Escort until October.

The RS-2000 has a stylish and well appointed interior with a comprehensive range of instruments, cloth trimmed reclining front seats with optional built-in head restraints and loop pile carpet.

There's a leather-padded steering wheel, vinyl topping on the roofline and six external color schemes, each with a broad stripe down the side.

To get as many of the available horses down to the road, the 2-litre has been specially tailored for installation under the Escort bonnet. An electrically operated and thermostatically controlled cooling fan helps (by eliminating the engine-driven fan) and gives the unit an extra two horses over the Cortina version.

As the car can be used for racing and rallying as well as long-distance high-speed cruising, a special baffled alloy sump has been fitted to prevent oil surge, and the unit is fitted with a

centrally mounted pump.

Modifications to the four-speed close-ratio gearbox from the Cortina include the raising of the pivot point for the single selector rail-shift mechanism to reduce gear lever movement between ratios.

The power really does fade out at 5700rpm, as I discovered during a short tryout on the high speed track and extremely tight esses of the Army proving ground at Cobham, just south of London.

The track is most suitable for comparison purposes, as Ford have selected it for each new uprated Escort release.

Compared with the new RS-1600 and the Mexico, the RS-2000 doesn't seem quite as easy to handle when you first start belting it around as a race car.

It is only after a few laps you get the message that this car has been set up by an expert in the art of building race and rally performance and handling in

It's got special paint, special trim and special appeal. The standard Escort has picked up a luxury finish, the 2-litre OHC motor and a good turn of speed to meet the requirements of European auto-bahns and highways. Dev spun out . . . fought back . . . and fell for it!

Escort RS 2000

a production car.

This person, of course, was Gerry Birrell the young Scottish racing and development driver who was unfortunately killed in practice at Rouen, two weeks before his latest **conversion**, the RS-2000 was released.

Drive the 2000 as you would on the road, and its manners are nigh on perfect. The car is no trouble for the man who wants something to drive fast on high speed roads, yet it is safe and nimble enough, though unfussy, for mum to drive to the local shops or to take the kids to school in.

Use everything it's got up to the 5700rpm limit (86mph in third, 60mph in second) around a race circuit and the back will come out on the really hard and tight corners.

At first I didn't think it handled as neatly or as precisely as the Mexico or the RS-1600, but after a few laps I wasn't certain that I didn't prefer the little heavier car. Certainly you could drift this car on its 5.5J rims and 165SR13 radials with a great feeling of confidence.

My first efforts through the tight esses nearly resulted in a spin on some of the tighter and more sweeping bends — something some of my colleagues didn't manage to prevent!

But most of us soon got used to controlling the rear end to get the best out of the car.

The main reason for early misapprehensions is that while the handling is really excellent, the car is far quieter than the Mexico or RS-1600. The lack of noise and roll are apt to lead the unwary into getting the tail hanging out. Not that this is anything to worry about, as on the circuit you can hold the correction and with a bit of practice drift nicely under control.

But compared with the Mexico, and in particular the RS-1600, the car seems, and is, more sophisticated in the suspension department, due to the efforts of Gerry Birrell.

Suspension is independent, using MacPherson struts with twin upper radius arms and semi-elliptic springs to give good location to the live rear axle.

Because the Germans need to be able to fit chains in winter, the rear drum brakes have been reduced in diamter from 9in and the width dropped from 1.75in to 1.5in.

The brake ratio front and rear has been revised, and the RS-2000 has a 30percent increase in spring rates over the Escort Mexico and RS-1600 models. At Birrell's suggestion, Ford reduced the shock absorber settings and lowered the ride height at the rear by using decambered leaf springs.

Rack and pinion steering and the wide sports road wheels shod with radial ply tyres are standard equipment.

The competition-developed type-49 heavy-duty two-door body (as in the Mexico and RS-1600) is used, and

ABOVE: The luxury seats are functional as well as good looking. They provide excellent support in all areas, stop movement of the occupants when cornering fast and are comfortable for long high-speed trips. Full instrumentation is provided to match the car's sporting capabilities.

both the front and rear wheel arches are flared to take the wide sports road wheels. The front suspension mounting points and the chassis side rails are specially re-inforced.

Laminated windscreens are standard as are the electrically heated rear screens.

I found the German version of the front seats (built for bigger German bottoms one presumes) a little too soft

riding, but Ford tell me the reclining seats will be made a little harder in all other markets.

Quartz-halogen headlamps, hazard warning flashers and a steering column lock are fitted as standard.

The finished product is a very good example of what I think a mass-produced body should be. For my money, this new Escort is well worth the price! ⓗ

ABOVE: The exterior features flared wheel arches, sports wheels and a distinctive wide-stripe paintwork treatment. The heated rear screen is standard.

Road Test:

Escort RS 2000

Yet another addition to Ford's Escort range will be available in Great Britain from the 11th of this month. This is the Escort RS 2000 and features the proven 1993cc Pinto engine installed in the heavy duty type 49 shell featured on both the Mexico and the RS1600 (which are both continuing in production). By using the old maxim of a big engine in a small body Ford's have produced a car that provides good performance without any stress on the motor or the driver. As such it is successful, although whether at £1500-£1600 the car is a little overpriced remains to be seen.

The engine has already seen plenty of life in the Cortina and Pinto range, and only two items are changed in its Escort installation.

A thermostatic electric fan is fitted and means that an extra two brake horse power is available, giving the RS2000 100 brake horse power. An alloy sump with baffles, and a central oil pick up prevents oil surge. The engine is generally quiet, but makes its presence felt with a flat roar at full throttle. At high revs (the red line is 6500rpm) the engine feels a bit rough, although on the test car (a left hand drive export model) we had problems with the plugs causing a misfire. However, the car is lively enough, and certainly both long journeys and motorways are covered at a rapid and prompt rate.

Power is fed to the wheels via a mechanically operated single plate 8.5 inches diameter diaphragm clutch, and a close ratio four speed gearbox. This is an adaptation of the Cortina 2000 box, and has a raised pivot point for the single rail shift mechanism to reduce gear lever movement. The gear shift seemed curiously notchy by the normally perfect Ford standards. Several people commented on it, and it stood out in a make of car where the gear shift is normally of a standard that other manufacturers should use as an example. Ratios are quite close, and fourth is a direct gear : with the 3.54 :1 rear axle ratio 18.7 mph per 1000 rpm means a long legged 90 mph cruising with little engine noise.

Suspension is the same as the Mexico and RS1600, although the front spring rate is 30% higher, and the rear shock absorber rates are reduced.The ride height at the rear has been lowered by using de-cambered leaf springs, and the results are excellent. The ride is firm, without being harsh, and cornering could be accomplished comfortably at high speeds with little or no roll. Pushed to the time limit initial slight understeer gives way to easily controlled oversteer, with the throttle playing its usual decisive part. On tight corners there is enough power to control the oversteer with the accelerator, but on fast corners more throttle means more understeer until the absolute ragged edge is reached. (By which time you've probably been arrested anyway!)

Braking via front disc brakes and smaller drum rears. is servo assisted with seperate circuits. There performance is excellent, and even our usual local test section (1000 feet drop through several hairpins in only 1½ miles) failed to cause any fade, despite the car being five up at the time.

Ford's smart new RS 2000 will be available in Britain from the 11th of this month, unfortunately without the super seats. (Below)

The usual delightful rack and pinion steering from the RS1600 is fitted, and a leather rimmed 14″ steering wheel is fitted, to the collapsible steering cloumn. A full range of instruments, hazard lamps and steering column lock are included in the specification.

The seats for the German market are rather super reclining jobs with padding up to the knees (literally!) and excellent support for the back. Fabulous though they may be, they do have a slight disadvantage—the rear of the car becomes acutely uncomfortable if not impossible, for anybody other than legless pygmies. The British models will have thinner seats, giving a more satisfactory situation for the rear passengers.

Other items in the specification include laminated windscreen heated rear window, and QI headlights.

Generally speaking we enjoyed our short aquaintance with the Escort RS 2000 On the production models a different exhaust will be fitted and we hope, different engine mountings. On our press car the sump was almost touching the rack, and seemed like a certain retirement looking for the first yump. When the car is homologated into Group One during next year, the real sales potential of the car will be realized. In the mean time the car will attract both road and competitive users—the former will get a well appointed long legged but smallish saloon car, the latter a good handling, quickish, and reliable car with good spares network. But at sixteen hundred quid? *N.I.J.*

Performance

Top Speed—
 109 mph (175 kph)—4th.
 86.5 mph (139.0 kph)—3rd.
 60 mph (96.5 kph)—2nd.
 32 mph (51.4 kph)—1st.
Acceleration—0-60 mph in 8.9 seconds.

FORD RS 2000

Jerry Sloniger drives the FORD ESCORT RS 2000, and finds it thoroughly acceptable even in these days of fuel economies. Sadly it's not available in Australia . . .

WE MIGHT AS well lead off with the admission that this Ford RS 2000 is a crazy mixed up kid in the car world — but you can't help liking its cheek.

It is a blatantly bestriped, hot machine at a time when such is supposed to be the original sin. Yet it is paradoxically a very logical way to have your whiff of fun and still consume relatively little fuel. So maybe Ford doesn't really regret launching the car just before the energy crisis after all.

The idea was simplicity itself. Digging into those near-bottomless parts bins, both English and German, Ford took an ubiquitous Escort shell which weighs a mere ton and stuffed in the ex-Pinto (and Australian Cortina 2000) single-OHC four to make a cheap goer with very low state of tune but the credentials of a hot sedan.

With 100 (DIN) bhp it falls between the Escort Mexico and race-engined BDA yet the power/weight ratio is such that it will outdrag the BMW 2002, go very nearly as fast in top, and costs 15-25 percent less. Being an RS Ford (which means it is only sold through selected dealers) it also benefits from Ford's infinite options list. Some of these items are essential.

All this for around $Aust2750 in Europe, and now that production has been taken away from those famous English non-workers, quality is acceptable too. The RS 2000s come solely from Ford's continental plant.

Obviously $A2750 isn't enough to eliminate all the compromises which may be traced to the original low-budget Escort. The interior is not plush and the back axle is still a crude beam.

In fact you can easily tell Ford of Britain did the suspension system. It goes around smooth corners like the painted line but rough bends throw it all around. A set of Bilstein shockers would help considerably since Ford gave up comfort and pothole-handling in favor of a lower stiffer and thus, safer, car.

Provided you remain within the limits of back end hop the handling is light understeer and provided, again that you are in the proper gear ahead of time, the tail may be hung on your accelerator pedal like a trophy.

On cobbles it remains an Escort. But an Escort with more than fancy stripes. For instance the dash holds a big speedo (five percent fast at 60) and a tacho but you don't get a tripmeter which should be standard in this class.

Ford did fit four extra instruments for fuel, water, oil pressure and volts and added a very nice, thick-rim leather steering wheel which blocks two or more of these at any one time.

Escort styling hasn't changed in the seven years it's been in production.

Minor controls are mostly left to tumblers along the dash where only an orang-outang could reach them with the standard three-point belt (inertia-reel belts are optional). This is particularly annoying in a light drizzle when you have to belt/unbelt every couple of minutes to get the wipers working. A stalk on the steering column would help. At least a foot-operated wiper (one wipe) is provided.

On the other hand Ford added a warning light to tell you if a brake circuit fails and gave it a tumbler with light to check the warning system itself. You also get a laminated screen and heated rear window. The car somes with good quartz iodine head lamps and two reversing lamps.

Yet there are no map pockets or glove boxes, only an open shelf. It's almost as if Ford costed the car by adding up options and using those.

One place where no corners were cut is the front seats, a pair of Scheel rally buckets which cost a fortune as extras and seldom appear in a standard car. Double credit to Ford. These have good long-distance comfort, fine lateral support, good adjustability and yet aren't hard to enter or leave.

About their only drawback is that they further cut already-marginal rear passenger space. Still, we managed four adults for half-hour jaunts.

Beneath the skin Ford was wholly true to its deep involvement with competition. It certainly improved this car. Suspension pickup points are stronger and Ford has fitted front discs as standard with booster from the heavier/faster 2.6 Capri. Vented discs are an option as is a limited slip diff.

Heavy striping distinguishes RS 2000 from more mundane Escorts.

Much the same as the GT 1600 unfortunately no longer available in Australia. Only the wheel is different.

FORD RS 2000

ENGINE: Single-OHC inline four, 1993 cm^3, bore 90.8, stroke 77 mm; 100 DIN bhp at 5700 rpm; torque 108 lb/ft at 3750 rpm, max revs 6500; compression 9.2:1.

POWER TRAIN: Ford Consul clutch, 2.6 Capri 4-speed gearbox. Final drive 3.54, gear ratios 3.65, 1.97, 1.37, 1.00, R 3.66.

CHASSIS: MacPherson struts front with stabiliser; beam rear axle with semi-elliptic springs. Rack and pinion steering. Dual-circuit brakes with Capri front discs, rear drums.

Wheels — 5½ in. steel rims with 165 SR 13 radials.

Wheelbase 92.7 in., front/rear track 73.8/74.5; overall length 156.9 in.; width 61.9 in.; height 57.8 in.

Ground clearance 5.5 in., turning circle 32 ft 2 in.

Empty weight 2020 lb, permitted load 850 lb. Fuel capacity 9 Imp gal, water 6.2 qt, oil 3.4 qt.

PERFORMANCE: Top, 112 mph at 5800 rpm; fuel consumption 26.6 mpg. Acceleration: 0-30 = 2.7 sec; 0-40 = 4.3 sec; 0-50 = 6.4 sec; 0-60 = 9.0 sec; 0-70 = 11.9 sec; 0-80 = 15.5 sec; 0-90 = 21.0 sec; 0-100 = 29.6 sec.

The RS 2000 is lowered an inch, has negative camber in front and is fitted with wider 5½ in. pierced steel rims with good wide radials. Steering is light and precise.

To handle the extra power of the large engine, Ford fitted the clutch from one of the mid-range Consuls and backed it up with the outstanding four-speed gearbox from the big Capri. Movements are very short, ultra-accurate and a constant pleasure.

Such newness may also have had something to do with a lack of elasticity.

One would expect two litres to pull from ground zero in such a light car, but there is nothing below 2500 and the only real action comes above 4000. From there it winds right on out to 6500 but gets very noisy indeed above 5000.

Part of the laggard feel is the Ford gearing which doubtless aids the car in reaching 110 mph-plus but only at the expense of mid-range pulling ease. The very low first gear masks this lack at stop lights but then there is a vast gap to second.

The car starts immediately from cold if the driver follows Ford's drill, and breathes easily, taking sudden throttle changes without a murmur.

Driving round town returned over 20 mpg while the 2000 did an easy 27 cruising in speed-limited Germany. Used hard, the car still returns some 23 mpg which renders the nine gallon tank size highly useful.

The body style has been around quite a while now but this one generated less wind noise than earlier models. Only turbulence from the outside mirror was really loud.

Just as it stands the RS 2000 from Ford is a fine way to feel sporting without feeling wasteful, it is taut, looks mean, and lets us recall the days of glory without overworking our ecological conscience. If competition should return to Europe it will be the budget racer's starting point.

Not bad for a hybrid collection of parts out of a common bin.   *

Above: If that engine looks familiar don't be surprised. It comes straight out of the Cortina 2000.

Above left: Full rally bucket seats provide a comfortable driving position but reduce rear seat room to a minimum.

HI HO PINTO!

First seen in the American Ford Pinto, the single overhead cam two litre engine seems to have overcome tuning troubles and now powers Roger Clark's cost-conscious rally car. David Hardcastle went to Boreham to try the car, which won first time out.

Photographs: Paul Skilleter

Although the back axle is pretty special, AOO shell is standard—so standard it had to be updated to '74 spec before its first event

ROGER shrugged and gazed into the distance with his head inclined at a slight sideways angle. From past experience I knew that I was not going to get a completely straight answer to my question "How do you feel, swopping a Group 2 BDA for an RS 2000 ?"

"It's just an RS 2000," he said, shrugging his shoulders in resignation, "I've had the lads screw me an extra interior mirror into it and we'll just have to wait and see."

The conversation took place at the Selby Fork Hotel, a few hours before the start of the Mintex Dales Rally, on May 17. One day and 150 stage miles later, Clark had been declared the winner by a mere two seconds over the BDA of Tony Drummond. The new interior mirror wasn't required—as usual Clark had had to move over for no one.

Although it was a shame that the RS 2000's first rally win should be both so close and controversial (Drummond would have won but for a crucial stage which was cancelled), it illustrated that Boreham at any rate have sorted out the tuning problems on the Pinto unit which had defeated several other engine builders.

Last year Harold Morley, fresh from his success as road-rally champion, started out with an experimental RS 2000 run by Crystals of Hull in selected stage rallies, but the car retired on several occasions with engine problems and now lies resting and rusting in Boreham's infamous compound.

Crux of the matter seems to be the solitary overhead cam, its bearing and lubrication. Ford's competitions engine man John Griffiths doesn't seem to lose any sleep over it, though, and the unit in Clark's car is made by Weslake and gives 60 thou more lift than the standard item. John does admit that at idling speeds, the Pinto unit tends not to have an effective oil spray on to the cam fingers and thus drivers of AOO are instructed not to let it idle too long.

Until news of Clark's performance on the Yorkshire stages got out, many fellow drivers had assumed that because the RS 2000's Group 1 homologation was imminent, this would be a shakedown session with a standard model. They were only half right !

The shell and suspension mounting points are absolutely standard—in fact this particular car is so old, relatively speaking, that apart from converting it from left-hand drive, the Boreham mechanics also

Clark moves his driving seat on from one car to the next.
Jim Porter nurses a large fire extinguisher under his knees

Twin Webers and special Janspeed manifold make
tight fit. The engine sits on a World Cup crossmember

had to update its rear suspension mounts from '73 Mexico spec to the '74 Mexico/RS2000 system. This entails fitting a transverse member at the fore-end of the boot floor, which can best be described as an internal cross-member, on to which the rear shockers locate. They are thus much nearer the ideal vertical position than before and mounted so that they will not punch holes in the floor, which is what non-turreted Escort shockers have acquired a reputation for doing.

But we were talking about the engine and that's a long way away from the glossy catalogue description. A total of 165 bhp at 6750 rpm and 152 lb ft torque at 4000 rpm is quite an improvement on the standard figures of 100 bhp at 5700 rpm (and 108 lb ft at 3500 rpm) and the aforementioned cam obviously has much to do with it. The head is polished, fitted with valves from the V6 Capri unit and given a 10.9:1 compression ratio.

As I said, the car has been around a fair while now and was subjected to several weeks of Hannu Mikkola doing an "assessment" in Finland earlier this year. It was the same engine, too, believe it or not, and was rebuilt back at Boreham just in time for Clark's outing.

Janspeed made up the exhaust manifold to Boreham's specification and the crank has been Tuftrided. Surprisingly, it's still an iron crank, but it is balanced, has a torsional vibration damper on the nose and uses a larger-than-normal cap. Forged pistons are mounted on steel rods but John feels that these may not be entirely necessary and may make the appropriate changes when he has gained more running experience with the unit. Carburation is by twin 45 DCOE Webers on conventional stub manifolds, which make for an extremely crowded-looking engine compartment. Other easy-to-spot components include the high capacity Lucas 16 ACL alternator (the metal mounting of its plastic strap to the block was the only thing to break on the Mintex) and Opus ignition. Sparks arrive courtesy of Autolite BF 22 plugs —one grade harder than normal.

Space problems on AOO have affected the clutch operation more than anything else. As a former left-hand drive car, the cable clutch wouldn't work in conjunction with the special exhaust manifold and the car thus runs an hydraulic Borg and Beck "white spot" clutch. The flywheel had to be modified to take this unit, though the ordinary aluminium bellhousing is retained, as is the four-speed gearbox—though it contains Rocket ratios.

Moving back down the drive train, a single-piece propshaft connects to the Taunus rear axle and 4.6 ZF limited slip differential feeds the power to Boreham's top-strength halfshafts.

We now seem to have moved into the province of Mick Jones, conveniently labelled Boreham's "chassis man" but better known to rally addicts as the white

wizard of the service team and chief scriptwriter to Tony Mason. Mick says that the new rear crossmember gives a damper position only 15 deg off the vertical. They are Bilstein units and are complemented by the usual AVO four-leaf cart springs and radius arms.

CD 6 rear springs with bigger eyes than normal are fitted and along with the Taunus axle come Capri-size drum brakes shod with VG 95 linings.

At the sharp end, Mick has installed Bilstein struts, Boreham springs (colour coded blue and white) and the now traditional World Cup crossmember which removes the danger of flattening the conventional wet sump on big yumps. The high ratio rack gives two and a half turns lock to lock on the 6in Minilites, which are shod with 175 x 5.50 hand-cut Dunlop rallycross tyres pioneered by John Taylor.

Front brakes are pretty special —in fact they're a straight pinch from Group 2, being 9½in Capri units, ventilated, of course, with Lockheed four pot calipers and Ferodo DS 11 pads. The braking effort is also easily adjustable front to rear in order to cope with demands of tarmac, and loose in a matter of seconds.

There seems to have been a change of heart at the competitions department regarding sump-guards, which may have gone unnoticed. The snug fitting Tech-Del unit with its intricate pattern of ribs on the upper side has given way to a plain sheet of bent Dural, half an inch thick and covered in aluminium cladding to take the scratches from sharp rocks. It's easier to fit, says Mick, and doesn't punch the chassis rails apart.

In the office of the forestry king is his usual throne, a high-sided Terry Hunter seat which Roger faithfully has transferred from one rally car to the next. In front of the reclining co-driver's model is a huge 5kg Pyrene extinguisher mounted on the floor, as the car does not have the sophisticated Fire-Eater system used on the Group 2 BDAs.

Safety Device's full roll-cage dominates the rest of the cab—until the engine is fired up that is, then the decibels take over. Company policy meant that I was unable to take the car on Boreham's excellent loose-surface track, which is now the sole province of the heavy goods division, so driving-in-anger had to be done round one of the overgrown airfield dispersal areas.

The car was exactly as it had finished the Mintex, with a soft shocker on the rear offside, which prompted me to do clockwise circuits and slides as often as possible out of sympathy. Although it was obviously a hard-worked car, AOO had an impressive amount of power, very useful torque and some exceptional rubber boots! Grip was surprisingly good on the rough concrete, directional control wasn't diverted by the odd clumps of grass and large patches of gravel (which normally send would-be

Roger gets it right on one of the Mintex Dales forestry stages : first win (and the last ?) for AOO

The new rear crossmember in the boot should prevent all the old Mexico problems of broken shocker mounts

Loud and lusty—the tuned Pinto unit which has previously defeated many a good performance specialist

rally heroes straight into the weeds) went almost unnoticed.

After many minutes' torture, I fully expected the Dunlop racers to be mere smouldering shadows of their former selves—yet they looked exactly as they had before I started. Rather battered yet capable of many more stages before being consigned to the pig bin! As usual with Escorts, the car was all oversteer and I gave thanks for the high ratio rack, without which I would have got completely out of phase.

The gearchange was the usual FoMoCo delight and it's easy to tell why those Rocket ratios are so desirable and sometimes hard to get. There is a cog for every occasion and usually a choice!

Roger had been told to keep the engine below 7500 rpm, so I did the same, but it was interesting to note how broad the power band was on this unit. It pulled strongly from very low engine speeds and felt like it would willingly go to well over the 8000 rpm line—a tribute to an excellent rally cam and a pretty unburstable building job.

For some reason the noise really was much more noticeable, even inside a helmet, than that made by Vic Preston's BDA in which I co-drove last year and, since there were no traces of deaf aids in the car, I can only assume that Messrs Clark and Porter have a very good intercom tucked away somewhere.

In spite of the limitations of my brief RS test, I was happy to grab the chance, since Ford have now decided not to enter it again for Clark in this form on national championship rallies. Roger admitted that he had to work harder than usual to go quickly in it, but enjoyed the change, so it doesn't sound as if he has given it the hard word. Tony Mason adds that when the twin sidedraught Solex carbs are homologated for Group 1 (hopefully in time for the Avon Motor Tour on July 11), they may field it with that spec for someone other than Roger.

Whatever happens, it looks like AOO has carved a small niche in Boreham's history during its brief spell in the limelight.

ROAD IMPRESSIONS
rs 2000

Try to analyse the individual features of the RS2000, and your conclusion is inescapable: it's a quick and well-engineered road car, with enough performance to keep it ahead of a BMW 2002 or an Alfa 2000 GTV — and a low enough price to keep it competitive with a Dolomite Sprint. Fine. Just what's needed. Or is it?

It's a week now, since I picked up the flame-red RS2000 from Ford's Brentford depot, but still I haven't made up my mind. Sure, it's what I expected. It's chuckable, great fun in the wet, torquey, it's got tremendous seats . . . and yet it's not everything it should be. Forget the cheap painted metal on the inside of the doors, the inoperative lock and the poorly sited instruments. You tolerate that. But what about the harsh ride, the remarkable understeer and the shallowness of the engine above 4,500 rpm. . .?

The RS2000 is intended to be an RS1600 for the masses, and in many ways it is just that. Providing a car's got a "sporty" feel, it seems, we shouldn't mind experiencing every nick in the road. Understeer, too, appears to be much in demand these days, although just why, we cannot think. Still, there's no doubt that the RS2000 is an inherently safe car. The overhead cam two-litre engine? It's got plenty of torque despite its breathlessness, and so right away the RS2000 emerges as an EASY car to drive.

Dont's get me wrong. There's nothing *bad* about the RS2000. It's just that it could have been a whole lot better had the formula not been so watered down. But as it stands, the RS2000 is still a very desirable package, and represents good value for money. Here's why:

The late Gerry Birrell played a hand in its development – with the handling, mainly, for the ease with which the car can be thrown into corners, or swerved midstream, never ceased to amaze. The power goes down well, too, while the brakes, which have been biased towards the front, are nicely balanced.

In coping with the extra weight of the two-litre engine, Ford's Advanced Vehicle Operations engineers have increased the front spring ratings by 30%, and correspondingly slightly reduced the rear dampers. The result is Understeer, a characteristic hitherto foreign to the Escort range, and there's no doubt that it takes a fair amount of the enjoyment away from Escort driving. The total predictability of the car allows you to give it an oversteer-inducing flick as you go into corners, but it's more of an effort than most people will want to use on the roads. Only in the wet or on slow turns can the power be used to tuck the front end in smoothly, but that, too, can be a bit too dramatic for road use.

In other respects, though, the RS2000's road manners are pleasant. The car remains unaffected by motorway cross-winds, and the steering has a nice feel to it – a happy compromise between lightness and sensitivity. At the beginning of our test, the car performed very well under braking, but in the last couple of days it developed an alarming tendency to dart left or right when the pedal was dabbed. Traction, as we mentioned earlier, is tremendous, and even in the wet the car accelerates briskly and cleanly. The ultimate road holding of the car is perhaps a little less than we expected – less than a BMW 2002, for instance – but although the big Dunlop SPs were probably partly to blame for this, we grew to like the tyres, particularly their lack of squeal.

The installation of the two-litre Cortina engine was no overnight job. The biggest headache centred around the bell housing, which doesn't fit under the Escort floor pan. In consequence, AVO designed a new alloy bell housing, and to complete the job cast some new steel engine mountings and an alloy sump. With space at a premium under the bonnet, an electric fan was placed in front of the radiator – a contributory factor to the slight power increase – while the only other modifications entailed strengthening the front cross-member and chassis rails . . . which should please the rally types.

The overhead cam two-litre remains in standard tune, in fact, but its 100 bhp can accelerate the 2015 lb car to 60 mph in just under nine seconds – marginally quicker than a BMW 2002 and Alfa GTV, and a shade slower than the four-valve Dolomite Sprint. Acceleration runs are undramatic, with a clearly defined surge coming in as each gear is selected – a pointer to the engine's good mid-range torque. For traffic use, the RS2000 need never be taken over 4500 rpm, and even then performance will be more than adequate. But wind it up on an open road, and the fall-off as the needle flickers past 5000 rpm is amazing, particularly in view of the fact that Ford claim maximum power at 5,500 rpm. Above 70 mph there is a marked boom period as well, and in this respect, the RS2000 owner would be well advised to fit some sound-proofing under the bonnet. Push it long and hard enough and you'll eventually see 109 mph on the clock, and although our RS was fairly noisy at this speed, it should be mentioned that its stability was first class – even a panic stop produced no untoward directional changes.

One of the reasons for the RS2000's comparatively sluggish top end performance is undoubtedly the 3.54 diff, which was installed to make the car far more of a long-distance tourer than is the RS1600. This it certainly is, although we wonder whether it was worth the drop in high speed response? The gearbox, incidentally, came right up to standard; more notchy than we remember it from other Escorts, it is nevertheless light and positive, and ideally located.

Beefed-up suspension and the long-legged two-litre engine. Two aspects where the AVO engineers have gone most of the way to developing a BMW-beater. The third? A luxurious interior, of course, although in this area we felt the boffins fell furthest from their aims. Having said that, though, we can't praise the seats high enough. They're not the big wrap-around sort fitted to the original left-hand-drive versions, but even so they are extremely comfortable. The steering wheel, of the flat rather than the dished type, has a thicker rim than the earlier version's, and thus does an even better job of obscuring the water temperature gauge. As on all performance Escorts since the twin-cam, the instruments are located in four small dials, with the speedo and tacho alongside. There is a clock, a useful console, a good rear-mounted radio speaker, but a lack of detailed appointments, like intermittent wipers or carpeting in the boot. Maybe we're just being super-critical, but for a car up in the £1800 class we thought there'd be a little more. Outside there are some reasonably discreet *RS2000* badges, some two-tone colouring tape – which personally I liked – and some 5½J sports wheels, which look good.

Overall, then, most people will be happy with the RS2000. It's got most of the attributes of the RS1600, but isn't as fussy, and is a lot easier to drive in the wet. You'll be able to show the way to most of the 2002s around, but you won't have the high-speed cruising ability or quality of finish that you'd get with, say, a Dolomite Sprint. Its handling is good, if not in the Escort tradition, and at 29 mpg, it's very cheap to run. So it's up to you. It wasn't everything we were hoping for, but by most standards it can be considered an extremely good sporting car.

FORD ESCORT RS 2000

FOR : sparkling performance ; excellent economy ; slick gearchange ; outstanding handling

AGAINST : uncomfortable ride ; engine harsh and boomy ; spongey brakes

It is exactly a year since right-hand drive versions of the Aveley-built Ford Escort RS2000 were made available in Britain after its German-market debut. Since then some 8000 have been sold and the car has registered its competitive ability, albeit as something of a homologation special, by providing Ford with a one/two win in the three-day Avon *Motor* Tour of Britain.

Equipped with a "cooking" 1993 cc sohc engine as fitted to the Cortina but with the benefit of an electric cooling fan (worth two bhp, making 100 bhp (DIN) at 5750 rpm) and a baffled sump (for competition use), the car, costing £1965, slots neatly between the smaller engined Mexico, at £1755 and the high performance 16-valve dohc RS1600 at £2394. It is a second slower to 60 mph (at 9.1 sec) than the twin cam and is down on maximum speed by 7 mph (at 106 mph) but in return offers less costly servicing, probably greater reliability, and better fuel consumption.

The engine starts readily on the automatic choke and pulls without hesitation immediately. The choke takes some time to cut out, though, and the engine generally is rather fussy. It also sounds harsh if pressed much above 5000 rpm, though it will rev freely to 6500 rpm and beyond (the tacho isn't red-lined) with a deep-throated growl typical of a sporting Ford.

Despite its larger engine the RS2000 is more economical than the RS1600 (25.5 mpg overall) and even the Mexico (at 27.8). Thanks to a higher final drive ratio (18.4 mph per 1000 rpm instead of 17.6 mph) the car did an excellent 28.7 mpg overall, returning 32 mpg at a steady 70 mph. Our computed touring fuel consumption figure is 33.2 mpg making the car good for nearly 300 miles on the nine gallon tank.

The RS's body is pure AVO type 49 (for the non-afficianados that means built by Ford Advanced Vehicles Operation centre) and as such is identical, except for minor cosmetics, to both the Mexico and RS1600 with flared wheel arches and specially strengthened front suspension mounting points and chassis side rails.

Mated to the 2-litre engine which, with its 107 lb ft (DIN) of torque at 3750 rpm provides lots of excellent mid-range pulling power (the 30-50 mph top gear time is a vivid 8.4 secs) is a superb, single selector rail four-speed all-synchromesh gearbox adapted from that on the Cortina

The Cortina's 100 bhp sohc 2-litre engine fits (just) under the Escort's bonnet and there's reasonable access to all the important service items. The battery is enormous

The cloth-covered high-back reclining front seats are particularly comfortable and afford an excellent degree of lateral support under hard cornering. When pushed forward to permit entry to the rear the seats don't lose their adjustment

2000. Changes are quick and precise with the short, stubby lever moving through a narrow, well defined gate. Only on very rapid changes was the weak synchromesh on second gear betrayed. The ratios are perfect, with first gear good for 32.5 mph at 6500 rpm, second a very useful 60 mph, and third over 86 mph. The clutch is rather· heavy with the characteristic feel of the RS1600 that suggests strong springs and ample reserves of strength. It showed no signs of wilting during almost a dozen standing start acceleration runs when we were popping the clutch at 6000 rpm. You can pull from as low as 1000 rpm in top, but not without some considerable boom from the body. In practice 1500 rpm, or 30 mph, is about the slowest anybody would want to travel in top, especially as the gearchange encourages liberal use of the lower gears.

The handling is largely unaffected by the extra weight of the 2-litre engine. The steering is a little heavier (particularly when you are parking) than that of either of the 1600 cc cars, but there the only noticeable difference ends. The RS2000 is as wieldy as Ford make them and is a delight to drive quickly along winding roads. Slight initial understeer gives way to a very progressive tail-end slide when driving quickly and the car can be held in such a pose through a corner with much satisfaction. Only on the bumpier bends at very high speed will the rear be thrown rather abruptly out of line. In short, it's extremely safe.

We were less enamoured of the ride which betrays its competition bias by being very firm. About this time last year Ford increased the front spring rates by 30 per cent and decreased damper settings at the rear. It was an unfortunate move. It is jiggly over uneven surfaces, and pot holes make the front suspension crash loudly. Surprisingly, most of these traits seem to disappear over really poorly surfaced roads taken at high speed. The front suspension system is the usual MacPherson strut set-up while at the

rear twin upper radius arms and semi-elliptic springs locate the axle well.

The servo assisted brakes were further cause for some concern. Built to German market specification (the car was available only in left hand drive form for the first few months of its existence) the rear drums are smaller than those on other Escorts (8 x 1.5 in instead of 9 x 1.75 in) to facilitate the fitment of snow chains—a prime requirement for the German market. Pedal travel is excessive and the pedal feels rather spongey. During some particularly hard cross country motoring involving heavy, frequent application of the brakes, they also faded quite noticeably and in characteristic Escort style, pulled to the left. The handbrake was most effective though.

Compared with many more compact fwd saloons the two-door Escort's accommodation isn't particularly commodious. The fully reclining black, cloth-trimmed front seats tilt forward easily without losing adjustment and access to the rear is only just sufficient. Two short adults can sit quite comfortably on the cloth covered rear seat ·provided the front seats aren't pushed fully back. The lidded glove box (an optional extra) is particularly large and the centre console (another extra) includes a useful oddments tray. There are roof-mounted grab handles for all passengers.

The driving position is excellent. The chunky, small diameter, leather rimmed steering wheel and pedals are at just the right distance for drivers of average height. The front seats are particularly comfortable and of the six rocker switches only that for the hazard flashers is not within easy reach. It's a pity that the long-travel brake pedal precludes easy heeling and toeing.

Instrument visibility is also something of a problem. The wheel rim obscures both the water temperature and oil pressure gauges and the console-mounted clock is more in the passenger's line of vision than the driver's. The instruments are the familiar

Throttle pedal offset should assist heeling and toeing but the long travel, spongey-feel brake pedal inhibits such footwork

Front quarter bumpers distinguish the RS2000 from other Escorts, as does the striped bonnet and side flanks. The transfers had begun to peel in places

The RS's facia carries all the options—console, wood grain dash and deep glove box plus radio. There's a useful map pocket in the driver's footwell. The carpets didn't fit too well on this particular car

T sextet with the rev counter calibrated to 7000 rpm) to the ft, the speedometer with kph crements in the centre and four upplementary gauges in a cluster the right. All are set in a ooded nacelle. In our opinion e optional wood trim facia is orth sacrificing because it eflects light quite badly, making e instruments sometimes awkard to read.

The heating and ventilation ystem is also the same as that und in other Escorts. The eater is particularly quick and fective with a fair range of ontrol, though while the ventilaon system is adequate at speeds ver 50 mph, its throughout round town is insufficient. On hot day you really need to open window. Unless both control vers are in the "off" position me warm air bleeds into the ockpit from the footwell vents nd the two stage fan is rather oisy.

As a clubman's car the body oom at several points throughout e rev range and the harsh noise e engine creates above 5000 m, may pass unnoticed, as will e tyre roar over certain coarse urfaces and the wind noise at peed. But we found the car ather wearing after longish eriods at sustained high rpm.

For a car costing around £2000 e fittings and finish are nothing pecial. The doors were awkward

he FAVO alloy road wheels and unlop Formula 70 rubberware are oth extra-cost options which nhance the car's appearance

close without a firm tug, the assenger's seat rattled when noccupied, the window winders ere stiff and the sun visors don't wivel round to shade the side indows. Furthermore there is no cterior mirror. In places the deep le carpet didn't fit closely and, erhaps worst of all, the toning olour panels on the boot, side d bonnet, are transfers which, one place, had already begun peel.

Perhaps most of these shortmings were peculiar to our car. s a national daily newspaper has ready announced, there is a w-look Escort scheduled for '75. Ford could improve the uncomrtable ride, spongey braking and or layout of the minor instruents the car should have even ore appeal to the driver who ants to combine business with easure.

MOTOR ROAD TEST No 51/74 ● FORD ESCORT RS2000

PERFORMANCE

CONDITIONS
Weather	Fine
Temperature	57-70 F
Barometer	29.7 in. Hg
Surface	Dry tarmacadam

MAXIMUM SPEEDS
	mph	kph
Banked circuit	106.6	172
Best ¼ mile	112.5	181

Terminal speeds:
	mph	kph
at ¼ mile	80.0	129
at kilometre	98.0	158
at mile	106.0	171

Speed in gears (at 6500 rpm):
	mph	kph
1st	33.0	53
2nd	60.0	97
3rd	87.0	140

ACCELERATION FROM REST
mph	sec	kph	sec
0-30	2.9	0-40	2.4
0-40	4.4	0-60	4.1
0-50	6.6	0-80	6.5
0-60	9.1	0-100	10.1
0-70	12.7	0-120	14.8
0-80	16.9	0-140	20.9
0-90	22.6	0-160	33.5

0-100	34.4		
Stand'g ¼	16.7	Stand'g km	31.4

ACCELERATION IN TOP
mph	sec	kph	sec
20-40	8.5	40-60	4.0
30-50	8.4	60-80	5.2
40-60	7.8	80-100	5.4
50-70	8.5	100-120	5.8
60-80	10.1	120-140	8.4
70-90	14.5		

FUEL CONSUMPTION
Touring* 33.2 mpg
8.5 litres/100 km

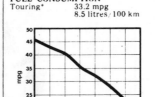

Overall	28.7 mpg
	9.8 litres/100 km
Fuel grade	97 octane
	4 star rating
Tank capacity	9.0 galls
	40.9 litres
Max range	299 miles
	481 km
Test distance	1560 miles
	2510 km

* Consumption midway between 30 mph and maximum less 5 per cent for acceleration

SPEEDOMETER (mph)
Speedo	30	40	50	60	70	80	90	100
True	28.5	38	47	56	65	74	84	93

Distance recorder 2.4 per cent fast.

WEIGHT
	cwt	kg
Unladen weight*	16.7	848.3
Weight as tested	20.4	1036.3

Distribution front/rear 58, 42 per cent
* with fuel for approx 50 miles.

Performance tests carried out by Motor's staff at the Motor Industry Research Association proving ground, Lindley.

GENERAL SPECIFICATION

ENGINE
Cylinders	Four in line
Capacity	1993 cc (121.6 cu in.)
Bore stroke	90.8 x 76.9 mm
	(3.58 x 3.03 in.)
Cooling	Water
Block	Iron
Head	Iron
Valves	Sohc

Valve timing
inlet opens	24 btdc
inlet closes	64 abdc
ex opens	70 bbdc
ex closes	18 atdc
Compression	9.2 : 1
Carburetter	W.ber DGAV 32/36
Bearings	5 main
Fuel pump	Mechanical
Max power	100 bhp (DIN) at 5750 rpm
Max torque	107 lb ft (DIN) at 3750 rpm

TRANSMISSION
Type	Manual four speed
Clutch	8.5 in. dia diaphragm spring

Internal ratios and mph/1000 rpm
Top	1.00 : 1	18.4
3rd	1.37 : 1	13.3
2nd	1.97 : 1	9.2
1st	3.65 : 1	5.0
Rev	12.96 : 1	
Final drive	3.54 : 1	

BODY/CHASSIS
Construction	Unitary, all steel, heavy duty Type 49
Protection	Phosphate dip, bitumen-based underseal to wheel arches and underbody areas

SUSPENSION
Front	Ind. by McPherson strut and double acting hydraulic shock absorbers plus anti-roll bar
Rear	Live axle, semi-elliptic leaf springs, radius arms and double-acting telescopic dampers

STEERING
Type	Rack and pinion
Assistance	None
Toe-in	1-3 mm
Camber	50' negative
Castor	2 18' positive
King pin	8 50'
Rear toe-in	Parallel

BRAKES
Type	Disc/drum
Servo	Yes
Circuit	Twin
Rear valve	No
Adjustment	Rears only

WHEELS
Type	FAVO 4-spoke light alloy
Tyres	175 HR 70 x 13 Dunlop SP Sport
Pressures	24 psi front and rear

ELECTRICAL
Battery	12V, 58 Ah
Polarity	Negative earth
Generator	35A alternator
Fuses	7
Headlights	55/55w halogen

COMPARISONS

	Capacity cc	Price £	Max mph	0-60 sec	30-50* sec	Overall mpg	Touring mpg	Length ft in	Width ft in	Weight cwt	Boot cu ft
Ford Escort RS2000	1993	1965	106.6	9.1	8.4	28.7	33.2	13 3.75	5 1.75	16.7	8.0†
BMW 2002	1990	2650	107.4	9.2	7.4	24.0	27.5	13 11.5	5 1.75	18.3	9.5†
Mazda RX3 Coupe	1964	1625	108.3	10.2	9.5	18.5	24.9	13 4.75	5 3	16.9	8.4
MGB GT	1798	1970	107.6	11.6	8.8	27.4	33.0	12 9	5 0	20.75	6.6
Opel Ascona 1.9 SR	1897	1732	98.7	10.5	9.3	25.2	28.9	13 8	5 5	18.6	10.5
Triumph Dolomite Sprint	1988	2293	112.7	8.4	8.0	23.0	26.1	13 6	5 1	19.8	9.4
Vauxhall Magnum Coupe	2279	1843	100.8	11.2	7.6	23.7	25.6	13 6.75	5 4.5	19.3	11.2

*in top/kickdown †measurements with boxes

Make: Ford
Model: Escort RS2000
Maker: Ford Motor Co Ltd, Warley, Brentwood, Essex.
Price: £1680.96 plus £138.07 car tax plus VAT equals £1964.55. Extras include FAVO alloy road wheels at £64.33, radio installation, £50.92, wood facia and centre console £33.04. Total as tested: £2112.84.

HOT ON THE HEELS OF A HOT DATSUN AND HOT LANCER, WE NOW PRESENT YOU WITH A
Hot Escort

WHEEL-SPIN AT 50mph in top gear? If your mind has started conjuring up some super or highly modified car, stop right there. It is only a standard but potent car. In fact, there is only one in Peninsular Malaysia, we are told.

The wheel-spin was experienced in a standard Ford Escort RS2000 while we were putting it through its paces in the dirt.

After all, the owner, Mr. Au Chee Hung, is a regular rallyman and motor enthusiasts may see his "Paprika" (orangey-red) super-Escort in the estate sections more than at the Selangor Racing circuit.

Basically, the RS2000 is a two-door type 49 body which has been strengthened by the boys at Ford Advanced Vehicle Operations (FAVO).

It is not that the normal Escort has a weak shell. It is only that those owning RSs and Mexicos are liable to drive the car very hard and over pretty rough roads.

Mr. Roger Clark's (and other rally) Escorts are given similar treatment.

At FAVO some of the things done include welding the seams and points where the most punishment is expected, enlarging the wheel spats and some strengthening of the suspension.

The front suspension has the same MacPherson struts as found in all Escorts. However, as the RS2000 has the Cortina 2000 SOHC engine in front, the springs have to be stiffened to keep the nose up.

To compensate for the reduced rear weight distribution, the rear semi-elliptical leaf springs are de-cambered to lower the rear while the shock absorbers have softer settings.

The belt-driven overhead camshaft engine does not get a hotter cam or carb to improve its performance. In fact, the two litre engine in a light body like the Escort is sufficient enough to produce respectable performance thanks to the excellent power to weight ratio.

The FAVO engineers increased the engine's maximum power by two bhp to 100bhp (DIN) at 5750rpm simply by using a thermostatically controlled electric fan in place of the belt driven unit.

Since the 2000 Cortina single-rail gearbox is one of Ford's best (designed in Germany), the whole engine and gearbox complete with the standard bell housing was transplanted into the heavy duty Escort.

Before you Escort owners start buying used Cortina 2000 engines and transmission units, please remember that the Escort RS 2000 has a different engine mounting.

The light alloy sump is also of a different

This is the view most other Escorts and makes will see when Au floors the throttle pedal.

design and is protected to a large extent by the cross member. It has baffles inside to prevent excessive oil surge during rough road work and a central oil pick-up point for positive engine lubrication.

Since June 1973, when the Escort RS2000 was launched in Germany, FAVO has been steadily producing about 30 units a day of this almost handbuilt Escort.

Our brief drive was in a car which is about 2½ years old but completely re-built in antica-pation of this year's rallies. Mr. Au was kind enough to let us have a bash at his almost completed super Escort even through some previous rally routes.

On getting into the car, the first impression is the very comfortable seat. Great effort has been made to provide the necessary support for the lumbar, thigh, and sides so that the re-clining seat is almost as figure hugging as the racing type but which does not hinder accessi-bility.

I was impressed by the fabric seat which enables the body to "dig" into the seat for that extra location when the going was rough.

The steering wheel is a flat leather bound stuff with a big boss. This boss is actually a convulated can which compresses like an accordian when there is an impact.

One can be forgiven if the RS dashboard is mistaken for the ordinary GT's. The instru-ment layout is the same except that the RS has 130mph (naturally) speedometer instead.

The two large instruments for the tachometer and the speedometer are located on the left of the oval while four small dials for the water tem-perature, voltmeter, oil pressure and fuel level are on the right.

As this was the old design dashboard, many of the instruments are obstructed by the steering wheel and the hands. (The new Escorts have the Award winning Cortina facia) the tachometer has no red line and ends abruptly at 7,000rpm. Does it mean that FAVO says we can rev up to that figure? Don't worry, Mr. Au, we didn't try

Starting the RS 2000 is just like the Cortina 2000. Au has removed some of the noise insula-

uarter bumpers and flared wheel arches are iginal equipment!

Simple yet effective. Ford shows how to drop a big engine into a small car.

on material since less weight is more important apparently) than keeping noise down in a rally.

The gearbox has one of the shortest throws I ave come across. Although the box is the same the standard Cortina, the changing makes a orld of difference.

The secret of the short throw is in the leverage ystem. Anyone can buy a conversion kit which aises the pivot point of the gear shift for racy ear swaps.

After a long rally, Au's left leg may be tired. I ound the clutch pedal heavy and the high thigh upport does not encourage frequent flooring of ne clutch pedal.

There is no drama in the engine such as spit- ack in the carburettors or rocking due to hot am. In fact, it is very gentle but can still do its b like wheel-spinning if you want it to.

The set-up seems more suited to our type of allies since big torque comes in at low engine evs (107 lb ft at 3750rpm) which means fewer ear changes.

In our estates, the tracks can change abruptly rom dry to muddy and the driver usually has no me to change down.

In fact FAVO is so confident of the two litre engine pulling the car easily that a fairly high final drive ratio of 3:54:1 is fitted (similar to the Ghia). This gives the RS a high cruising speed at low engine revs or 33mpg as claimed.

Au grinned when I asked what would happen if the 4:125:1 GL diff was used.

As it is now, Ford claims an acceleration time of nine seconds from rest to 60mph which I do not doubt. Au's car was at the final stages of a rebuild and I did not want to break his heart by undoing his hard work.

One thing which impressed me was the very good handling even when zipping between rubber trees. Despite the shock absorbers being old, the RS could be chucked around with confidence.

When the tail swings back after being deliberately swung out of line, its does not go much beyond the line of travel.

On the other ''hot'' cars I have so far tested, the tails seemed to enjoy wagging.

This may be dramatic to look from the spectators's point, but valuable seconds are lost while the driver fights for control or while the rear wheels fight to regain traction.

Stopping the RS is not a hot point. The brakes are heavy and not as positive as a ''hot''

"Special message for you. If you wanna' send a reply, I'll be waiting at the finish line—"

car's should be. Perhaps the brake linings were tired too.

Mind you, the RS can reach a top speed off 110mph casily! (The RS is about 90 lbs lighter than the current Ghia series.)

When Au goes to the starting line in the next rally, his RS would not be the same in some ways. For instance, the rear may have the turret conversion kit installed.

This changes the rear shock absorbers to a vertical location for apparently better handling. Then the front cross-member will be the World Cup (marathon) rally type which is a strongly re-inforced job which should mow down some of the obstructions.

Au is even contemplating a twin-cam engine. His industrious mind never stops at just what he has. Anyway, all the best to you and thank you for that nice drive. LK

Brief Specifications

ENGINE

Capacity	: 1993 c.c.
Bore	: 90.82 mm
Stroke	: 76.82 mm
Compression ratio	: 9.2:1
Valve gear layout	: S.O.H.C.(Belt driven)
Carburettor	: One progressive twin choke downdraught
Maximum power	: 100 bhp (DIN) at 5,750 rpm.
Maximum torque	: 107 lb ft (SAE) at 3,750 rpm.

TRANSMISSION

Gearbox	: Four speed, floor shift, fully synchromeshed.

High final drive ratio encourages high speed cruising at low engine revs.

DIMENSIONS (ins/mm)

Wheelbase	: 94.5/2400
Front track	: 51/1295
Rear track	: 51.7/1313
Overall width	: 61.8/1570
Overall length	: 156.8/3983
Overall height	: 54.8/1341
Kerb weight	: 2015 lbs. 915 kgs.

SUSPENSION

Front : Independent, MacPherson struts, coil springs, telescopic dampers, lower arms, anti-roll bar doubling as radius arms.

Rear : Live axle, semi-elliptical leaf springs, telescopic dampers, radius arms.

FUEL CONSUMPTION

As claimed: : 33mpg 8.55 l/100k

PERFORMANCE

Max. speed in gears (claimed)

1st	–	32 mph	51.4 kph
2nd	–	60 mph	96.5 kph
3rd	–	85.4 mph	139 kph
4th	–	110 mph	177 kph

ACCELERATION

0-60 mph	–	9.0 secs

The hot one

Take chilli con carne, add a dash of tequila, and the mixture's still cool compared with the small Ford that won the 1970 World Cup Rally, and then predominated in all-round sport for most of the decade.
Brian Bennett analyses this recipe for success and tastes the joys of driving a mint-condition Mexico

FORD "CASHED-IN" on their World Cup Rally win of 1970 almost before the victorious car had passed the finishing post in Mexico more than one hour in front of its nearest rivals. Although it was not an exact replica of the winner, and was not blessed with all the works "goodies", the production Escort Mexico was based on a similar compromise to that used by Ford to win the rally. This was achieved, in the case of the road car, by taking an RS1600 (which in 1970 had replaced the original Escort Twin-Cam as the basis of Ford's onslaught on the world of rallying) and replacing its fragile twin overhead camshaft, sixteen valve BDA engine with the more reliable and easily maintained pushrod 1600 GT unit from the Capri.

The outcome of this opportunist marketing was a big success for Ford. The Mexico fitted neatly into their range, providing more relaxed performance than the Escort GT while being more manageable than either the Twin-Cam or the RS1600. It was the ideal club rally car, being an excellent platform for accommodating the many Rallye Sport options that were available. Mexico challenge and championship races became popular and the Mk. 1 continued to win these even when competing against Mk II Escorts.

Ford Advanced Vehicle Operations announced the Escort Mexico in November 1970. It could then be purchased for £1,150, which represented very good value for money. Of course, this basic price could soar if extras such as the Rallye Sport Clubman pack were specified. This pack consisted of four quartz-halogen auxiliary lamps, uprated springs and struts at the front, gas filled dampers all round, map reading lamp, bucket seats, and a rollover bar. It should be borne in mind when buying a Mexico, that if these options have been fitted it is highly probable that the car has been raced or rallied.

In 1973 the Escort RS2000 was introduced. Like the Mexico and RS1600 it used the Type 49 body-shell with its flared wheel arches and strengthened suspension mountings and chasis rails, but its motive power was provided by the ohc 2 litre engine already

The Mexico can be distinguished from its lesser brethren by the twin front bumpers, flared wheel arches and fat tyres. Below: handling can still be classed as good and can cope with wide variations of road surface

used in the Cortina. This combination gave a level of performance close to that of the RS1600 while still having the advantages of low-cost servicing and reliability of the Mexico. However, for bargain-basement performance motoring the Mexico was still unrivalled.

With the introduction of the Mk. II Escort in 1975 Ford temporarily stopped the practice of using reinforced bodyshells for their performance-orientated Escorts. Resultingly, the 1600 Sport was not such an attractive proposition to the budding racing/rally driver as the Mk. I models, although the accommodation was rather more comfortable and appealing. In fact those Mk. I versions continued to

be embarrassingly successful in competition well after the Mk. II version was launched!

Technically, the Mk I Mexico is not very exciting. The front suspension is by MacPherson strut with the geometry altered to give more negative camber than the "normal" Escort saloons. At the rear, a live axle is used, with semi-elliptic springs, and the addition of radius rods. Steering is, of course, by rack and pinion and the $5\frac{1}{2}$J section 13 in. wheels are equipped with 165x13 radial tyres. Braking is by the same servo-assisted setup used in the RS1600, with bigger diameter front discs and rear drums than its more mundane stablemates.

The 1600 cc "cross-flow" engine is a simple cast iron, push-rod ohv unit which produces 86 bhp at 5500 rpm and 92 lb ft at 4000 rpm. This is achieved with a 9:1 compression ratio and a Weber twin-choke carburettor. These power figures can be improved by drawing on the wide range of tuning equipment that is available, and the car we drove in connection with this article did benefit from a hotter camshaft as well as a limited slip differential.

It is the property of Gordon Bruce, a former member of *Motor*'s editorial staff, and despite having covered more than 70,000 miles it is still in beautiful condition. Thankfully, this example is not afflicted with the gaudy stripes which were a delete option on Mexicos when they were originally purchased. As a result, it has a purposeful "Q" car feel, rather than that of the boy-racer.

On the road the Mexico fulfils its intended function, which is to get from A to B as briskly and entertainingly as possible without too much regard for comfort. Subjectively it perhaps feels faster than it is, although the 101 mph top speed and 0-60 mph time of 11.5 seconds obtained from our original (standard) test car do indicate that it is pretty quick. Certainly, its stability and performance allowed me to keep pace with much more exotic (and expensive!) cars.

Swift progress is aided by a slick gearchange, which cannot be faulted even when compared to more modern gearchanges. However, the clutch is rather fierce and heavy. This is uncomfortable in slow traffic but when the Mexico is in its proper environment — winding country lanes — it works very well.

Handling and roadholding were classed as superb in the original test, but understandably enough our car was beginning to feel a bit tired in this respect; perhaps the dampers on this example were past their prime, but in any case general standards in this area have improved enormously since the Mexico was new. Even so, the stability is good and the superbly direct steering, with lots of feel, lets you know exactly how the car is behaving.

A significant advance in suspension design has been the ability to

obtain a good ride without compromising the roadholding and handling. Here the new front-wheel drive Escort should score significantly over the old version, especially in the case of the Mexico, the ride of which can only be described at best, as lively.

Stopping is no problem in the Mexico, but the long pedal travel and spongey feel are typical of Ford brakes of that era. Certainly this is one area where Ford have made a useful improvement with the latest Escort.

Another area where it shows its age is in noise levels. There is a plentiful helping of wind and road noise, but engine noise is the most significant when the upper rev range is used. This does tend to make motorway cruising a bit tiresome, even when travelling at no more than a strictly legal 70 mph.

These particular criticisms against noise and ride should be weighed against the fact that the Mexico is a no-frills sporting machine, and when viewed in this context these facets of the car actually contribute towards its overall enjoyable and purposeful feel.

Accommodation is fairly Spartan by modern standards, with areas of bare, painted metal and non-reclining (though comfortable) seats. Adjustment is limited, but a comfortable driving position can be found due to the well-positioned pedals, which facilitate easy heeling and toeing. In "our" car, this was further aided by an extension to the throttle pedal.

Comprehensive instrumentation is partially obscured by the handsome leather-bound steering wheel, although this is not too much of a drawback since they are difficult to read because of reflections, anyway! Switchgear is typical of that period. There is only one column stalk, which controls indicators, horn and dip/flash. Wash/wipe is operated via a floor control which takes some skill to work efficiently, but becomes convenient with use. The rest of the controls are spread indiscriminately across the facia.

Heating and ventilation are not up to modern Ford standards, but are still competitive when compared with some other systems used today. Generally speaking, in its interior appointments, the Mexico compares well with many modern cars. Everything necessary is present, even if the layout and presentation is not up to current standards.

Overall, the Mk. I Escort Mexico achieves the objectives set for it. It is a sporting car which has sufficient performance, roadholding and handling and these qualities can be further enhanced (to the owner's requirements) by purchasing the appropriate "goodies" or, alternatively, by going for the more powerful Twin Cam, RS1600 or RS2000 models which share the same strengthened bodyshell and uprated suspension and brakes as the Mexico.

It's a fair bet that a good example of any of the AVO-built Escorts will at least hold its value, if not actually appreciate, as well as pro-

viding a great deal of enjoyment for the owner. When you're buying, though, make sure that the car offered for sale is the genuine article, for there are a good many "ordinary" Escorts running around which have to a greater or lesser degree been modified to Mexico or RS specification, and which sellers may try to pass off as the real thing. Similarly, by their very nature, even the genuine ones are likely to have been modified and, of course, are also likely to have had a hard life in small-time competition or fast road use. So, apart from the usual checks you'd make for rust on any Escort getting on for ten years old (front wings, rear wheel arches and the front strut mounting plates are particularly vulnerable), take extra care over looking for signs of repaired accident damage.

With the exception of those Twin Cam and 16-valve engines, Escorts are mechanically simple and robust, with no special weak points to look for other than the usual checks you would make on any car of that age. The Mexico

and RS2000 engines are, respectively, the same as those of the (earlier) Capri 1.6 and the Cortina Mk 3/4, and so should not cause any particular worries. Be wary, however, of the Twin Cam and, especially, the RS1600 units; the former is basically tough, but sensitive to ignition and carburettor maladjustment which can at best cause poor running, and at worst lead to burnt-out exhaust valves or pistons. Do check the compressions, which should be at least 150 psi, and look out for oil leaks, particularly from the cam and timing covers.

Much the same holds true for the RS1600, but additionally be wary of alloy-blocked versions. These had a reputation for distorting the cylinder walls — a fault which would manifest itself in heavy oil burning, particularly at high revs. Look also for signs of water in the oil (or oil in the radiator) and head gasket leaks. Some people also found that the cylinder head on the 16-valver was prone to cracking across the valve seats.

SPARES (Prices excl. VAT)

	£
Air Filter	3.83
Set front brake pads	12.18
Set rear brake shoes	11.96
Front wing	24.02
Starter motor (exchange)	51.03
Windscreen	14.69
Oil filter	3.45
Clutch assembly, complete	46.87
Front damper (exchange)	28.95
Rear damper	16.78
Exhaust system, complete	54.55
Short engine	326.38

PERFORMANCE

MAXIMUM SPEED	Mexico	Twin Cam	RS 1600	RS 2000
Lap	101.0	111.3	114.4	106.6
Best ¼ mile	104.7	116.9	—	112.5

ACCELERATION

mph				
0-30	3.9	3.0	3.2	2.9
0-40	5.9	4.4	4.5	4.4
0-50	8.3	6.4	6.4	6.6
0-60	11.5	8.7	8.3	9.1
0-70	15.8	11.8	11.5	12.7
0-80	21.5	15.6	15.0	16.9
0-90	30.9	21.6	20.0	22.6
0-100	—	29.5	29.9	34.4
Standing ¼ mile	18.4	16.9	16.5	16.7
Standing Km	34.3	—	30.7	31.4

IN TOP

mph				
20-40	9.7	9.3	10.5	8.5
30-50	9.3	9.1	8.8	8.4
40-60	9.7	9.1	8.9	7.8
50-70	10.3	9.5	9.7	8.5
60-80	11.6	10.6	10.3	10.1
70-90	15.4	12.7	11.8	14.5
80-100	—	16.3	16.2	—

FUEL CONSUMPTION

Overall	27.8	23.4	25.3	28.7
Touring	32.3	23.6	25.5	33.2

GENERAL SPECIFICATION

ENGINE

Cylinders	4 in line
Capacity	1600 cc (97.51 cu in)
Bore/stroke	80.98 x 77/62 mm (3.19 x 3.06 in)
Cooling	Water
Block	Cast iron
Head	Cast iron
Valves	Pushrod ohv
Cam drive	Chain
Compression	9:1
Carburetter	Weber compound twin-choke
Bearings	5 main
Max power	86 bhp (DIN) at 5500 rpm
Max torque	92 lb ft (DIN) at 4000 rpm

TRANSMISSION

Type	4-speed manual,
Clutch dia	7.5 in
Actuation	Hydraulic

Internal ratios and mph/1000 rpm

Top	1.000:1	17.6
3rd	1.397:1	12.6
2nd	2.010:1	8.8
1st	2.972:1	5.9
Rev	3.324:1	
Final drive	3.77:1	

BODY/CHASSIS

Construction Unitary

SUSPENSION

Front	Independent by MacPherson struts with coil springs and anti-roll bar.
Rear	Live axle located by radius arms; leaf spring suspension

STEERING

Type	Rack and pinion
Assistance	None

BRAKES

Front	9.6 in discs
Rear	9.0 in drums
Park	On rear
Servo	Yes
Circuit	Dual
Rear valve	No
Adjustment	Manual

WHEELS/TYRES

Type	Pressed steel
Tyres	165-13
Pressures	24/24 psi F/R (normal)

**Instrumentation is comprehensive but spoilt by reflections and the thick rim of the steering wheel which hides three of the minor gauges.
Below: the pushrod engine provides sufficient and reliable power**

Hannu Mikkola and Gunnar Palm celebrate their Mexican World Cup Rally win with Ford team-mates in 1970, left. Their famous victory inspired the production Mexico, which is now a covetted keepsake Ford, along with the Mk1 RS2000, as Graham Robson explains

Classic choice

ESCORT MEXICO

and Mk1 RS2000

HOW do you produce a silk purse from a sow's ear? Ford thought they knew how, when developing the Lotus Cortina early in the Sixties, but they weren't entirely successful. With the RS Escorts of the late Sixties and early Seventies they made no mistakes. Twenty years ago, no motoring enthusiast would have believed it possible, but now there is no doubt. Thousands of specialised Escorts, some for competition, some merely for fast road use, surely now qualify as modern classics.

Ford's development of a performance image had begun in 1962, and the hot Cortinas which raced and rallied with great success were the first fruits of the policy. With the Escorts, and particularly with the foundation of the specialised Advanced Vehicle Operation, it came to maturity.

First, though, let's establish the family tree. The original 'hot' Escort was the Twin-Cam of 1968-1971, a car which combined Lotus Cortina mechanical components (including the Lotus Ford Twin-Cam engine) with the heavy-duty Type 49 version of the two-door Escort bodyshell. This was always built at Halewood, on Merseyside.

Ford then decided to build derivatives of the Twin-Cam, one with a pushrod ohv engine, and one with the even more complex 16-valve BDA unit. To do this, redundant Ford factory building at South Ockendon in Essex was re-equipped as a small assembly facility, and in November of 1970 it was officially opened, with Ray Horrocks (now chairman and managing director of BL Cars) as its manager. The BDA-engined car, known as the RS1600, had already gone into production at Halewood, but assembly was transferred immediately to Ford AVO at South Ockendon.

Commercially, the first series-production RS Escort to be built at AVO was the Mexico, which was effectively a Twin-Cam-RS1600 in all respects *except* for the use of an 86bhp pushrod ohv 'Kent' engine of 1599cc, almost exactly as used in the Capri and the Cortina GT models. Announced just before the end of 1970, Mexico remained in production until the AVO facility was closed down in January 1975, a victim of falling demand for cars in the wake of the 1973/1974 energy crisis.

Although the Mexico became very popular, and was always good value (it cost a mere £881 basic in 1970), it was never really fast enough, refined enough, or well-enough equipped to satisfy everyone, particularly Ford's European customers. As a result, another derivative called the RS2000 was developed, and put on sale in mid 1973 (UK supplies did not begin until October 1973). This was yet another version of the same basic design for the RS1600 and Mexico cars remained in production at AVO. Inside the same rolling shell it had the 2-litre Pinto sohc engine matched to the latest German four-speed gearbox (very different from the RS1600 Mexico gearbox), a much better equipped interior, including sumptuous seats and a lot more sound deadening. All told, it was a much more refined car. Better yet, it was almost as fast as the RS1600, with a top speed of 108mph, and its maintenance held no terrors for Ford garages or resourceful private owners. Like the Mexico, it remained in production until the AVO facility closed down, though hundreds of Mexicos and RS2000s were actually registered later in 1975, months after production had ceased.

These, then, were the definitive AVO-built RS Escorts, and they have had no successors. All the Mk 2-shape RS2000s, RS1800s, and RS Mexicos were built at Halewood or Sarrlouis (in West Germany) on mainstream production lines.

Enquiries at Ford have failed to produce definitive production figures for the Mexico and RS2000. However, both the Mexico and the RS2000 were eventually homologated into FIA Group 1, which means that Ford certified they were being built at the rate of more than 5000 cars a year. I believe that the RS2000 began to

Above, the standard Mexico interior as shown here was functional, but cars with reclining custom pack cloth seats were more comfortable.

outsell the Mexico almost as soon as it was put on sale in 1973, and that production of the 16-valve RS1600 was very restricted indeed, especially towards the end of its life.

Development changes

In the short life of the RS2000 Mk 1 there were no important changes to the specification, though it is worth noting that a good many of the cars built had the optional cast-alloy road wheels, and the optional centre console between the front seats and footwells. A few cars had the optional (and costly) twin-downdraught carburettor kit (Solex or Weber instruments), developed for competition use, which could boost peak power to over 140 bhp if the appropriate camshaft was fitted.

Regarding the Mexico, from September 1972,

the battery (which had originally been placed on the boot floor, like that of the RS1600) was relocated in the engine bay, the spare wheel then being mounted upright in the standard Escort position, while at the same time sculptured steel sports road wheels were standardised, and the trim specification improved, to include carpets on the floor instead of rubber mats.

Maintenance and Restoration

The most encouraging news for owners (and potential owners) of Mexicos and RS2000s is that Ford dealers, particulary those designated as RS or Rallye Sport dealers, are well equipped with parts and expertise to ensure that no car will deteriorate through lack of factory support. The

➔

Spares and prices

There is no spares problem, but we recommend that Mexico and RS2000 owners always consult one of the 70-odd Ford Rallye Sport dealers in the UK for assistance. Special sections of the Parts Manuals are devoted to these cars, for in many detail ways they differ from 'mainstream' Escorts.

There are two specialist clubs, both of which welcome Mexico and RS2000 owners. If only for the fellowship, but especially for the access to special information on the cars, an owner should join either the RS Owners Club or the Ford AVO Owners Club. Contacts in each case are: RS Owners Club: Membership Secretary, David Bennett, 22 Hurst Road, Hinckley, Leicestershire LE10 9AB.
Ford AVO Owners Club: Secretary, Mark Smith, 20 St. Catherines Court, Aylesbury, Bucks.

Mexico (1970-1975)

Engine: Kent 4-cyl with 5-bearing crankshaft, in cast-iron block. Overhead valves operated by pushrods and rockers from camshaft in cylinder block. Cast-iron cylinder head, but combustion chambers formed in piston crowns. Bore and stroke 80.97 × 77.62mm, 1599cc (Homologated for sporting purposes as 1601cc). Max power, 86bhp (DIN) at 5500rpm. Max torque 92lb ft at 4000rpm.
Transmission: 4-speed all-synchromesh manual gearbox, with remote control change. Diaphragm spring clutch. Hypoid bevel rear axle. 3.77:1 final drive ratio.

Suspension: Independent front, coil springs, MacPherson struts, anti-roll bar; live rear axle, half-elliptic leaf springs, twin radius arms.
Steering: Rack and pinion.
Brakes: Girling hydraulic, disc front and drum rear, with vacuum servo assistance.
Wheels: Four-stud pressed steel, with 5.5in rims and 165-13in radial ply tyres.
Performance: Maximum speed 100 mph; 0-60mph 10.7 sec; 30-50 through gears 4.0sec.
Overall mpg: 27.5.
Production: Total figure not available. Max build rate about 6000 cars a year.

RS2000 (1973-1975)

Basic layout as for Mexico, except for:
Engine: Pinto unit. Overhead valves operated by fingers from camshaft mounted in cylinder head. Cast iron cylinder head, with flat-top pistons. Bore and stroke 90.8 × 76.95mm, 1993cc. Max power, 100bhp (DIN) at 5750rpm. Max torque 108lb ft at 3500 rpm.
Transmission: 3.54:1 final drive ratio.
Wheels: As Mexico, or optional cast-alloy wheels (fitted to most cars).
Performance: Maximum speed 108mph; 0-60mph, 9.0secs; 30-50mph through gears 4.0sec.
Overall mpg: 26.6
Production: Details as Mexico.

How much? Mexico prices run from £500 for a rough example, to £1600; RS2000s start at around twice the price, £1000, and fetch £2300 or more for a really clean one.

thoroughbred & classic cars july 1982

Ford Mexico

cars, after all, have only been out of production for seven years, and major components such as the Kent and Pinto engines, the British and German types of gearbox, and the common Timken-type of hypoid bevel rear axle, are all still in production.

There are, however, problems which occur with the cars, and our experience is that you should look out for the following:

Bodyshell

Mexicos and RS2000s share the same heavy-duty Type 49 two-door saloon derivative of the normal Escort shell. All have circular headlamps, and officially there never were any estate car or four-door versions of these cars, though one or two prototypes and special order models were built. The 'heavy duty' differences really amount to stiffening around the MacPherson strut locations, to the 'chassis' legs, and in the provision of rear suspension radius arm mounts. Theoretically the front wings are also slightly flared, to clear the wider wheels, but I know of many cars which have been rebuilt after accident damage with normal wings, needing no more than local modification to the wheel arch flanges to give enough clearance.

Although the Mexicos and RS2000s received extra attention in the paint shops at the Ford AVO facility (the bodies were delivered by transporter from Halewood in a painted and trimmed condition), their corrosion-resistance was no better than that of most Fords of the day. By now the oldest Mexico will be more than 11 years old, so look carefully for rusting under the sills between front and rear wheels, at the edges and on the faces of lower front and rear panels, on the sharp edges of doors and opening panels, and along the weld lines between panels, especially where stone clipping may occur.

In particular these Escorts are very vulnerable to corrosion around the top mountings of the MacPherson struts, which can be seen by opening the bonnet panel and looking into the engine bay. On cars used for competitions (and many of them have been), an extra patching panel may already have been added to deal with this. If not, it would be advisable for you to consider doing the same. Look, too, for deterioration of the panel attachment line between inner and outer front wheel arch panels, also visible by opening up the bonnet. Corrosion in these areas is accelerated by the heavy flexing caused by suspension stress reversals from the MacPherson struts.

Although the bodies of these cars can put up with a lot of abuse, such as rallying or use by fast-driving enthusiasts, they last well, especially if looked after and rectified where appropriate. Don't worry too much if trim panels are torn, missing, or non-standard, because most of them can still be found, especially through RS dealerships.

How do you know if a car has been used in competition? Look for all the tell-tale signs of extra holes, slots, plugs, louvres, and stiffening panels which may have supported roll cages, extra lamp brackets, instruments, special seats and so on. Look, too, for evidence of over-spraying of older non-standard or even complex sponsors' colour schemes. Some cars may have had extra flaring of the wheel arches to allow extra-wide tyres to be fitted, and there's no harm in that, but rally cars often give themselves away by having damaged or rippled floor panels, and scuffed or even distorted 'chassis' legs. Jacking points are often the first items to suffer assault from under-floor rocks.

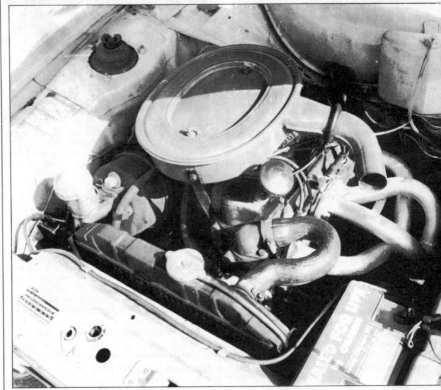

Suspension, steering, brakes

Quite a lot of the Escort's detail fittings have to be considered as consumables, including components like anti-roll bar bushes, radius arm bushes, brackets, leaf spring pick-up points, and the bushes supporting shock absorbers, not to mention the mountings for the steering rack itself. Have a really good look round the underside of the car, especially where worn pivots might affect steering or suspension geometry. Suspension rubber bushes tend to become contaminated with oil, and can be 'squeegeed' out of position.

A look at spring conditions and damper performance is always worthwhile, though in general the steering should be in good condition — light, precise, and positive. If the car you are looking at has pressed steel wheels, check that all of them (including the spare wheel — you'd be amazed at how often horror stories are hidden away in the boot!) are still round, and free from damage and distortion. Cast-alloy wheels should be corrosion free (but check), and should run true, though they may have damaged rim edges, and perhaps even small pieces chipped away from those rims. If you're worried, get an impartial garage to look at the wheel: replacements will cost you a great deal of money.

Tyres are no problem, but our advice is always to use top-grade radials, and not to 'over-tyre' the car with wider sections on the same rims.

Apart from keeping a check on rust or stress deterioration of the MacPherson strut bodywork top mountings, the most important suspension check point is the condition of the struts themselves. Check that the geometry is still right (it is possible to distort the hubs after a kerbing incident on these cars), and that damping efficiency is unimpaired. It may not be necessary to replace the entire strut to restore the suspension to full health, as inserts are available. As in all things Escort, check that you are taking delivery of the correct part for the appropriate model, for there are so many variations in spring lengths, damper settings, and other details between the various models. Do not be fobbed off with the remark, "They're all same". It just isn't true.

You should have few problems with the brakes, but make sure that the handbrake mechanism is undamaged under the car, and that the adjustment mechanism of the rear drum brakes is working properly.

Engines and transmissions

The good news here is that both engines are still in production, and that spare parts are therefore plentiful. Both have very strong bottom ends, with crankshafts which are just about indestructible if the oil ways have been kept well supplied and the engines not been grievously overrevved.

The Mexico's Kent engine is particularly long-lasting if it has been properly maintained, though

Top, l to r, original Cibiés on this Mexico show signs of lens corrosion; not all Mexicos had flashy stripes; check the spring hangers and under floor for damage — this car is good; non-standard tyres have forced the owner to put the spare on the boot floor — all pre-1973 cars had the spare on the floor; post-1973 battery position was under bonnet — look for corrosion in this area. Above left, this owner has the rare World Cup manifold. Above, an unusually well-preserved example, this Mexico.

continuous over-revving is not good for the valve gear, camshaft, and general well-being. It is not particularly highly tuned, and should produce vigorous torque from fairly low speeds. Signs of old age include noisy valve gear in general, and a rise in oil consumption. It is very rare that such a 'Kent' engine has to be scrapped — it is nearly always worth rebuilding, as the unit is simple, and parts are freely available.

The 'Pinto' engine of the RS2000, with its single overhead cam layout, is a bit more finicky, but the early and well-known problems, relating to camshaft wear, loss of profile, noisy behaviour, and loss of performance, seem to have been more prevalent on Cortinas, and on earlier models. Once again, a properly maintained RS2000 engine should give sparkling performance with very reasonable fuel consumption, but it certainly doesn't like to be revved as highly as the Kent unit. If you're RS2000-shopping, see if you can get a look under the cam cover, at the condition of the camshaft lobes themselves, and the fingers where they rub on the lobes. If all is well there, the engine is normally quiet, and power output is correct, the rest of the engine should be in acceptable condition. Cam drive is by cogged belt, and it many be worth enquiring if this has ever been changed — on a high-mileage RS2000 such a change is usually advisable, but make sure the valve timing is not disturbed in the process!

Both the transmissions — the British' gearbox used in the Mexico, and the very different 'German' gearbox used in the RS2000 — are good and strong, widely used in other contemporary (and, in some cases, current) Ford models, simple, and straightforward to rebuild when necessary. There is nothing unusual in their behaviour, so apart from the examination on purchase for oil tightness, synchromesh wear, and the condition of the change linkage, there is nothing to fear. For an accomplished mechanic, dropping the transmission from an Escort is simple enough, and all the parts are readily available.

The same type of rear axle, and hypoid bevel differential, is used for both cars, the basic difference being that the faster car (the RS2000) had smaller drum brakes! Illogical but true — the smaller RS2000 brakes were specified not only to provide clearance for snow chains (an essential provision on Continental Europe), but to modify the brake balance from the Mexico, which was a touch too strong at the rear.

The axle itself is a Ford family unit, in production for at least 20 years, and with impressive reserves of torque capacity. In this connection, however, check that the correct final drive ratio (3.77:1 for the Mexico, and 3.54:1 for the RS2000) is still fitted, that there are no undue oil leaks, and that the unit is not noisy and beginning to make expensive protests.

Interiors

Remember that both cars, no matter how sporting, were built down to a price and, in fairness, were still modified 'bread-and-butter' Escorts. In some cases the trim and seating will have become scruffy with age, but it should be possible to renew such items. On the RS2000 in particular, the special body-hugging seats should still be in place.

When buying a pre-1973-model Mexico, with battery in the boot and spare wheel mounted on the boot floor, you should beware that this limits the amount of luggage which can be carried. All later Mexicos and all RS2000s had normal luggage provision like other 'mainstream' Escorts.

Most door furniture details such as chrome handles, fittings, and glass, were the same as those of standard Escorts, as was much of the soft trim and carpeting, but it is best to consult the very detailed Parts Manual which every RS Dealer holds, to make sure you buy precisely what you need. The actual layout of the instruments is the same as that of the more mundane Escort GTs and late-model Escort Sports, but the instruments themselves are special. The steering wheels are special 'RS' components, but, if necessary, replacements are still available. △

The first time British buyers saw the RS2000 was at the October 1973 Motor Show, though it had been announced that July

Rather Special

Made in England but initially sold only in Germany, the first Escort RS2000 allied 110mph pace with possible 30mpg frugality. Jeremy Walton recalls the details

Independence Day – July 4 – 1973 was the official birthdate of the Escort RS2000. A product of the compact 250-employee Ford Advanced Vehicle Operations plant at South Ockendon, Essex, the first RS2000s were sold only in Germany. In October of the same year, though, the Earls Court Motor Show proved the platform from which Ford announced that the car would be sold in rhd "from approximately £1500" according to early press pronouncements.

The distinctively striped 2-litre Escort ended production with the other Mk1 Escort RS products when the Ockendon plant was officially closed in the second week of December 1974, although some were finished in 1975. Sales, naturally, continued until stocks ran out. It is probable that some 3500 RS2000s of the first series were made, roughly half as many as its successor – the beak-nosed Mk2 – of which 5939 were manufactured in Germany. We have to say "probably" because Ford claim to have no records covering production of the original RS2000 series.

With its £1500 target price, the RS2000 fitted neatly between the September 1973-priced RS1600 at £1700 and the sub-£1300 Escort Mexico in the FAVO line. In comparison, the similar looking Escort Sport 1300 from Halewood's mass production lines was little over £1000. The RS2000 soon reached £1800 and was priced at £1965 by its demise.

Although the original British road tests and launch had to be conducted with lhd examples, the concept of a bigger engine in a well sorted Escort chassis received a deservedly warm welcome.

All the components were well proven, but it had proved a squeeze to get the Cortina/Pinto 1993cc unit into the engine bay of the Type 49 Escort bodyshell. The 49 shell consisted of a normal Escort unitary steel construction plus flared wheelarches front and rear, extra thickness chassis side rails, and double plating for the top pick-up points of the MacPherson front suspension legs. Such bodies were produced for the Mexico and competition-inspired RS1600 at Ford's Halewood plant, arriving at South Ockendon fully trimmed, electrically complete and with all glass in place. All that was basically needed

was the installation of running gear, unless a special order exception had been made.

For RS2000, the 90.82mm by 76.95mm sohc unit had a number of important ancillary changes. An electric fan had to be squeezed in front of the radiator, because the unit was just too long for comfort with the normal mechanical cooling fan so close to the radiator. This saved a little on noise and officially boosted the power output from 98bhp to 100bhp at 5700rpm. Maximum torque was quoted at 107lbs ft at 2750rpm. Incidentally, it was the later Beak Nose RS2000 that gained the twin downpipe exhaust system as standard, Ford claiming 108bhp for what was still basically a Cortina/Capri 2-litre motor.

Panics with blown engines

The original RS2000 also gained a cast aluminium sump with central oil pick up point, the same material being used for the clutch bellhousing. While the normal Ford 8.5ins diameter single plate clutch remained, hydraulic operation was dispensed with, being replaced by cable operation. Those alloy sumps did cause some initial panics because swarf got into the first batch and caused a number of engines to go 'pop' before the cause was speedily discovered!

The gearbox certainly came from the Cortina, complete with caravan towing first gear (3.65) and more reasonable subsequent ratios of 1.97 for second; 1.37 for third and a direct top. The latter was allied to a 3.54 final drive; enough to give a then tallish 18.7mph per 1000rpm. That rear end was not entirely happy when attacked by an enthusiast, its ancestry going back to 105E days, but uprating work over the years left the halfshafts usually able to cope. Location was via the normal RS upper links with multi-leaf springs while the later Mk2 "Brenda" floorpan back dampers – which mount almost vertically – should be present in 1974 models. The earlier Escort had distinctly angled rear dampers but the layout for the later cars was put into production long before the Mk2 was announced, echoing a similar introduction pattern as was followed with the Capri: new underpinnings, old body.

The gearbox was modified in respect of its change quality with a new spacer providing a shorter shift arc for the single rail Cortina box.

In the original press releases Ford spoke of competition drivers helping the development of the RS2000 and this was not company jargon for "whose name have we got on a contract at the moment?" Promising young Scottish driver Gerry Birrell genuinely *did* sort out a stiff front (30 per cent up on Mexico) and slightly softer rear damper settings for RS2000 and the car was notably good under track conditions in its first form. Tragically, one of Gerry's last public engagements was to attend the car's press launch, for later in June 1973, he died in a French Formula 2 race.

RS2000 brakes were the usual servo assisted 9.6ins discs at the front, but the rears were 8.0×1.5ins drums instead of the normal RS 9.0×1.75ins. This was attributed to the need for German homologation and the use of rear snow chains in safety, but the brake bias on RS2000 was another area in which hard drivers like Birrell were able to influence matters so that the bias of effort shifted forward.

Inside the lhd drive cars were a pair of expensive and rather cumbersome Scheel reclining seats. These did not find universal road test favour when the scribes were trying the machines, so an alternative UK-sourced seat of broadly similar look was introduced. These proved very satisfactory to the accountants *and* the customers, a rarity indeed!

A three spoke flat sports steering wheel of FAVO origin (much better in crash tests than the original dished sports wheel that was always favoured on Boreham competition cars) sat in front of comprehensive instrumentation. These dials were based on the kind of information Escorts had always offered in sporting trim, including oil pressure, rpm (6500 was the maximum allowed), water temperature, battery condition, speed and fuel contents. Interior options included wood finish and a push button radio. A Ford executive told me recently: "We found the Mexico had been selling

Autosport's road tester, John Bolster, smokes a tyre on one of the original left-hand drive launch cars

The 2-litre Pinto unit developed 100bhp giving the RS2000 a good power-to-weight ratio

Interior of the left-hand drive launch cars. Neat and functional cockpit was a model of efficiency

well with more interior features, such as the Comfort and Custom Pack type with better seats and trim, and so the RS2000 started off with many of these features included."

Externally there was no mistaking the RS2000 in its launch guise. They had those odd side body stripes that looked as though a child had allowed a transfer to slide halfway down the panels, front to rear. Later on you could opt out of such gaudy finishes and solid green, red or extra cost black became a regular sight, alongside the yellow, orange, white and blue shades that were offered as basic colours with mild extra badgework and striping. However, one of the original launch cars in white with blue stripes could have historic value: it should be lhd, of course, and have an XVX 300 numeral Essex registration with L suffix.

Alloy wheels of the four spoke FAVO type were *not* standard, but a widely fitted option. They replaced charcoal grey and silver two-tone steel wheels, which were offered as production equipment. Dimensionally they were the same 5½J×13ins.

As with any Ford Escort of the period the sports options were almost limitless. You may well discover a car with the first homologation special carburation layout: twin downdraught 40/42 Solexes, which were used to such good effect, amongst other

modifications, to bring Roger Clark and Gerry Marshall home first and second against powerful Vauxhall and BMW opposition in the 1974 Tour of Britain. Clark's car – PVX 445M – offered 138bhp.

The later Webers were a much better bet for power and road manners though. Also homologated for Group 1 competition were Bilstein dampers, single leaf rear springs, a twin pipe exhaust system, limited slip differential and the close ratio Rocket gear set within the standard casing. Many more goodies, including ventilated front disc brakes and a 'quick' high ratio steering rack, were allowed for the Mk2 RS2000. Such features could easily be incorporated on a roadgoing Mk1, along with 165 docile bhp if required . . . if you can afford the cost of a blueprinted engine and extra parts.

Delight for a keen driver

Wider wheels, up to 7J in the FAVO four spoke series, could be fitted under the steel wheelarch extensions offered through Ford's Rallyesport network. The 7J wheels were rare, but worthwhile from a looks viewpoint with the big arches.

These cars should delight any keen driver. The combination of 110mph – some tests recall 112mph as the maximum – and 0-60mph in 9secs, or less, went with prompt brakes and a stiff ride. The steering was a little heavier than on the Mexico/

RS1600, but unless the road was wet, when the extra torque could lead to excessive wheelspin on Pirelli CN36 or Dunlop SP68 production 165 SR radials, it was hard to fault the 1973-75 RS2000 series.

As collectors cars for Ford fans, the first RS2000 series has more to commend it than any other sporting Ford. Spares are easily obtainable and not unreasonable, although you might well find that some parts unique to the Mk1 are harder to come by. The performance is thoroughly up to date and even hard drivers used to get 27mpg fairly easily, which is not a bad price to pay for reliable performance. Newer Mk2s might be a better – if more expensive – road bet, but the Mk1 will always have a valuable place in British sporting history and comparative rarity on its side.

You can reckon it will cost from £1000 to £1700 to buy a Mk1 RS2000. There were six such cars in the pages of a recent sporting weekly and competition examples were on offer at similar prices.

If you want to go a little more deeply into the subject there is an RS Owners Club, run by David Harrison from 21 Middlemarch Road, Coventry, Warwickshire. There is also a book covering the subject. And for further reading try *Ford Escort RS* by Graham Robson (Osprey), an account of Escort Twin Cam, RS1600, RS2000 and Mexico and thoroughly worth £6.95.

Clark yumps his way to a fine win in the 1974 Tour of Britain, a mixture of racing and rallying

Bolster hurls the RS through a favourite corner. Gerry Birrell helped in the car's development

Clark, 1974 Tour. The RS2000 proved the dominant car on the event finishing first and second

SUPER-ROO ESCORT *Continued from page* 42

Lights and washers all needed attention on the test car. It was fitted with the optional GS pack, which gives you the sports steering wheel, rally stripes, Super Roo decal, external color-keyed mirror, lights and special wheel covers. The optional driving lights are imported quartz units but rate in the also-ran quality compared with the Cibie Type 45 and Hella rectangular quartz driving lights available here now. We believe Ford will soon be using the Hella lights for the Escort and Capri options.

On the test GT both the normal headlights and driving lights were poorly set, which did not enhance the overnight Melbourne-Sydney run. The windscreen washer union also came adrift leaving the Escort with a very murky screen on a drizzly night. The wipers, however, are excellent and on full speed must be the quickest in the business. Even in a heavy Sydney shower, "slow" is sufficient. On "fast", and well lubricated by rain, they go into frenzied action.

We found the Escort's simple lines and majority of sealed glass made washing easy.

Considerable design effort has gone into the Escort's panelwork by Ford's chief engineer, Harley Copp, in a battle against the NVH factor (Noise, Vibration, Harshness). The Escort side body panels are pressed as one unit. This makes alignment easier, reducing the wind noise element. It also has made the rear window quite small in an effort to keep up torsional strength.

The doors, which are also two single pressings — an inner and an outer skin—are welded to hinges instead of bolted. This takes out the human element of individual alignment to take up manufacturing inaccuracies but, in fact, the doors do not fit well. The rear extractor vents do not have non-return flaps and catch water in their plenum chamber.

While the Escort does not have the variation of the Capri's Aeroflow ventilation system, it is very good. The Escort has sealed quarter vents and for Australian conditions the fresh air flow for really hot days is inadequate. Two easily understood controls in the dash direct hot or fresh air to the footwells with hot and/or fresh to the dash vents which act as personal vents as well as windscreen demisting.

One deficiency which showed during our Sydney-Melbourne hike was the lack of touring range. The fuel gauge shows empty after eight gallons (nine-gallon tank) and 200 miles is an unsatisfactory range out here. We believe an 18 gallon tank will be optional for the GT soon and standard on the Twin Cam. That should be good range for the Bathurst race too. Funny about that!

The tank is stored behind the wheel arch in that space which is normally so unusable. The spare occupies the opposite side, aft of the arch. This gives the boot a healthy clear space for luggage and by small car standards it can swallow a huge amount.

Good as the value is, we feel many owners, especially in the GT market, would like to see a few improvements and be prepared to pay the extra. Reversing lights, for instance, which aren't even offered as an option; better seat adjusting mechanism to make it more comfortable for the lanky ones; bigger fuel tank (that's covered), wider wheels and tyres and power washers.

But for $2445, the Escort 1300 GT GS is a complete package and, on today's car prices, no one could argue it isn't value-for-money. In fact, we'd even go so far as to say that for our money — it's a little gas! #

INSTANT RACER—*continued from page* 55

in behind him when, with a lap to go, he got the chequered flag—in theory he had a lap start. So it was all over and we slackened our pace and were all beckoned back to the grid for the presentation. In fact, the chap in the Mini had exceeded his practice time by too large a margin and thus fooled the handicappers so he was disqualified, as was a BMW 2002 driver. So I was really cheated out of an extra lap.

There was considerable deliberation by the officials while we all talked excitedly about how we almost had accidents and J.W. told frightening tales of his throttle sticking open at the *chicane*. The winner turned out to be Formula Ford driver Richard Leach driving one of the just-announced Toyota Celicas, but J.W. upheld Standard House honours by finishing an excellent third. I was placed down in 19th spot, which I suppose is a start if nothing else, while Cutting had worked his Escort up to sixth place off the same handicap. Anyway, I received a consolation of a Contour long-playing record for my efforts, the car was in one piece and I had really enjoyed myself. The aftermath included legs, and particularly arms, which ached for about two days after and a very nice mention in the race report in *Autosport* which said I was cheered on at the *chicane* by a band of enthusiastic followers, apparently mainly the F3 boys, who I know well. Actually I was trying so hard I never saw them.

Naturally I want to have another go and see if I can go faster next time, for I can assure everyone there is a world of difference between track and road driving. It looks as if Group 1 racing has a big future in Britain, although the present handicap system is not very satisfactory. What could happen, however, is that Group 1 will become big business and the novices will not stand a chance. I would advise those wanting to start racing on a limited budget to buy a car primarily for racing rather than attempt to use a road car as I had done. The advertisement columns of the racing weeklies have plenty of quite competitive second-hand cars at under £750, particularly smaller-capacity saloons, modified sports cars (Sprites, etc.), or Clubman's cars. One can then learn the ropes fairly quietly over a season and then decide whether to carry on into single-seater racing and/or more professional classes. Incidentally, MOTOR SPORT is always willing to offer advice to prospective racing drivers.

The day after Thruxton I went to Castle Combe to report and there was a race in the Escort Mexico Challenge series. I was sorely tempted to try for a late entry but as Ford had no prior knowledge decided I had better not. Escort Mexico racing is decidedly hairy and there have already been multiple pile-ups. The great majority of the drivers are very experienced and all determined to do well and consider it to be far from a beginners' class as was originally intended.

So I have made my racing debut and maybe I will have a chance to try again. Thanks should go particularly to AVO, first for lending us the car but second for producing a machine which makes a terrific road car yet far from disgraces itself at club race or rally level.—A. R. M.